GEOGRAPHIES FOR ADVANCED STUDY

EDITED BY PROFESSOR S. H. BEAVER MA

THE TROPICAL WORLD

GEOGRAPHIES FOR ADVANCED STUDY

EDITED BY PROFESSOR S. H. BEAVER MA

THE

TROPICAL WORLD

ITS SOCIAL AND ECONOMIC

CONDITIONS

AND ITS FUTURE STATUS

BY

PIERRE GOUROU

*Professor at the Collège de France
and at the Free University
of Brussels*

TRANSLATED BY

S. H. BEAVER
& E. D. LABORDE

LONGMAN

LONGMAN GROUP LIMITED
London

*Associated companies, branches and representatives
throughout the world*

New edition © *Longman Group Limited (formerly Longmans,
Green & Co. Ltd) 1958, 1961, 1966.*

*First published 1953
Fourth edition 1966
New impression (sixteenth printing) and first
appearance in paperback 1973
Second impression in paperback 1975*

ISBN 0 582 48163 5

*The original edition of this work was published
by Presses Universitaires de France, Paris*

*Printed in Great Britain by
Lowe & Brydone (Printers) Ltd, Thetford, Norfolk*

PREFACE TO THE FOURTH EDITION

The eighteen years that have elapsed since the publication of the first French edition of Pierre Gourou's *Les Pays Tropicaux* have witnessed enormous changes throughout the tropical world. The first English edition of this book appeared in 1953, translated by Dr E. D. Laborde. It proved extremely popular with English students because of its broad scope and the clarity of its style. A second edition with revisions was published in 1958 and further amendments were incorporated in the third edition in 1961. By this time, however, with so many tropical countries having achieved political if not economic independence, and as a result of the far-reaching effects of technical progress in many directions, but particularly in medicine and agriculture, it was obvious that the book could no longer be tinkered with; it must be virtually rewritten. This Professor Gourou has now done; in the first six chapters there are still some recognizable passages from previous editions to be found, but the rest of the book is almost completely new. Unfortunately the original translator, Dr Laborde, died in 1962, so this new edition is the work of the Editor of the series. Professor Gourou has performed a great service in recasting this work, and in enriching it with the fruits of his personal experience and his immensely wide reading of the vast mass of literature on the tropical world that has poured out in many languages and in many books and periodicals during the last decade or so. The editor is proud to have been associated with such a work.

S. H. BEAVER

University of Keele
August 1965

CONTENTS

MAPS

PLATES

Photographs are by the author unless otherwise acknowledged

CHAPTER 1

Density of Population

HITHERTO lands with a hot, wet climate seem to be less favourable than the temperate belt as an environment for man. The problems connected with the use of natural resources are not presented in the same way in the two belts, for hot, wet lands have their own special physical and human geography.

The following pages deal with lands which have no month with a mean temperature of less than 65° F and get rain enough for agriculture to be possible without irrigation. (The minimum is about 20 inches, but irrigation might well be useful with such a total.) This definition is not meant to be rigid and may be departed from in special cases; and it includes both the equatorial and tropical climates. For the sake of brevity the term 'tropical' will often be used to denote countries with a hot, wet climate.[1]

---

1. It is futile to attempt to draw linear boundaries (unless, very exceptionally, the landscape itself provides them). In general we are dealing with gradual transitions. A monthly mean of 65° F is suggested above; a lowest monthly mean of 60° F would almost involve the possibility of frost, but we should hardly consider omitting Hanoi (North Vietnam) from the hot wet lands simply because its coldest month has a mean of 62 degrees. As for rainfall, it is impossible to name a precise isohyet beyond which agriculture demands irrigation; in earlier editions of this book a figure of 27½ inches was proposed, but now it seems that 20 inches might be more appropriate, for millet is harvested north of Lake Chad with only 14 inches (concentrated, it is true, into a short season), and in any case the actual area lying between the 20- and 27-inch isohyets within the tropics is not large. A very useful map has been presented by F. R. Falkner in 'Die Trockengrenze des Regenfeldbaus in Afrika' (*Petermanns Geogr. Mitteilungen*, 1938, pp. 210–14); see Fig. 9 on page 70. See also the same author's thesis, *Beitrage zur Agrargeographie der Afrikanischen Trockengebiete* (Basle 1939, 76 pp.). W. B. Morgan, 'The distribution of food-crop storage methods in Nigeria' (*Journal of Tropical Geography*, 13, 1959, pp. 58–64) suggests that 'a rainfall of 16 inches annually may be considered as the minimum normally necessary for agriculture'.

A recent attempt to delimit the 'humid tropics' is that of F. R. Fosbey, B. J. Garnier and A. W. Kuchler, 'Delimitation of the humid tropics' (*Geogr. Review* 1961, pp. 333–47) which has two maps (Climatic criteria, Vegetation criteria). It may be noted that 'humid' is not synonymous with 'rainy', and this explains certain rather surprising features of the maps of climatic criteria. In the context of human and economic geography with which we are here concerned, it matters relatively little whether the air is more or less humid, but it does matter whether it rains. Agriculture does not depend on relative humidity but on rainfall. Our point of view could be altered, of course, if it were proved that the physical and mental activity of man were notably modified by a greater or less amount of humidity in the air—but in our opinion this is not so (see p. 4, note 3).

1

Thus defined (see Fig. 1), the hot, wet regions have an area of 16 million square miles: 3 million in Asia and the East Indies, 1 million in Melanesia, Australia, and Oceania, 6·5 million in Africa, and 5·5 million in America. This is a considerable fraction of the earth's dry land and an even more remarkable proportion of its useful parts. In fact, if the area without value to man is estimated at 17·4 million square miles, the hot, wet belt covers rather more than one-third of the useful portions of the earth's surface.

Most hot, wet lands are sparsely peopled. This fact is surprising at first sight, for these regions support a luxuriant natural vegetation, which seems to betoken conditions favourable to agriculture. But in about 1958 the hot, wet parts of America had a mean density of

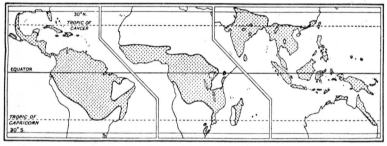

FIG. 1. The belt of hot, wet lands

18 persons to the square mile; those in Africa approximately 25; New Guinea between 2·5 and 0·5; whilst those in Australia were, at any rate outside the east coast of Queensland, almost uninhabited.

The vast Amazon region[1] is practically empty (see Fig. 2). The Brazilian State of Amazonas has a population of 600,000 to 710,000 square miles (a density of 0·8), that of Mato Grosso one of 400,000 to 500,000 square miles, the Amazonian territories of Venezuela, Colombia, Ecuador, and Peru are scarcely better off, and the Peruvian Province of Madre de Dios in the Amazon valley had a density of 0·06 in the census of 1940. The basins of the Orinoco and Amazon are uninhabited wastes of dense vegetation.[2] British Guiana contains 5 persons to the square mile, Dutch Guiana 4, and French Guiana 0·8, whilst the Brazilian territory of Amapá, which is adjacent

1. On this subject see the following articles by P. Gourou, 'L'Amazonie: problèmes géographiques', *Les Cahiers d'Outre-Mer*, Bordeaux, 1949, pp. 1–13; 'Observações geográficas na Amazônia', *Revista Brasileira de Geografia*, 1949, pp. 355–408, and 1950, pp. 171–250; 'Le pays de Belem', *Bull. de la Soc. Belge d'Etudes Geogr.*, 1949, pp. 19–36.
2. They are well described by Earl Hanson, *Geog. Review*, 1933, p. 578.

to French Guiana and has a population of 40,000 on 54,000 square miles, gives a good idea of the size of the population in the interior of Guiana. But the territory of Rio Branco do Norte in Brazil is still less densely peopled for it has a population of 20,000 on 96,000 square miles, or a density of 0·16.

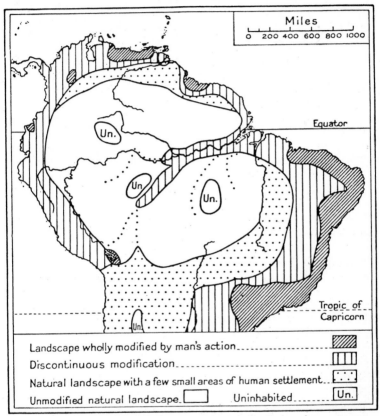

FIG. 2. Man's influence on nature in South America

(After F. Jaeger, 'Versuch einer Anthropogeographischen Gliederung der Erdoberfläche' *Petermanns G. Mitteilungen*, 1934)

In Central America and Mexico there are uninhabited expanses like the region aptly named *El Desierto*[1] in the east of the Mexican State of Chiapas, a region continued with similar features into northern Guatemala. The country has a moderately broken surface-relief, fine rivers, many lakes, mineral resources of sulphur and iron ore, a magnificent vegetation in which mahogany and wild cacao

1. *Geog. Review*, 1937, p. 28.

flourish, and a plentiful fauna including many species, like turkeys, pheasants, tapirs, wild boars, deer, antelopes, agutis, and edible fish from Lake Miramar. Yet it is almost uninhabited.

Tropical Africa has a population of 165 million on its 6,500,000 square miles of surface, i.e. 25 persons to the square mile. As a whole the centre of the continent seems to be the most thinly peopled part with 30 million persons to its 2,000,000 square miles or 15 per square mile. Congo-Léopoldville has a density of 15, Angola 9, Gabon 4, Congo-Brazzaville 5, Central African Republic 5. East Africa, with an area of 1,050,000 square miles, has a population of 28 million and owes its higher density (27) to a few small thickly peopled areas,[1] for outside these the population is no denser than in the central region. West Africa is better off, having a population of 70 million on 1,600,000 square miles, and a density of 40. Yet vast expanses are very thinly peopled.[2] Thus, the density of the hot, wet parts of the Sudan hardly exceeds 20. In the tropical parts of southern Africa densities are generally low; Southern Rhodesia, for instance, has 5 persons to the square mile and Madagascar 13.

The 13 million square miles of the hot, wet regions outside Asia contain some 300 million people, i.e. 10 per cent of the world's population on 28 per cent of its exploitable land surface, giving a density of 23 to the square mile. Furthermore these 300 million belong to nations which are economically poor, badly provided with roads, railways, and industries, and in which agricultural productivity is low, in terms both of crop yields and of human labour. We may well enquire whether this low population density and this poverty are a direct result of the hot, wet climate which limits man's physical and mental activity. The abundant literature on the subject[3] does not lead to a definite answer; and we may suggest that the direct effect on the human body and mind of the tropical climate is not great enough to be regarded as a major geographical factor. But the indirect effects of climate, acting through tropical diseases and the peculiarities of tropical soils, merit much greater attention.

The hot, wet parts of Asia, with their teeming populations and much higher degree of civilization, prove that it is unwise to expect a tropical climate to be a direct cause of low population density and poverty. The 3 million square miles of tropical Asia contain 800

1. See below, pp. 103–6.
2. See below, pp. 106–15.
3. Summarized by Max. Sorre, *Les fondements biologiques de la géographie humaine*. Paris, 1943. See also D. H. K. Lee, *Climate and Economic Development in the Tropics*, New York, 1957. It is possible, even probable, that man originated in the tropics; and if so, is it not paradoxical that he should be enfeebled by the tropical climate?

million people, that is a quarter of the world's population on 8 per cent of its exploitable area, and a density of 267 to the square mile.

Do the physical conditions for development present themselves in a different form in tropical Asia? It would not seem so. It must be recognized at the outset that the traditional civilizations of the Asiatic tropics have raised themselves to a high level: their production techniques, and their systems of land-use control have been perfected, and they have mastered the art of writing.

Is tropical Asia a physically different world, or simply a similar environment in which well-developed civilizations like those of India and China have blossomed?[1] Was not the growth of these civilizations itself influenced by the most favourable environmental conditions to be found in Asia? The question must be asked, although the development of the high civilization of the Mayas shows that it is unwise, in a survey of the level of civilization, to oppose tropical Asia and the rest of the tropical world.[2]

The sparsely peopled areas and the densely peopled areas of the tropical world have one thing in common: they are all 'under-developed'. In the tropical world all aspects of underdevelopment are to be found, such as areas sparsely occupied by a very poor population (e.g. central Africa and Amazonia), and areas densely settled by a poor population (e.g. eastern Bengal, Java, the plains of Vietnam, the Si Kiang delta, Barbados). The territories exhibit all the usual stigmata of underdevelopment, such as low per capita income and low energy consumption, widespread lack of education, poor national equipment in the shape of roads, motor vehicles, telephones and industry.[3] The only tropical land enjoying a high standard of living is the Hawaiian islands, which, in income, actually rank twentieth or twenty-first amongst the fifty States of the U.S.A. Are there specially favourable natural conditions here? Certainly there is no malaria. Or is it merely the transplantation of American civilization, with high per capita income, due to an historical accident and an enormous inflow of American money?[4]

It would thus be rash to assume that the human geography of the sparsely-peopled parts of the hot, wet lands was due simply to the unhealthy climate and the poverty of the soil. The striking contrast between tropical Asia and Hawaii underlines the fact that there is no such determinism in the tropical world. However, the physical conditions are not without their influence on men and civilization.

1. See below Chapter 10.
2. See note on the Maya civilization on p. 52–5.
3. E. Staley, *The Future of Underdeveloped Countries*, New York, 1954, observes that there are no well-developed countries in the tropics.
4. See below, p. 153.

At a certain level of technical accomplishment in the use of natural resources, unhealthiness on the one hand, and the peculiarities of tropical soils on the other, help to explain the small numbers of people, the low standard of living, the cultural stagnation, and perhaps also the decay of such civilizations as have existed, e.g. those of the Maya, of Angkor or of Anuradhapura.[1]

One thing is certain, that the development of the tropical world has been much delayed since the industrial and scientific revolution. Progress in the conquest of infectious diseases and in the maintenance of soil fertility has been realized in the temperate zone, through the agency of research workers born and living in the temperate zone; such discoveries have been but slowly transferred to the tropical zone, because the natural conditions are there so different. Scientists of tropical origin have been rare, and those from the temperate zones have needed much time to accustom themselves to the conditions of the tropics.

This book examines the central problem of geography, the relation between human communities and the natural (in this case tropical) environment in which they live. These relations are by no means simple, for the very existence of human communities modifies the natural conditions (which can then no longer strictly be called 'natural'), and each community sees and utilizes the natural environment, not as an orderly collection of resources to be systematically developed, but in the light of the techniques, customs and tastes which characterize its own particular civilization. The civilizations, which changed but little during the life-span of the individual and were therefore largely heritages of the past, were simply systems of land-occupancy which had but limited scope and were only concerned with a part of the possible field of exploitation; each one had its blinkers, which prevented it from seeing and utilizing the whole range of opportunities. In some of them the accent was on agriculture, in others on pastoralism, whilst still others developed the arts of metallurgy and writing. In view of this diversity it would be inappropriate to attribute responsibility to the 'natural' environment. All cultural landscapes result from the application of a certain form of civilization to a certain natural environment, and in this book we shall study both. It is within the framework of the tropical world that will be posed and repeated the questions that the geographer addresses to the landscapes that it is his mission to understand.

1. See below, p. 61.

CHAPTER 2

Unhealthiness of the Hot, Wet Regions

HERE is a portrait of an African village, not far from Accra in Ghana.[1] It lies in a forest region suitable for cocoa; it is relatively prosperous because it grows its own food (maize and manioc) and can easily sell foodstuffs, cacao beans and firewood by reason of its closeness to a good road. The relative wellbeing is apparent in the neat houses. However, the village is unhealthy: malaria is (or was) firmly rooted, for 45 per cent of the inhabitants had enlarged spleens, and 32 per cent had parasites in their bloodstream. The most widespread parasite is *falciparum*, which causes 'tropical' fever, so that malaria is endemic —a not surprising fact in view of the presence of the mosquito *Anopheles gambiae* in most of the houses. In addition there is a good assortment of intestinal parasites—amoebae, hookworms (in 44 per cent of the inhabitants), threadworms (in 76 per cent), and whipworms. Vesical bilharzia, derived from contact with the neighbouring river, affects 9 per cent of the population. Filariasis is very widespread (21 per cent of the inhabitants) but the parasite which causes it (*Dipetalonema streptocerea*) creates little havoc. The Guinea worm (*Dracunculus medinensis*), though rare at the time of the study, had affected half the population. Three-quarters of the people were affected by yaws, the cause of many troubles, embarrassing but not unduly serious.

This is a weighty pathological list, but it might be even longer, for there is almost no sleeping sickness (though the tsetse fly is abundant) no tropical ulcers and almost no yellow fever. As for the worldwide diseases that are not confined to the tropics, there is no tuberculosis, no leprosy, no trachoma, and few venereal diseases. The birth rate and the death rate are both high, particularly the child death rate (up to age 10). From the point of view of modern hygiene this village of Kwansakrom is in a bad way: yet its population is increasing, and we are told that 'despite their burden of serious sickness, the people of Kwansakrom are animated by infectious good spirits'.

We who live in temperate lands find it difficult to realize that the water in streams, and even the soil, may swarm with dangerous

1. M. J. Colbourne, G. M. Edington, M. H. Hughes, A. Ward-Brew, 'A medical survey in a Gold Coast village', *Trans. R. Soc. Trop. Med. and Hyg.* **44**, 1950, pp. 271–91.

germs, and that myriads of blood-sucking insects may inject deadly microbes into the human body.

Man is not the only victim of the unhealthiness of the tropics. Close examination of animals in hot, wet regions shows that they are attacked by serious diseases of various kinds. For instance, the gibbon is in a poor state of health in Siam and is found to be infested with parasites.[1] Cattle are subject to trypanosomiasis in equatorial Africa, and sheep do not easily thrive in hot, wet regions; the huge animal burial places found in Africa are probably due to trypanosomiatic diseases.

This unhealthiness is connected with the climate. The steady high temperature, the humidity of the air, the many water surfaces fed by the rains are necessary for the continued existence of pathogenetic complexes in which man, an insect, and a microbe or parasite are closely associated.

Malaria is the most widespread of tropical diseases. Though it occurs in certain temperate regions, its main spheres of action are in the hot, wet belt. It attacks (or did until recently) something like one-third of the human race, but in practice all the inhabitants of the hot, wet belt may be considered to be more or less infected.[2] Malaria weakens those whom it attacks, for the bouts of fever sap their physical strength and make them unfit for sustained effort. Hence agriculture does not receive all the care it needs, and the food supply is thereby affected. In this way a vicious circle is formed. Weakened by insufficient nourishment, the system offers small resistance to infection[3] and cannot provide the effort required to produce an adequate supply of food. The malarial patient knows quite well that a bout of fever may be the unpleasant reward for hard work. In a period of six months a hundred work-men from a healthy district suffered the following casualties in unhealthy road work in Vietnam (1931):—25 men were eliminated by death or evacuation; those remaining had, owing to temporary indisposition, lost 25 per cent of their capacity for work;

1. See the account of researches by M. Schultz of Baltimore, *L'Anthropologie*, 1939, p. 211. It may console mankind to know that the gibbons suffered from abscesses on their teeth. Besides, they were found to have many malformations, hernias, atrophied arms, extra fingers, etc.

2. The densely peopled regions of tropical Asia present special conditions; see below, p. 118.

3. The malaria epidemic which ravaged Ceylon in 1933–4 was fomented by a famine due to drought and already raging. The official report on the epidemic states: 'Even if the population had been well fed and prosperous, there would have been a malaria epidemic, but the vicious circle in which malaria and physical weakness mutually favour each other would not have been established, the death-rate would have been lower, convalescence would have been quicker, and there would have been fewer relapses.'

and the capacity for work of the group had fallen off by 50 per cent.[1]

Malaria carries off a great many infants who are infected from birth. It may kill adults through general debility, pernicious and cerebral attacks, and blackwater fever; and it prepares the way for the development of other diseases. It may take epidemic form and ravage districts previously little affected. In the years 1931 to 1935 Ceylon was hard hit, more than 100,000 persons dying of malaria, and the consumption of quinine rose to three tons a month.

Malaria normally requires heat and standing water. The haematozoa in the body of the anopheles die if they are subjected to temperatures below 60° F. several nights running, and the mosquito likes heat for itself and its larvae. The latter, which develop in water, have precise requirements which differ according to species. Certain of them prefer shady water; others, more numerous, favour running water warmed by the sun. In Serra do Mar in Brazil certain anopheles even go so far as to find for their larvae little pools of water which collect in the leaf-bunches of epiphytic Bromeliaceae. Thus, owing to the myriads of these tiny hanging aquaria, certain trees being able to carry as many as three thousand of the species of Bromeliaceae called *gravata* in Brazil, what may be termed Bromeliacean malaria is started. Hence, throughout the area covered by the hot, wet regions the anopheles finds conditions favouring its rapid multiplication.

The seriousness of malaria varies with the species of anopheles carriers. The most dangerous of these insects is probably *Anopheles gambiae*, an African mosquito; the larvae of this creature are not particular as to the quality of the water in which they develop, and the female insects are very greedy for human blood. Another African, *Anopheles funestus*, is also very dangerous, but less widespread. In southeast Asia *A. minimus, maculatus,* and *umbrosus* are no less deadly; Brazil has the relative good fortune to owe its malaria mainly to *A. darlingi*, a creature that is somewhat less to be feared, because its larvae are more delicate and because it does not wholly concentrate on human blood.[2]

Undoubtedly, malaria is largely responsible for the poor health, small numbers, and absence of enthusiasm for work of tropical peoples.[3] The decadence of certain districts in the Mediterranean at

1. It is estimated that in India, between 1901 and 1931, malaria was directly responsible for 30 million deaths. Indirectly, by opening the door to other diseases, it killed many more. But the most disturbing fact is that one death from malaria means at least 2,000 days of illness and absence from work.
2. See below, p. 157.
3. Does there not exist, however, a sort of immunity or inurement to malaria? Several points are worth noting: (1) It has often been noticed that individuals living in a malarial region and not attacked by it develop violent fevers if they

the end of the Roman Empire has been attributed to the spread of malaria due ultimately to political troubles which disorganized the drainage system. The disease is far more able to check the development of population in hot, wet lands, where marsh fever rages virulently all the time. The depopulation of the district of Anuradhapura in northern Ceylon was preceded by political troubles which ruined the network of irrigation canals and the ricefield system, and so helped the countryside to run wild and malaria to develop. If the northern borders of Angkor in Cambodia are almost deserted today, the causes for it are much the same. The former occupation of the area is proved by irrigation dams. But the work was ruined and the district abandoned owing to Siamese invasions, after which it became infested with malaria. Certainly today the progress of chemotherapy and the development of insecticides have made it possible to conquer malaria, provided that these efforts are backed by administrative efficiency.[1] A new development in human geography is now possible at little cost, whilst in the past the measures taken against malaria demanded great efforts undertaken purposely or incidentally. Examples of such operations will be given later.[2]

Intestinal diseases also contribute largely to weakening man in the tropics. The intestine of an inhabitant of Yucatan, when seen under a microscope, is a terrible 'museum of horrors',[3] in which such a large number of organisms is found that immunological prophylaxis seems to offer no remedy. Improvement in sanitation would alone be effective. So common are intestinal diseases in the country that the Mayas have little fear of them; and it would take a long time to teach this people hygienic habits. The number of deaths

migrate to another malarial region (this happened to Congolese soldiers in Nigeria during the last war); the explanation is perhaps that they are inured to certain strains of plasmodia but cannot resist others. (2) The theory has been held that newborn children in malarial regions have a certain innate resistance to malaria, but this resistance must be maintained by a daily puncture made by an anopheles infected with *Plasmodium falcoparum*; if this daily dose ceases for a time, a new insect bite starts an attack of fever. (3) Persons attacked by *drepano-cytosis*, that is, having sickle-shaped red corpuscles, are in a peculiar situation: in the first place they do not get malaria, for the plasmodia do not attack their red corpuscles; secondly, how is it that the whole population does not have this condition, which is inherited and which confers an obvious advantage on the individuals? Thirdly, however, homozygote victims of drepanocytosis, that is, those who have a double inheritance of sickle-shaped red corpuscles, quickly die of anaemia, and it is the heterozygotes who survive and resist malaria. See P. Gourou, 'Une humanité noire', *L'homme*, Paris, 1961, pp. 90–4. All in all, the facts of immunity and inurement have but few geographical repercussions.

1. During the military operations in 1951 in the malarial area of Hoa Binh (Tonkin), 14,000 men, protected by anti-malarial measures, were completely free from malaria after two months, but in a neighbouring sector 7,000 men, not so protected, developed 500 serious cases in two weeks.

2. See below, pp. 122–3, 137 and 175.

3. See a medical report published in the *Geog. Review*, 1935, p. 346.

due to intestinal diseases is certainly astonishing, but it is even more surprising that in such conditions man can survive the age of infancy.[1]

Tropical Africa offers an almost complete collection of intestinal diseases, especially amoebic and bacillary dysentery, which are serious, even deadly, and at the very least extremely weakening; maladies contracted by drinking water or eating raw vegetables; and ankylostomiasis, which is due to worms whose larvae penetrate into the human body through the skin of the foot, and so is caught by mere contact with the soil. The settlement of a number of hook-worms in the duodenum brings on anaemia through intestinal disorders and much haemorrhage. Altogether, anyone who harbours plasmodia in his blood and a rich collection of amoebae and dysenteric bacilli, hookworms, tapeworms, schistosomes of bilharziasis, and various other parasites in his intestines—as do most of those who dwell in the hot, wet regions—must certainly be debilitated, unfit for hard physical work, and incapable of great mental effort.

In certain conditions of the environment intestinal diseases may be more virulent than malaria. This is the case in Yucatan, which, being composed of a block of Pliocene limestone, has no surface drainage.[2] Ground water rarely comes to the surface, and then only at the bottom of certain *dolines* in ponds called *Cenotes*. The climate is sub-arid, with a severe dry season and a wet season which brings only 31 inches of rain. These conditions do not exclude malaria, but restrict its ravages, making it less widespread here than in the rainier districts to the south, like the Guatemaltecan province of Petén. On the other hand, intestinal diseases have become terribly prevalent. Perhaps this is due to the fact that the ground water is infected and that in this limestone country the streams are not filtered, but circulate easily through a widely meshed network of channels.

Other diseases peculiar to warm latitudes overwhelm man in the tropics. Bilharziasis of the bladder is especially deadly in Africa, and kala-azar causes considerable havoc in India. Man's vitality is further sapped by filarial diseases, elephantiasis, Guinea worm (dracontiasis), transient Calabar oedema, and onchocerciasis. This last affection, which sometimes causes blindness, is transmitted by sand-flies whose bite is enough to make it disagreeable to stay in some parts of Uganda. The N'Ghan tribe in the Bavule district of the Ivory Coast owes its name to the general lameness caused by the

1. Similarly, when R. E. Crist studied the population of the middle São Francisco River in Brazil he thought it wonderful that so many of the inhabitants reached adult age (*Geog. Review*, 1944, p. 605).
2. *The Peninsula of Yucatan*, by G. C. Shattuck and various collaborators, Carnegie Institution Publication, No. 431, Washington, 1933.

presence of Guinea worm in the lower limbs. Yaws is endemic on the coasts of the Gulf of Guinea. This is a disease which is suspected of being a cause of the terrible deformity of the bones known as goundou, or anakhrë, and is often fatal. Tropical ulcers, leishmaniasis, and relapsing fevers complete this short list, the horror of which is increased by sleeping sickness and yellow fever, both deserving of special notice.[1] Of course, no mention is made here of diseases of the temperate belt which are widespread in the tropics.

Yellow fever is confined to the hot, wet parts of Africa and America; of African origin, it was spread by the black slaves and has not yet reached Asia. Both the virus and the insect vectors (*Aedes*) require high temperatures. It was formerly thought that in Africa the disease was restricted to active endemic centres on the Gulf of Guinea, but recent work has shown that it extends, in a more or less dormant form, as far as Uganda. Perhaps there is a relationship between the viruses of yellow fever and of poliomyelitis. For a long time it was thought that man was indispensable to the survival of the amaril virus, but again, recent observations have indicated that it can exist in certain species of monkey, and be transmitted to man by mosquitoes. Thanks to inoculation, however, yellow fever no longer presents a difficult problem.

Sleeping sickness is peculiar to black Africa; the microbe and the tsetse flies that carry it and are indispensable to its development are only found within the African tropics. There is one small exception in that the tsetse has been seen in the vicinity of Aden, but the vast expanse of the Arabian desert has prevented its spread into Asia. If African slaves infected with the disease were transported to America, they were unable to spread their trypanosomes since there are no tsetse flies in the New World. The limits of the tsetse fly are perhaps the most accurate indication that can be given of the extent of the hot, wet regions of Africa. Sleeping sickness causes many deaths and physically and mentally weakens the persons it affects. It was noted in the Cameroons in 1923 that 42 per cent of the population of the district of Akonolinga were infected, and in the Nupe district in Nigeria it was found in 1936 that the percentage was as high as 70. The disease has grown worse in black Africa owing to the movements of population which have resulted from European colonization.

---

1. This list of tropical diseases does not pretend to be complete. It could easily be lengthened by the addition of pyomyositis (muscular suppuration due to a *Pasteurella* or a *Micrococcus* and occurring in the upper Senegal and upper Niger) and of porocephalosis (a parasitic disease caused by porocephales, Arachnida which infest the windpipe and lungs of snakes, and are transmitted to persons who eat badly-cooked snake flesh). *Cf. L'oeuvre des Pastoriens en Afrique noire* by Dr. C. Mathis, Paris, Presses Universitaires, 1946. See p. 352.

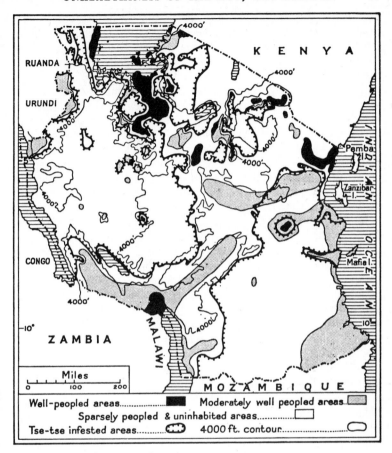

FIG. 3. Distribution of population in Tanzania

(After C. Gillman, 'A Population Map of Tanganyika Territory', *Geog. Review*, 1936; and E. Weigt, 'Schlafkrankheitsbekampfung in Tanganyika', *Petermanns G. Mitteilungen*, 1938)

Sleeping sickness, like many other tropical diseases, and malaria in particular, is a disease of uncivilized or half-civilized countries. The tsetse fly, which is very exacting as regards conditions of temperature and humidity, finds the necessary shelter in uncleared forest or woodland. In other words, the complete 'humanization' of a district involves the complete disappearance of the tsetse.[1] In Tanzania[2] the tsetse is not responsible for the low density of population; rather, it is the low density that causes the abundance of the pest. If the

1. See below, p. 63, for methods of fighting sleeping sickness.
2. See Gillman, *Geog. Review*, 1936, p. 354.

population were numerous enough to master nature completely, that is, not to leave any spontaneous vegetation in which the tsetse might take shelter, the insects would disappear. There is thus a threshold population density beyond which sleeping sickness cannot exist.

Before the development of modern medicine man was subject, in the hot, wet regions, to many infectious diseases which limited his health, his activity and his breeding.[1] Whilst with us the open country and the woodland evoke ideas of health, in tropical lands the healthiest place is the town, where contact with untouched nature is broken and hygienic measures are easily taken. The life of pioneers in the wildernesses of Siberia, Canada and New South Wales was rough but healthy; but in tropical lands the pioneers, whatever their race, have paid a heavy toll to disease.

In the pre-scientific age, men kept the most serious infectious diseases in check by organizing the total occupation of the land, thus eliminating the breeding-places of the mosquito. Such occupation demanded a high density of population and a complete control of land use, and hence the interdependence of a highly organized agricultural system (itself a function of soil quality, reliable climate and a certain degree of technical competence), a dense population and an advanced political organization. Such a concatenation of circumstances is hardly necessary today, for it is relatively easy to control both parasites and insects. But this scientific revolution, born in the temperate zone, is only slowly spreading to the tropical world and is only just beginning to show results.

1. On the Ivory Coast in 1925 a medical board passed only forty out of 336 young men as fit for military service.

CHAPTER 3

Tropical Soils

ILL-INFORMED writers are fond of calling to mind 'the inexhaustible wealth' of tropical soils[1] which, they suppose, nourish the irresistible luxuriance of the equatorial forest. This forest is supposed to be an 'invincible' obstacle to man, because it is said to grow up again as fast as it is cut down. Overwhelmed by the forest, and lost in the 'green hell', man is thought to be deprived of air and light—which does not prevent him from having a black or dark-coloured skin. This touching picture is inaccurate.

Forests in the hot belt are rarely virgin, but more often secondary, that is, forest which has grown again after being cleared by man.[2] They have no more vitality than the temperate forest, because they usually grow in very poor soil. The fertility of Trinidad is a myth

---

1. Earlier descriptions of the tropical environment were not all infected with such optimism. For example, in a penetrating analysis published in 1783, W. Marsden, *The History of Sumatra*, London, 1783, wrote (p. 68): 'Notwithstanding the received opinion of the fertility of the Malay islands, countenanced by the authority of Le Poivre, and other celebrated writers . . . I cannot help saying, that I think the soil of Sumatra is in general rather sterile than rich. It is almost everywhere a stiff, red clay, burned nearly to the state of a brick, where it is exposed to the influence of the sun. The small proportion of the whole which is cultivated, is either ground from which old woods have recently been cleared, whose leaves had formed a bed of vegetable earth, some inches deep; or else swamps, into which the scanty mould of the neighbouring hills has been washed. . . . It is true that on many parts of the coast, there are, between the cliffs and the beach, small plains of sandy soil, probably left by the sea . . .; and such are found to prove the most favourable spots for raising the productions of the western world. . . . Every person, at first sight, and on superficial view of the Malay countries, pronounces them the favourites of nature, where she has lavished all her bounties with a profusion unknown in other regions, and laments the infatuations of the people, who neglect to cultivate the finest soil in the world. But I have scarcely known one who, after a few years' residence, has not entirely altered his opinion.'

2. Too much stress has often been laid on the barrier presented by 'virgin' forest to human activity. The equatorial forests that cover such vast expanses remain not so much because of their own resistance as because of the feebleness of the human attack on them. Sumatra, Java, and southern Nigeria were completely forested before the arrival of agricultural people. Foresters say with some justification that the African savanna quickly erodes the forest after it has been attacked by cultivators. Thus we have two contradictory opinions—that the forest is resistant and that it easily yields; and the second appears the better of the two. The existence of the equatorial forest is simply a proof of the absence of a population interested in its destruction. The forest does not 'resist' if groups of cultivators wish to take its place. That the forest grows on poor soil does not hinder the pioneers, for the products of the forest—humus and wood-ash—give fertility to the cleared patch.

based on the fine appearance of the forest.[1] But equatorial forest may thrive exceedingly on infertile soil. In fact, the finest forests in Trinidad, forests of *Mora excelsa*, grow in sterile sands. The 'virgin' forest demands scarcely anything from the soil and lives in a state of equilibrium. Mineral substances extracted from the soil return thereto, organic matter fallen from the trees constitutes the humus, and everything that the forest produces goes back to the forest. Clearing causes unpleasant surprise, for instead of deep humus sand is found, and the forest may have the greatest difficulty in growing up again once man's exploitation has exposed the underlying sand. Expanses of brushwood in Trinidad are eloquent in this respect. Similarly, in Central Congo the sandy beds at Lubilash bear a fine open forest in their original state; but on being cleared the soil rapidly becomes exhausted.

Hence it must not be inferred from the luxuriance of the vegetation, that the soil in hot, wet lands is rich. Besides, analysis shows that, apart from rare exceptions, tropical soils are very poor in assimilable bases and phosphorus, and ill supplied with humus. The deficiencies are such that soils of similar composition would be barren in a temperate climate. A piece of cultivated land of average quality on the Red River delta which yields two crops of rice a year contains the following elements making for fertility: lime, less than 5 per thousand; magnesia, less than 2 per thousand (there is no possible comparison with temperate soils, which are basic and not acid); potash, less than 0·1 per thousand (in temperate lands soil with less than 0·5 per thousand is not cultivable)[2]; phosphoric acid, less than 0·1 per thousand (in temperate lands soil with less than 0·2 per thousand is not cultivable). The content of humus and nitrogen will be examined later.[3] According to J. Baeyens, the pedologist,[4] much of the land occupied by profitable plantations in the lower Congo valley would, if transported to Belgium, be heath or utterly barren moorland.

So great is their poverty in bases that tropical soils are acid, a condition unfavourable to good use of the humus. But cultivated tropical plants are adapted to acid conditions, and tropical agriculture

1. J. S. Beard; *Land Utilisation Survey of Trinidad, Farm and Forest* (Ibadan), Dec. 1941, p. 133. A very suggestive study of the relations between tropical or equatorial forest and the soil is given in G. Mangenot, *Etude sur les fôrets des plaines et plateaux de la Côte d'Ivoire* (Institut Français d'Afrique noir, études éburnéennes, IV, 1955, pp. 1–83).
2. G. Wiegner, *Anleitung zum Quantitativen Agrikultur-Chemischen Praktikum* Berlin, 1926.
3. See below, p. 21–2.
4. J. Baeyens, *Les sols de l'Afrique centrale, spécialement du Congo belge*, vol. I; *Le Bas-Congo*, pub. by INEAC, Brussels, Supplement No. 6, 1938, p. 22. For these pedological problems see also E. C. J. Mohr and F. A. van Baren, *Tropical Soils, a critical study of soil genesis as related to climate, rock, and vegetation*, The Hague, van Hoeve, 1954, p. 498.

is satisfied with the poorest soils, provided that they have a suitable physical texture, that is to say, that they are sufficiently friable.

Is the poverty of tropical soils reflected in their crop yields? It is tempting to think so, for statistics show that the yield per acre of rice or maize is much lower in tropical than in temperate lands, and a comparison of Java with Japan seems to clinch the matter, for in the former the rice yield is 1,650 lbs. per acre and in the latter 4,460. But perhaps it would be better not to make such comparisons, for almost inevitably the items in question will not be strictly comparable.

Thus in the case of Java and Japan, the Javanese paddy field never receives any chemical fertilizer, and little organic matter either, whereas the Japanese rice crop is deluged with all sorts of stimulants to growth, both organic and inorganic; it is thus difficult to attribute the difference in yields to natural soil fertility. Other comparisons encounter similar difficulties; besides, are not the cultivated fields very largely what man has made them? Intensive methods can transform poor soils into heavy yielders, as the Flemish peasants have done in the fields of Flanders and the Chinese in Malaya. The latter, at the cost of immense labour and the application of abundant organic manure, have even transformed the sterile wastes of the tin dredgings into market gardens.

One might expect that, given equal fertility, tropical soils would give better yields than those of temperate lands. Tropical agriculture benefits from higher temperatures and a year-long growing season; only drought (which can be countered by irrigation) can cause a stoppage in the cycle of agricultural operations, and harvests can be reaped in every month of the year. But are these real advantages? The answer is not as clear as it might appear at first sight. Account must also be taken of the influence of daylight (and the absence of the long days of higher latitudes) and of the extent of cloud cover, which greatly reduces insolation during the rainy seasons. These influences have been the subject of various interpretations; some authors have considered that they lower crop yields[1]; it seems, however, that no advantage in insolation can be claimed for the temperate lands around the 50th parallel where very high wheat yields are obtained. An ingenious comparison of soya bean yields under excellent temperate climatic conditions and in an equatorial climate does not prove that the latter is better.[2] Nevertheless, it ought to be possible in a tropical

1. E. Fukui, 'Climatic superiority of the middle latitudes', *Proc. I.G.U. Regional Conference*. Tokyo, 1957, pp. 112–16. E. Bernard, *Le climat ecologique de la cuvette centrale angolaise*, Brussels, INEAC scientific series, 1945.
2. P. Sapin 'Le soja a Yangambi', *Bull. Inform. INEAC*, 1958, pp. 105–16.

climate to obtain two or even three harvests of soya (or some other crop) in twelve months, given irrigation and manure, and this would certainly not be possible in temperate lands.

Soils in the rainy tropics are usually poor in mineral matter that can be utilized by plants, such as lime, magnesia, potash, phosphates and nitrates. This generalization however, should not obscure the great variety of soil that exists; as elsewhere, there are rich soils and poor soils, clay soils and sandy soils, thin soils and deep soils. A large-scale map would show a mosaic in the tropics just as in other parts of the world. In East Africa pedologists have recognized a succession of varied soils—a 'catena'—from hill-top to valley-bottom, each with different agricultural potential. In south-west Nigeria the cacao plantations are to be found on soils derived from the weathering of crystalline rocks; they do not succeed on the Benin sands, further south and in a climate actually more favourable to the cacao tree. But rubber will grow here.

Tropical soils are also usually very poor in soluble elements, for the copious warm rains lead to the rapid and deep leaching of the soluble elements in the soil which are derived from the alteration of mineral particles and from the mineralization of the organic matter. The warmer the water and the greater its acidity, the greater is its power of hydrolysis. In the equatorial regions the streams and percolating waters lead to rivers which are very poor in both dissolved and suspended matter, thus confirming the state of exhaustion of the soils from which they have drained. This is as true of the Congo as of the Amazon. In the latter river, the quantity of dissolved matter in samples taken three feet below the surface at Obidos averaged 0·0545 grammes per litre (of which 0·0146 was carbonate of lime and 0·0122 silica); the quantity of suspended matter was 0·1966 grammes per litre, consisting of silt, fine quartz sand, diatomaceous debris and vegetable matter. The amount of silica both in suspension and in solution is noteworthy and corroborates observations made on other tropical rivers, such as the Niger. It is thus not surprising that, given this abundance of quartz sand and diatom spicules, the deposits of the Amazonian floods are not generally good alluvial soil but more often *tijuco*, which is a kind of tripoli stone or diatomaceous earth; in the lower reaches of the river these *tijuco* deposits become dangerous quicksands (*areias gulosas*) at low tide.

Whilst the Amazon transports 0·1966 grammes per litre of suspended matter, the Congo, near its mouth, carries only 0·0385 g. This might be due to the existence of the quiet waters of Stanley Pool above the rapids of the lower valley; but on the other hand it seems that the river is equally poorly charged above the Pool, where in any case the current is far from being negligible, and that the alluvia of the lower valley were derived from the basin above Léopoldville. The suspended matter carried out to sea by the Congo amounts to 47 million tons a year as against 600 million by the Amazon. The Congo thus resembles the *rios negros* of the Amazon basin; the inhabitants of the latter recognize a distinction between the *rios brancos*, with turbid waters, slightly opaque and of red or whitish colour, and the *rios negros* or *pretos* which have dark limpid waters, slightly coloured brown by minute quantities or iron-stained organic matter. The Amazon itself, a *rio branco*, carries 0·1966 grammes per litre in suspension at Obidos, but its tributary the Xingu, a *rio negro*, has 0·0875 g. above Porto de Moz, and the Tapajós, another *rio negro*, 0·0912 at Itaituba.

The Amazon, as we have noted, carries 0·1966 grammes of suspended matter per litre; the Congo carries 0·0385 g, the Mississippi 0·638 g, the Yangtse-Kiang 0·930 g and the Hoang Ho 4·8 g. The basins of the true tropical rivers have soils which are too leached to yield large quantities of silt and soluble products. It is significant that at the beginning of the rainy season there is a rapid multiplication of plankton in the waters of the Amazon; once the rains have commenced, the plankton population reverts to normal. This is because the first rains, running over and through the soil after the dry season, carry small quantities of organic matter and even of mineral substances, which stimulate the plankton; once the first flush is over the percolating waters resume their habitual poverty.

Rivers in equatorial regions are incapable of building great alluvial plains of rich earth. The Amazon, with an annual mean flow of 200,000 cubic metres a second, has entrenched its valley between sandy terraces. The valley proper is only a few miles wide, and where the river itself broadens, as around Gurupá and Obidos, to something over five or six miles, the waters wash the edge of the bounding terrace, reducing the alluvial plain almost to nothing. The enormous expansion of the Tapajós above Santarem is a lake without any alluvial plain. The mouth of the Amazon is not a true delta, for the islands in between the distributaries—like Marajó—are ancient terraces left stranded by the deepening of the Amazon branches. A somewhat similar false delta appears at the mouth of the Congo.

Tropical soils are generally formed from the upper part of a thick mantle of altered rock. The solid rock is always 30 feet down, and sometimes as much as 100 feet or more, particularly if it consists of coarse-grained granite or gneiss which is very susceptible to chemical weathering by tepid waters that are heavily charged with carbonic acid, nitric acid (derived from thunderstorms) and humic acids. Just as the rains cause the rapid leaching of the soil, so they attack the rocks beneath.[1] This sort of thing is very widespread, for by a remarkable coincidence a large part of the tropical world is occupied by ancient plateaus—Guiana, Brazil, intertropical Africa, peninsular India and northern Australia.[2] They are composed of pre-Cambrian rocks, often granitic in character, and up to 4,000 million years old. These ancient massifs have shown a remarkable stability throughout geological time; they have been warped, uplifted, downfaulted and broken, but never folded; the crystalline basement is usually exposed, for sediments and lavas have only in places covered it.

Stable and emergent, these ancient plateaus have been levelled by successive erosion surfaces, from which only here and there rise *inselbergs* which have resisted planation either by reason of a hard rock outcrop or because of a wider mesh of joints that has locally slowed down the rate of water penetration and solution. These inselbergs are sometimes reduced to a chaotic mass of blocks severed along the joints. The peneplain surfaces of the crystalline massifs are not only accidented by the upstanding inselbergs, whether these be of 'sugarloaf' form or piles of blocks; they are also seamed by systems of flat-bottomed valleys with convex sides and amphitheatres at their upper end. On a map the pattern of these valleys is like the veins of an oak leaf or the antlers of a reindeer; the valleys are outlined by ribbons of forest whilst the interfluves carry savannas.

The erosion surfaces which have planed these old massifs are covered with very ancient soils which are worn out with age. They all consist, from the oldest to the youngest, of pure quartz sands that are the final residue from the decomposition of the crystalline rocks. Such sands, sometimes hardened into sandstone, form monotonous coverings to some parts of the tropical massifs, as in Roraima in the Guianas and Umpata in southern Angola; they give rise inevitably to poor and sandy soils. In some places where climatic action has been at work for a very long time on the tropical massifs the end-product has been the formation of a lateritic crust, as we shall see later on (p. 24).

The ease of leaching is due in part to the feeble capacity for adsorption of tropical soils; they cannot retain fertilizers because they are poor in humus, because their clays have an unfavourable structure and because they have a tendency to accumulate inert lateritic elements.

1. The rapidity of rock-weathering is not necessarily a disadvantage, for it also means that soils suitable for agriculture are quickly formed. Thus in St Vincent, in the Antilles, the ash from the Soufrière volcano was converted into soil capable of bearing forests and crops in less than thirty years. (F. Hardy, 'Soils and soil erosion in St Vincent', *Tropical Agriculture*, 16, 1939, pp. 58–65.)

2. A penetrating study of the relief and soils of these ancient tropical plateaus is that by G. Rougerie, *Le façonnement actual des modelés en Côte d'Ivoire forestière.* Dakar, 1960.

1. A mosquito haunt. A mangrove swamp through which the River Pachu runs on the island of Choiseul in the Solomons. Note the roots of the mangroves and the stillness of the water.

2. Malaria control. Cleaning the banks of the Milk River so as to remove mosquito-breeding pools.

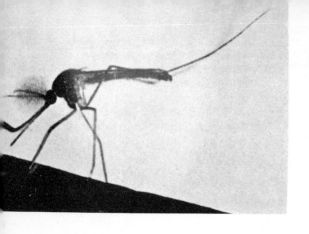

3. *Anopheles quadrimaculatus* with its proboscis plunged into man's arm.

4. A tsetse fly (*Glossina palpalis*).

5. A Madrasi boy suffering from elephantiasis ("Barbados leg").

Even in the forest humus blackens the soil to a depth of only a few inches; but the quantity of organic matter deposited is considerable. It has been estimated at Yangambi in Congo-Léopoldville at between twenty and twenty-five tons of leaves, twigs, lianas, and branches per annum per acre.[1] But in these forests the deposits do not enrich the soil, for they are offset by equivalent losses, with the result that the soil contains at most 1·8 per cent of humus, whilst fertile soil in temperate regions often contains more than 10 per cent.

The explanation is that organic matter is quickly decomposed and reduced to the condition of soluble minerals and easily lost to the soil. First of all it is broken down by countless insects, the most active being termites, some species of which feed on humus and thus destroy it.[2] Insects and microbes rapidly transform organic matter and humus; in Java the humus content of the surface-layer of the soil was shown to rise from 5 per cent at an altitude of 1,000 feet above sea level and a mean annual temperature of 76° F (24·5° C) to 14 per cent at an altitude of 3,250 feet and a mean temperature of 68° F (20° C). The organic nitrogen is soon transformed into nitrates which, being in too great a quantity for the needs of the forest trees, are dissolved by the water and finally lost. This is one of the great differences between

1. A. Beirnaert, *La Technique culturale sous l'Équateur*, I. *Influence de la culture sur les réserves en humus et en azote des terres équatoriales*, pub. INEAC, Technical Series, No. 6, 1941, p. 12.

2. The effect produced by termites is various. Though termites are great destroyers of organic matter and humus it is agreed, on the other hand, that termitaries are often more fertile than the soil on which they stand. On the light, sandy soil of eastern Siam termitaries give soil that is heavier, more clayey, and neutral or basic, whilst the natural soil is acid. Rich crops of cotton, tobacco, mulberry, beans, pineapples, or sugar cane may flourish on termitary soils (R. L. Pendleton, *Geog. Review*, 1942, p. 323). Elsewhere the advantages of the termitaries are less certain; it all depends on the nature of the subsoil. If the subsoil is fertile, it is useful to have it brought to the surface, but if it is poorer than the surface soil, it is a hindrance to have it covering the latter. Thus conditions vary greatly from one place to another. The genus *Odontotermes*, that cultivates fungi in a central chamber, ensures a great concentration of both organic and mineral matter, but when the termitary is abandoned this quickly disappears. See P. Grassé, 'Termites et sols tropicaux', *Rev. Bot. Appliquée*, 1937, pp. 549–54; also Ph. Boyer, 'De l'influence des termites de la zone intertropicale sur la configuration de certains sols', *Rev. de Géomorph. dynamique*, 1959, pp. 41–4. The termitaries can be very useful if they occur on a lateritic crust, since they cover this with light soil. But these termite mounds can also present quite an agricultural problem by obstructing the movement of ploughs and tractors. They must be knocked down and their soil strewn over the field; but this is rough work. In the open forest of Katanga there are about three giant termite mounds to the acre, covering 6 per cent of the area; their destruction would cover the entire acre to a depth of 8 inches. The complete clearance of such an area would require 150 man-days for clearing the forest, six days with a tractor to remove the tree stumps, seven hours with a bulldozer to level the ground, five hours with a deep plough to extract the roots, at a total cost of 11,000 Belgian francs per acre in 1959. (M. Jottrand and E. Detilleux, 'Le problème des termitières dans la région d'Elisabethville', *INEAC Info. Bull.*, Brussels, 1959, pp. 112–29.)

the humid tropics and the temperate belt; for, whilst temperate agriculture must overcome the slow rate at which organic nitrogen places itself at the disposal of plants, tropical agriculture must, on the contrary, worry over the waste of nitrogen. The loss of nitrogen is reckoned at between 60 and 70 lb per acre per annum in the loams of temperate regions and at between 170 and 270 lb in hot, wet lands. A rise in temperature favours the loss of nitrogen. Above 79° F a rise of one degree in the temperature of the soil leads to an increased loss of humic nitrogen amounting to between 15 and 25 lb per acre per annum, which is equivalent to between 100 and 125 lb of sulphate of ammonia.

It is easy to verify the fact that an application of manure in the tropics makes its effect felt for far less time than in the temperate regions: a few months only, instead of two or three years. Roots left in soil cleared for cultivation disappear far more quickly in tropical lands.

The equatorial forest does not increase the quantity of humus, but maintains it. If the forest is destroyed, the soil no longer receives the organic matter indispensable for making humus, whilst the processes by which the humus is decomposed continue to act and are even accelerated because lack of cover makes the temperature of the soil rise. Whilst the surface-layer of soil does not exceed 77° or 79° F (25° or 26° C), under forest, it may reach 104° F (40° C) after the bush has been cleared away. Now, the rate at which humus (and organic nitrogen) deteriorates increases with the temperature.[1]

It should be added that bare soil is subject to great alterations in dryness and damp, and the alternate penetration of air and water into the macropores of the soil is harmful to it. What happens is that the water drives out the carbon dioxide before being replaced by air. Thus, the oxygen is continually being renewed, which is favourable to the combustion of the humus during the midday heat, and this combustion adds to the effect of bacteria. Turning up the soil with the hoe as well as with the plough aggravates the situation still further by favouring a rise in temperature.

The destruction of the forest and the denudation of the soil have another disadvantage, for percolation is greater through the bare soil than underneath the forest cover, and the percolating waters leach the nitrates and bases from the soil. Evaporation from bare soil has been

1. According to E. C. J. Mohr, who is quoted by Baeyens on p. 101 of the work mentioned above on p. 16, n. 4, when the temperature of the soil remains about 77° F (25° C) equilibrium is established in tropical regions between the production of green matter and its mineralization. Below that temperature an accumulation of humus takes place; above it, humic matter gradually disappears. The optimum temperature for chlorophyll assimilation is between 68° and 77° F (20° and 25° C) and the optimum for microbic activity between 86° and 95° F (30° and 35° C).

estimated[1] at about 40 inches in the equatorial zone between the equator and latitude 10 degrees, whilst a dense cover of vegetation transpires at least 60 inches; consequently there is much more water available for percolation and leaching in bare ground than under forest.

The impoverishment of the soil in humus results in weakening the 'adsorbent complex'; and the structure of tropical clays contributes to the same effect. Clays in temperate latitudes are *montmorillonites*; detailed analysis shows that the hydrated silicate of alumina has a foliated micro-crystalline structure, with alternating plates of silica and alumina. The spaces which separate these plates play a vital role, for they greatly increase the surface area that can attract and retain such elements as potash, ammonia, lime and magnesia; and clays are thus important agents in preserving soil fertility in temperate lands. In contrast, clays in tropical lands, as a result of chemical actions that are linked with climate, have lost a large part of their silica (which appears as we have noted in the river water) and are in effect *kaolinites* which, though containing material with a foliated micro-structure, as described above, also have a large proportion of hydroxides of alumina and iron in very minute crystals, and these are disposed in such a way as to hinder the retention of the fertile elements.[2]

Tropical soils thus have a tendency to contain a large quantity of inert matter, which on the one hand contributes nothing to the fertility and on the other does not help to prevent the loss by leaching of the fertile elements that are present. Amongst these inert elements are quartz-grains, fragments of hydroxide of iron or of alumina, and an appreciable proportion of kaolinite. The copious and tepid percolating waters will thus soon dissolve and carry away the fertile elements that the deficient clay and the all too rare humus are incapable of holding back. Tropical soils are thus quickly exhausted once they are cultivated; as an example, the yellowish leaves of the Congo oil palms show an extreme deficiency in magnesia.[3]

The rapid leaching is less harmful if the mineral particles of the decomposing rock beneath quickly liberate the nutrient salts that

1. C. Coster, 'De verdamping van verschillende vegetatie vormen of Java', *Tectona*, 1937, p. 28.

2. M. C. Gastuche, 'La genèse des minéraux argileux', *Rev. des questions scientifiques*, Louvain CXXX 5 e, session XX. 1959, pp. 63–92; G. Waegemans, 'Introduction a l'étude de la latéritisation et des latérites du Centre African', *Bull. agr. Congo Belge*, 1951, pp. 13–53; 'Latérites et bauxites', *id.* 1951, pp. 567–74; 'Latérites mésolithiques et scoriacées', *id.* 1952, pp. 735–49; *Les latérites de Gimbi (Bas Congo)*, Brussels, INEAC, 1954.

3. M. Ferrand, 'La carence magnésienne dans les palmeraies de la cuvette central congolaise', *A.R.S.C. B. séances*, 1958, pp. 531–46.

they contain; this is particularly the case with dark minerals such as olivine. Sometimes such mineral particles are present but their rate of decomposition is too slow to compensate the losses by leaching; but more often the country rock has no such minerals at all.

The capacity to retain fertile elements is finally reduced by the increase in the proportion of iron and aluminium hydroxides in the soil, that is, the tendency to lateritization. This kind of process is not, it is true, confined to the tropics, for the temperate lands also show soil impoverishment in the case of the 'podsols', consisting of grey quartz sand from which the clay and the bases have been leached, whilst the hydroxide of iron accumulates below as a hard-pan. But in the tropics the process of lateritization is much more in evidence. A soil may become encumbered with lateritizing substances either by the loss of its non-lateritic components (bases, silica and silicates) or by the addition of iron hydroxide from elsewhere, most likely from the upper layers.[1]

So long as the soil, full of lateritic elements, remains loose, it can be used for agriculture; and it can continue to be cultivated even if the lateritic elements have coagulated into small gravel,[2] though it should be noted that since in such a case part of the soil has become inert, good crops can only be obtained if the rest of the soil is deep and rich.[3] The cassava plantations on the terraces of Travancore in southern India are quite successful even though the pebbly lateritic soil looks just like railway ballast; for there is loose soil underneath the pebbly layer, from which rainwash has removed the finer particles; the concentration of lateritic gravel has at least the advantage that it protects the layers underneath from erosion.

Over vast areas of the tropical world, laterite is in the form of a concretionary crust, which is formed either by the agglomeration of gravels through the agency of lateritizing solutions, or by the formation from such solutions of a spongy, vesicular rock, reddish-black in colour, which may in fact be almost an iron ore.[4] The formation of these lateritic crusts is the result of a long pedological evolution which has been accomplished on very ancient peneplain surfaces; and it is thus not surprising that the senile morphology of the vast crystalline massifs of the intertropical zone has been fossilized by these lateritic carapaces.

1. J. d'Hoore, 'L'accumulation des sesquioxydes libres dans les sols tropicaux', Brussels, *INEAC série scientifique*, No. 62, 1954.
2. J. Baeyens, *op. cit.*
3. It should also be noted that in many cases the presence of hydroxides of alumina or of manganese may hinder the use of certain chemical fertilizers which would form salts toxic to plant life.
4. Bauxites, which are alumina-rich laterites, are rare and of great economic value; another peculiar variety is the phosphatic laterite of the Thiès region of Senegal, which is worked as phosphate rock.

So long as the crusts remain buried, they do no great harm to agriculture; this is the case with the lateritic horizons which are seen to jut out on the sandy-clay scarps that overlook the valleys of Amazonian tributaries such as the Rio Pará, the Tapajós, and the Rio Negro. But unfortunately the crusts are at the surface over vast areas, for the loose soil which covered them has been removed by erosion. This erosion may have been due to soil creep, to changes of climate or to the influence of man. Such lateritic crusts, called *bowal* in Guinea, *khoai* in west Bengal, are sterile and forbidding wastes, covered with a black patina; the slabs of laterite are impermeable and collect pools of water after rain. The crust is often broken by a network of fissures, which result from the subsidence of the ground immediately underneath. A little soil accumulates in these fissures, and trees growing therein can help to split the crust still further. The crust is also sapped at its projecting outcrops on the sides of valleys, so that eventually it may disappear. In the hinterland of Santarem, in Brazil, such a crust has indeed almost disappeared, leaving occasional *buttes-témoins* which are the only upstanding features on an otherwise flat and dreary landscape.

The crystalline plateaux of Madagascar are usually covered with a thick mantle of decomposed rock, sometimes reaching a depth of 300 feet. The upper part of the mantle is heavily lateritized, though without the appearance of a crust. The lateritic surfaces of these *tampoketsa* are hard and impermeable. The Merina and Betsileo people build the walls of their huts and gardens of puddled laterite; such walls are almost completely avoided by vegetation, neither moss, nor fungus nor any higher form of plant life taking root thereon, though plants grow readily on walls of baked brick.

This Malgash laterite is so completely impermeable that the peasants make store pits for grain in it simply by digging holes with spades; once the crust is pierced they can make their silo in the earth underneath. This is exactly the process by which erosion, having made a gully in the lateritic bed, enlarges the excavation into a wide hollow or *lavaka*.

True lateritic crusts may end up by becoming harder than most rocks; they can be quarried, and the laterite actually hardens still further on exposure to the atmosphere. This fact is noticeable in certain Khmer ruins. The Khmers used to build their magnificent edifices of laterite, covering the laterite with a veneer of sandstone. Sandstone lends itself to carving, whilst laterite cannot be chiselled owing to its cellular structure. It has been found that sandstone is less resistant than laterite to the agents of erosion; e.g. in the temple of Ban Gu near Roi Esh in north-eastern Siam the sandstone base of a door-frame has been eroded by the salts which rise by capillary attraction during the dry season, whilst the immediately adjacent laterite remains intact.[1]

The clearance of the forest is probably responsible for the surface outcrop of many laterites, for once the forest has gone the covering of loose soil which concealed the crust is rapidly removed; this is probably what happened in the *khoai* of western Bengal, where the removal of the forests of *sal* (*Shorea robusta*) set erosion in motion.

The *terra rossa* that covers limestone rocks can also give rise to lateritic soils. But the evolution of the land forms in limestone terrain under a rainy tropical climate can give rise to bizarre relief that is unfavourable to human occupation. An extreme case of this hostility to man is found in the district of Ke Bang on the borders of Annam and Laos between lat. 17° and 18° N. Here the Uralo-Permian limestones are completely uninhabited over an area of from 2,000 to 2,300 square miles. There is not a single inhabitant in a district as big as a French department, although the rainfall is 60 inches a year and the altitude is moderate, rising no higher than 3,000 feet. But the relief consists of an infinite series of steep-sided peaks crisscrossed with narrow cracks (*lapiés*). The peaks, up to 600 feet high, touch each other at their bases and give no room between them for flat-bottomed valleys or enclosed hollows filled with *terra rossa*. There are no streams, for the drainage percolates through the rock; nor is there any path, and one's progress is an exhausting succession of ups and downs over rough rocks fortunately covered with trees on which the hand can find a hold.

Only a few clay-bottomed hollows on the borders are inhabited, and even so one reaches them only by a hazardous crossing by means of ladders over ramparts of limestone. The pigs and buffaloes in them have been carried thither in their owners' arms when quite young and cannot escape from these vertically-sided amphitheatres.

To explain this kind of relief certain special conditions must be taken into account. The very hard limestone has been greatly folded and has been exposed for a long time to the action of erosion. The fact remains, nevertheless, that this type of relief which is utterly hostile to man has been caused by the tropical climate with its warm, heavy rain laden with carbonic acid. The Ke Bang district is the world's largest expanse of desert exclusively connected with the nature of the rock and with the relief—a low relief at that. The same facts are found again, though on smaller areas, in other parts of North Vietnam, Laos, Siam, eastern Burma, in the *magotes* of the Guani-

1. R. L. Pendleton, 'Laterite and its structural uses in Thailand and Cambodia' *Geog. Review*, 1941, pp. 177–202.

guanico Hills in Cuba,[1] in the islands of Japan and Waigeu,[2] in the neighbourhood of Coban in the district of Alta Verapaz in Guatemala, and elsewhere. Java's Duizendgebergte ('Thousand Mountains') are a milder form of the same type of landscape. In temperate lands limestone never gives rise to forms so hostile to man at a low altitude.[3]

Those parts of the tropics that are fortunate enough not to consist of ancient plateaux, and not to be afflicted with the kind of limestone surface described above, have one great advantage, the possibility of being covered by soils which are freshly developed on terrain of immature relief. Orogenic movements and volcanic eruptions have rejuvenated the soils and hindered the formation of crusts. But the rebirth must have been quite recent, for even the alluvia of Pleistocene terraces are already leached and lateritized, as in the jungle of Madhupur in eastern Bengal, and in the Biên Hoa district of South Vietnam. On the other hand, rivers flowing from alpine fold-mountains are charged with fertile alluvium which builds up into rich deltaic lands like those of the Red River, the Mekong, Menam, Irrawaddy, Brahmaputra, Ganges and Indus. Thus south-east Asia is exceptionally favoured, for in addition to these deltas there are the recent volcanic soils of Java, as well as the limestones of low relief in Madura which are no less cultivated and just as densely peopled as the Javanese volcanoes.[4]

Tropical soils that are well protected by a vegetative cover, whether of dense forest or of savanna, suffer but little from sheet or gully erosion. The intervention of man, however, may have disastrous consequences; forest clearance, cultivation, over-grazing and the treading of flocks and herds expose the bare soil to the tropical rainstorms, particularly on sloping land.[5] In the inter-Andine region of Ecuador, for example, between Loja and Cuence, three-quarters of

1. H. H. Bennett, 'Some geographic aspects of Cuban soils', *Geog. Review*, 1928, pp. 62–82.
2. L. E. Cheesman, 'Two unexplored islands of Dutch New Guinea', *Geographical Journal*, 1940, I, pp. 208–17.
3. See G. Lesserre, *La Guadeloupe*, Bordeaux, 1962, pp. 58–91, for an excellent discussion of the problems of limestone morphology in the rainy tropics.
4. A study by I. W. C. Dames, *The Soils of East Central Java*, Bogor. Contributions of the general agricultural research station, 1955, shows that one cannot determine the fertility of the soil by the number of people it supports. The mean density in the area of 5,800 square miles investigated in eastern Java was 958 per square mile; however 36·7 per cent of the area gave poor agricultural yields, 12 per cent low yields and 33·5 per cent only average yields.
5. In the Pabbi mountains in the Punjab, M. Maclagan Gorrie *Congr. internat. de géog.* Amsterdam 1938, *Géographie coloniale*, pp. 405–16, noted that in rainfall of average intensity, the run-off from a slope covered with dense forest was 1·1 cub. m. per second per sq. km.; from a slope covered with bush, 6·6 cub. m.; from a grassy slope with occasional trees, 11 cub. m. and from a slope bared by over-grazing, 18 cub. m.

the original cultivated area has had to be abandoned owing to soil erosion.[1]

The removal of the fertile topsoil and the creation of a network of gullies is a disaster. But is it any worse than in the Mediterranean regions or in the loess area of northern China? It does not appear that the rainy tropics are particularly ill-favoured, and indeed it is possible, though a little paradoxical, that in large parts of the tropics erosion would be a good thing rather than a danger, and one can envisage with satisfaction the wholesale sweeping away of the lateritic crusts, the hard lateritized soils, the sandstone pavements and the leached sands. That good may come from what appears to be bad is not surprising—but it can hardly happen in a day.

It is possible to counteract soil erosion. The construction of banks and horizontal furrows along the contour lines is widespread in eastern Africa and in Rwanda-Burundi, but it is a method that has its limitations, for when the slope gets steeper than about 15 degrees the fields become very narrow, thus ruling out the possibility of substituting machines for human labour and condemning the peasants to a life of toil; and it involves bringing to the surface undesirable materials from the subsoil. It is little wonder that the African peasants themselves question the wisdom of these anti-erosion measures, for they reckon that the damage caused by the occasional and accidental breaking of one of the banks is greater than the erosion that would occur if there were no banks and ditches at all.

From the moment of his rather belated discovery of the tropical world, European man developed an exaggerated idea of the fertility of the hot, wet lands, from which came first the traditional spices, then later on sugar, tobacco, coffee and cocoa. Disappointment has led to a modification of these views—but what is now the balance of opinion? An appreciable part of the tropical lands is devoid of agricultural value, either by reason of rock outcrops (limestone karst, sandy tableland, crystalline inselbergs) or more commonly of lateritic crusts; this sterility is sometimes concealed by the desperate eagerness of men to cultivate the odd pockets of arable soil. But political changes may cease to fix these people to the soil, as has been seen in the case of the Dogons of the Bandiagara plateau, the Kabré in Togoland the Kirdi in northern Cameroon.

The greater part of the tropical lands consists of very mediocre soils, mainly sandy, poor in humus, in clay and in fertile elements, but sufficiently friable for cultivation. Conditions vary very widely, and whilst the sands of the Kwango and Kwila plateaus in Congo-Léopoldville are of extreme poverty, the sandy soils of southern Nigeria are much better.

1. *Geog. Review* 1944, p. 64.

Only a small part of the tropical lands is naturally very fertile; such areas are those of recent formation in which the processes of leaching and lateritization have not yet had time to evolve—soils derived from basic volcanic ash or from basaltic lavas (like the *roxas* of São Paulo), recent alluvia charged with fertile materials, or forest soils developed from the deep decomposition of crystalline rocks rich in dark-coloured minerals. These are only some of the possible types, and there is an immense variety; though the zonal or latitudinal tendency for the rapid leaching of bases, humus and clay is a very real one, local diversity based on the underlying rocks and on the surface relief makes the detailed soil maps bear some resemblance to contour maps on the one hand and to geological maps on the other.

The soils of the humid temperate zone have many advantages over those of the humid tropics: the temperate soils develop more slowly and so preserve for a much longer time their nitrogen, their bases and their clay fraction, whilst the alternation of frost and thaw at the beginning and end of winter contributes to their friability. The winter season, indeed, is of much more value than the dry season, which is the equivalent 'close-season' for agriculture in the tropics. Furthermore, in temperate oceanic climates the regular and gentle rains provoke but moderate erosion of the surface soil, whilst the temperate regions as a whole have often inherited from Pleistocene periglacial conditions loams of a richness that is seldom encountered in the tropics.

As a whole, tropical soils are poorer and more fragile than those of temperate lands. To harness them for a stable agriculture, capable of regular annual harvests, thus requires careful and refined techniques which have more respect for the soil and for its enrichment than is the case in the temperate zone. Since such techniques have been but rarely applied in the tropical lands, it is not surprising that the density of population is often low and that civilization suffers through lack of mastery of the thin and unstable soil. But the primary responsibility for this state of affairs lies with civilization rather than with the soil, for Asiatic paddy culture can assure an adequate food supply for an extremely dense population. This rice cultivation is a development of the civilizations concerned and does not depend on the soil, for one can find it equally on the steep slopes of Luzon and on the deltaic plains. Similarly, modern agronomic methods can give large and regular yields in many tropical areas, such as 13,000 lb of cane sugar per acre per year in Hawaii, over 4,000 lb of palm oil in the plantations of north-eastern Sumatra, and over 2,000 lb of rubber in the Malay peninsula. On the other hand, however, extensive agriculture practised on the poor and fragile soils which are most common in the tropics can only be unstable and insecure, and such conditions are unfavourable to the development of a high civilization. The low population density and the poverty that characterize the greater part of the tropical world are due to a combination of civilization and soil; but this combination, so widespread as to be a major geographical characteristic, is not inevitable.[1]

1. A broad examination of the problems created by tropical soils will be found in *Comptes rendus de la deuxième conférence inter-Africaine des sols*, Léopoldville, 1954, 2 vols. (Brussels, Ministère des Colonies).

CHAPTER 4

The Characteristic Agriculture of the Tropics

OVER a large part of the rainy tropics agriculture conforms to the same general technological pattern, the object of which is to produce carbohydrates, the basis of human food, by shifting cultivation without the aid of irrigation. The forest trees are felled with axes, and when dry the vegetation is burnt; after the crop harvest the patch lies fallow and the forest regains control until it is once more burnt. The axe is more useful than the hoe; often the soil is not tilled at all, and no manure is added. This form of agriculture is known under many different local names—*ladang* (Indonesia), *ray* (Laos), *caingin* (Philippines), *taungya* (Burma), *jhum* (Assam), *bewar* (Central India), *podu* (Telugu-speaking parts of India), *milpa* or *coamile* (Mexico), *conuco* (Venezuela), *roça* (Brazil), *masole* (lower Congo). Here we shall use only *ladang*. We shall discuss later the relations between this agricultural system and the natural environment; here we may merely note that ladang is appropriate for poor soils, for the cultivated crops benefit from the fertility given by the wood-ash. Other forms of agriculture are also possible however, in the rainy tropics, such as flood-irrigated rice cultivation, rubber plantations, and so on. Ladang is not imposed by natural conditions but corresponds to a certain level of civilization; indeed, as we shall see, it may actually be more productive in terms of labour than more advanced techniques.

The cultivator marks out a piece of forest, regularly chosen for its special fertility. This quality is indicated by certain plants. In Brazil preference is given to land in which grow *padræs*, or tree-guides, especially *Gallesia gorasema*. In the Cameroons the Bulus like soils which favour *Thaumatococcus danielli* and *Cassia abata*. In Dahomey the cultivator tastes a pinch of soil to test its fertility.

Then the undergrowth is cleared and the big trees felled. The biggest trees, and those which yield edible fruits, may be spared, for they are useful for fixing the soil and protecting it from erosion; or it may be thought sufficient to kill them by ring-barking. Usually the trees are felled about six feet from the ground, because in hot lands trees generally have buttresses which widen their bases, and so to cut them off at ground-level would be labour wasted. In consequence of all this, the ground remains bristling with trunks and presents a hirsute appearance.

31

As the natural vegetation would not burn without it, clearing is necessary. When the Light and Power Co. wished to destroy the forest which was to be flooded by their dams in the State of São Paulo, they had to spray it with mineral oil in order to burn it, as they did not wish to go to the expense of felling the trees.[1]

When the trees and branches are dry, they are burnt.[2] At the end of the dry season columns of smoke rising in every direction indicate the work of clearing. Destruction by fire is easier than any other method when one's only implements are the hoe and an inadequate axe.[3] If necessary, some precautions are taken to prevent the fire from spreading to the rest of the forest, but this is generally unnecessary, since the rain forest contains little combustible material. The soil is enriched with ashes from the fire. To secure greater fertility in the very poor soils of their open forests the Bembas and Lalas in Zambia pile up on the chosen patch branches collected from all around; and in doing this they remove the vegetation from an area six or eight times larger than that of the patch. The havoc caused by their *chitimene* is therefore considerable, though it is less than it might be, since they are satisfied to use the boughs and do not fell the trunks, so that the trees are able to sprout again. Climbing the trees to cut off the branches is a sport that calls for plenty of pluck. The men display great rivalry and daring; and accidents are frequent. The women pile up the branches in heaps about three feet high.[4]

The firing of the patch cleared is an operation of dubious value, if the effects are carefully weighed. It leaves fertile ashes, but destroys per acre between 250 and 450 tons of organic matter which would

1. P. Deffontaines, in *Bull. de la Société de Géographie de Lille*, 1939, p. 58.
2. On the subject of these bush-fires here and farther on, see G. Kuhnholz-Lordat, *La terre incendiée, essai d'agronomie comparée*, Nîmes, 1938. See also H. H. Bartlett, *Fire in Relation to Primitive Agriculture and Grazing in the Tropics*, Annotated Bibliography (Supplement to Background Paper No. 34, Wenner-Gren Foundation Internat. Symposium: Man's Role in Changing the Face of the Earth, Princeton, U.S.A., 1955).
3. The Amerindians in the Amazon basin used to burn the trunks little by little so as not to use their wretched stone axes more than necessary. Hence, the arrival of iron implements with the Europeans caused a considerable technical revolution. 'A very few strokes of the steel axe were enough to modify the conditions of labour, to increase the area felled, and double and even treble the harvests.' Hence, after the discovery of America there was among the Indians a thirst for iron as great as that felt by Europeans for gold. Iron gave an assurance of superiority over one's enemies. (A. Métraux, 'Le caractère de la conquête jésuitique', *Acta Americana*, Jan.-March 1943, pp. 69–82.)
4. A. I. Richards, *Land, Labour, and Diet in Rhodesia*, Oxford, 1939, p. 288. See also M. D. U. Peeters, *Land Usage in Serenje District, Rhodesia*, Livingston Paper No. 19, Oxford, 1950. In the Serenje plateau, each Lala family destroys 18 acres of open forest, piling the branches and trunks on 1¼ acres; the cultivable surface is about 60 per cent of the total area, and since the fallow period lasts for twenty-two years and there are 6·7 persons to each family, the population capacity of the land under this *chitimene* system is 8 persons per square mile.

have been more profitable in the form of timber, firewood, wood-pulp, leaf manure, and products from the distillation of wood. Between 600 and 900 lb of nitrogen per acre go up in smoke; the potash is reduced to a very soluble form of carbonate which is leached away by the first showers; and the humus and bacteria are badly misused.[1] But could the tropical cultivator, within his present technical and economic framework, do otherwise than he does? The method he employs is quick and gives him in a short time the area required for subsistence. The unavoidable deficiency in the means of communication in sparsely peopled countries prevents the systematic exploitation of the forest; and the tropical forest is not easily exploited.[2] (See plates 10–14.)

Very often the soil is not turned up. There is scarcely any need for it after the fire, since forest soil is naturally friable and, moreover, fire has the fortunate effect of making it more friable still.[3] Besides, it might be dangerous to turn up the soil too much, lest it should become a prey to erosion.[4]

In the Brazilian *roça* the various operations described above are named thus:

Brocar	=to cut down the undergrowth with a bush-knife, or *terçado*; and perhaps to place the bush on the ground in a layer called a *facho*.
Derrubar	=to fell the big trees with an axe.
Picar	=to pile up the trunks in order to burn them.
Aceiro	=space carefully cleared and weeded round the patch to be burnt. This is to prevent the fire from spreading. In the State of Rio de Janeiro the name *bambe* is given to a forested strip between two patches.
Queimar	=to burn.
Encoivarar	=to make little heaps of trunks and branches not yet consumed in the *queimada* and to burn them again.

1. See *Agriculture et élevage au Congo belge*, Oct. 1936, p. 157. From accurate measurements made at Yangambi, near Stanleyville, it appears that one hectare (2·47 acres) of virgin forest produces the following quantities of organic matter: 30 tons of litter and dead wood, 39 tons of leaves, 55 tons of twigs, 364 tons of branches, creepers and stems of small trees, 210 tons of trunks of average diameter, 266 tons of large boles, a total of 964 tons. (Beirnaert, *La technique culturale sous l'Equateur*, I, p. 40.)

2. See below, pp. 90–7, for details of the forest problem.

3. Sir A. Howard, *An Agricultural Testament*, Oxford, 1943, p. 32, points out that in western India cultivators use fire to make the soil of their seed-beds friable. At the end of the dry season the earth is too hard to be dug, and yet the seed-beds must be set before the coming of the monsoon. To overcome this difficulty the cultivators pile branches on the space to be used as a seed-bed and burn them. The heat breaks up the lumps and gives the soil a friable texture which makes digging possible.

4. The introduction of the plough into tropical countries is not necessarily an undisputed blessing. See below, p. 190.

Sowing begins after the first rains. A few seeds are put into a hole made with a stick and filled in with the foot. The Kuoys of northern Cambodia have simplified this task by using a tube which allows them to sow the seed without stooping.[1] As a general rule several kinds of seeds and tubers are planted, since in this way are obtained both a main crop which supplies carbohydrates and subsidiary crops which give the wherewithal for making sauces to accompany the boiled vegetables. The variety of combinations is infinite. For example, it has been observed in yam patches in southern Nigeria that 99 per cent of the lots had pumpkins as well, 93 per cent had maize, 92 per cent groundnuts, 90 per cent red pepper, 80 per cent beans, and 24 per cent cassava.[2] Owing to the mixture of crops the ground is covered over with a thick mantle of cultivated plants, which to some extent protects it from erosion.

The cleaning of the ground is so formidable an operation that it is often dispensed with; in this mixed cultivation it is thus often necessary to grub up by hand the undesirable plants which are inextricably mixed with the crops. Besides, there were few weeds in the forest, and in any case their seeds will have been destroyed in the burning. Nevertheless, let us make no mistake: weeds and shoots of trees, creepers and ferns are often so abundant that without their removal, cultivation is impossible.

The crops must be protected against the ravages of ruminants and birds. Green corn crops attract wild herbivores, and these are frightened away. The Bembas of Zambia keep them off by putting up palings. The flights of birds which dart down on the ears of corn are driven off by shouts or volleys of stones. A network of strings is set up over the crops to enable a watchman perched on a platform to sound clappers to frighten away the birds. Certain ingenious Mois have even invented water-driven devices for making protective noises. The cultivators must often leave their villages and temporarily live near the plantation so as to keep a more effective watch. In these ways the crops are saved, unless they attract the attention of a herd of elephants. Patches of cassava have the advantage of not needing such close supervision, since animals do not eat the leaves or roots of this plant. But we should not be too sure on this point, for it is reported that peccaries plunder the cassava crops of the Kuikuru in the Amazon basin.[3] (See plate 15.)

1. In Urundi the women fill their mouths with beans and, without stooping, spit them with amazing accuracy into holes they dig with their sticks.
2. Lord Hailey, *An African Survey*, 1938, p. 888.
3. R. L. Carneiro, 'Slash-and-burn cultivation among the Kuikuru and its implications for cultural development in the Amazon Basin', *The evolution of horticultural systems in native South America: causes and consequences*. Caracas, Sociedad de Ciencias Naturales La Salle, 1961, pp. 47–68.

All agricultural work is usually accompanied by a grand display of magic. That of the Banhar Reungaos in the mountains of Annam has been particularly well described.[1] Christians in Brazil are not free from these superstitions, and the *caboclos*[2] invoke St Andrew to secure a wind favourable to their fires. The anxiety of the peasants is great, for if the trees have not had time to dry, they will not burn; and if the cultivator is too late with his fire, he runs the risk of being caught by the first rains. The clearing will have been in vain, and famine is inevitable.

The harvest ends the series of agricultural operations, which, taken by and large, have demanded only very little trouble, the heaviest toil being that of clearing the forest. Estimates of the duration of the work required by the ladang are very varied. This diversity is in the nature of things and is increased by the difficulty of observation. For example, the Bembas of Zambia do about four months' agricultural work in the year, the day's work lasting about four hours.[3] In Brazil some think that clearing alone (*brocar* and *derrubar*) takes twenty-five days' work per hectare. In the Belem district the cultivator works about sixty days a year on a hectare of cassava.

The technique of the ladang may be complicated by the use of the hoe. In forest clearings hoeing is not indispensable the first year, but becomes so in the second; it is nearly always necessary in savanna clearings. The fire does not destroy the rhizomes of the giant grasses or of more or less woody plants like *Landolphia*, the rubber vine of the Téké areas of the two Congo republics; and the cultivator has to take them out with his hoe to prevent them from stifling the corn crops.

In the lower Congo the agricultural worker (usually female) piles up the haulms and rhizomes into heaps and covers them with earth; the heaps are then fired, and the slow burning removes all possibility of renewed growth and helps to break up the soil.[4] The use of the hoe is required to break up the soil when the ladang is cultivated for more than one year. The ridges and heaps of earth in which the tubers and cereals are planted are made with the hoe. Hence very few tropical cultivators do not use the hoe and have not passed beyond the stage of

1. Rev. Father Kemlin, 'Rites agraires des Reungao', *Bull. de l'École française d'Extrême-Orient*, 1909 and 1910. See also G. Condominas, *Nous avons mangé la forêt*. Paris, 1957.
2. Brazilian peasants.
3. A. I. Richards, *Land, Labour, and Diet in Northern Rhodesia*, p. 397.
4. A peculiarly rudimentary form of agriculture persists amongst the Zande and Nyangwara peoples of the Sudanese savannas; they sow eleusine (a small variety of millet) between the large tufts of grass, and when it develops they pull up the grasses; the yields are very poor. See P. de Schlippe, *Shifting cultivation in Africa; the Zande system of agriculture*, London, 1956.

the digging-stick.[1] The Nupes in Nigeria have two hoes, a big one for making the ridges and heaps, and a little one for weeding and other light work. So have the Umbundus of Angola. But throughout the hot, wet regions, with the exception of certain parts of southern Asia, none of the cultivators has progressed beyond the hoe. Either for lack of draught animals or through ignorance of the technique of harnessing, they have not adopted the plough; besides, the ladang is always encumbered with tree debris which hinders the use of a plough. Although predominantly European by blood and civilization, the cultivators in vast expanses of Brazil have not yet adopted the plough, but use the *enxada* (hoe).

In 1920 there were only 141,196 ploughs in Brazil, 73,403 of which were in Rio Grande do Sul alone. The State of Ceará had one plough for every 2,030 people working on the land, and the State of Pará one plough for every 5,600. Besides, the digging-stick is still used in the *sertão* of Bananal in the State of São Paulo, and in Peruíbe. It is called *chuço, soquete,* or *estaca de cavar.*

The work of hoeing and weeding is often done communally. Neighbours and relatives assemble and work together, and in Africa south of the Sahara the work is done to the rhythm of drums and songs. The slaves carried the custom to Haiti, where it is known as *coumbite*. Brazilian cultivators practise the *mutirão*, which is not appreciably different.

If the same patch is cultivated several years in succession, tropical cultivators may employ a system of rotation. For instance, among the Nupes of Nigeria yams, cotton, and groundnuts are always the first rotational crop, whilst sorghum and millet are planted in the second year. The Tivs of Nigeria plant yams the first year, millet (Pennisetum and sorghum) the second, and sesame the third. The crops planted between these are beans, *voandzu*, various hibisci, water melons, sweet potatoes, and cassava.[2] (See Plates 16, 17.)

After a varying number of years the patch is abandoned and relapses into forest, or into savanna if the area is burnt at the end of every dry season. The promptness with which it is abandoned mainly

1. The digging-stick remains the only agricultural implement in certain parts of the Toma district on the lower Ivory Coast, whilst the hoe is used in neighbouring areas. This is a curious example of the juxtaposition of different technical levels. The hunting spear used for turning the soil by the mountain cultivators of New Guinea is not incompatible, on the other hand, with more advanced agricultural techniques involving irrigation and the use of manure, so that it is not quite correct to regard the digging-stick as the hallmark of primitiveness in agriculture. See J. Barran, 'Subsistence agriculture in Melanesia', *Bishop Museum Bull.,* 219, Honolulu, 1958; P. Brown and H. C. Brookfield, 'Chimber land and society', *Oceania,* 30, 1959, pp. 1–75; P. Gourou, 'Un terroir de Nouvelle Guinée', *L'Homme,* 1962, pp. 102–5.

2. G. W. G. Briggs, 'Soil Deterioration in the Southern District of the Tiv Division, Benue Province', *Farm and Forest* (Ibadan), 1941, June, pp. 8–12.

6. Laterite at Panjim north of Nova Goa in India. A hard layer of this rock covers most of the surface of the Goa district. When a little soil remains on the layer, thin low forest may grow; otherwise, there are merely patches of poor grass. The pools caused by recent rain indicate the impermeability of the laterite and the tendency of this rock to form enclosed hollows.

7. A laterite terrace at Gurupá on the Amazon.

8. Lateritic soil in Travancore. A crop of cassava is growing in soil, the greater part of which consists of lateritic pebbles. The plants are raised on little mounds which look like heaps of road metal.

9. A termitary in Katanga near Elisabethville. These ant-hills are often as high as fifteen feet and, as there may be four or five to the acre, they reduce the cultivable area considerably.

depends on the exhaustion of the fertility (the *terra acabada* of the Brazilians). In the south of the province of Ilorin in Nigeria a savanna patch is used for one year only, whilst a forest patch is cultivated for three years.[1]

The excessive growth of weeds may be more decisive than the exhaustion of the soil; but the latter is very rapid, not so much by reason of the nutritive elements that the food crops extract from it as because of soil-wash, leaching and oxidation. The rapid lowering of the percentage of organic matter in the soil reduces its ability to retain bases and nitrogen.[2] The exuberance of the vegetation and the exhaustion of the soil are the main reasons for the abandonment of a clearing and its return to secondary forest; but tradition and habits acquired in different natural circumstances may sometimes explain differences of behaviour. Thus the Lalas in Zambia abandon their *chitimene* after one harvest, whilst the Bembas remain for four or five. The Ibans of Sarawak work desperately hard to cultivate paddy fields on their steep mountain sides, under an equatorial rainfall régime that every year renders doubtful the drying-out and burning of the clearings.[3] Their agricultural system, which would be appropriate if there were a regular dry season, appears absurd when there is not a single dry month. Might it not be that these Ibans, who are the greatest of the forest clearers, and who have moved northwards from the interior of Borneo, brought their methods to perfection in a climate less equatorial in character?

After the last harvest, the occupiers having decided not to sow or plant any more crops, the clearing remains fallow. Certainly the cultivators may return to collect fruit from trees that have been planted or left to grow, and they may also in case of necessity dig up a few cassava roots, so that a kind of penumbra of production separates the cultivation from the forest; this sort of thing has been well described in Mindoro, in the Philippines.[4]

If the ladang has been created from forest, the latter very quickly resumes possession of the ground. Colonizing plants come in, and shrubs are succeeded by softwood trees like the umbrella tree and then by slower-growing species. The forest slowly restocks the soil with organic matter and nitrogen and even mineral substances; and at the same time it hinders soil erosion. Thus it comes to resemble a

1. J. W. Costello, 'The Forest Conditions of South Ilorin', *Farm and Forest*, 1943, Dec., p. 194.
2. Cf. Beinaert, *op. cit.*, pp. 28, 46.
3. J. D. Freeman, *Iban Agriculture: a report on the shifting cultivation of hill rice by the Iban of Sarawak*. London. H.M.S.O. 1955.
4. H. C. Conklin, *Hanunoo agriculture in the Philippines*, Rome, F.A.O. 1954; also 'An ethnological approach to shifting agriculture', *Trans. New York. Acad. Sci. Series II*, 17, 1954, pp. 133–42.

fallow in a very long rotation. In some cases, though rarely, the forest fallow may actually yield a crop: the cultivation of vanilla (the only edible orchid) is an example.[1]

Bush fires do not generally hinder the re-establishment of forest or the abandoned ladang; but the situation is otherwise if the cultivators attack the forest systematically all along its margins, and if they persist in cultivating their patches as long as they will yield a crop. A situation may thus arise in which there are patches of exhausted soil too far from the forest edge for recolonization to take place. This sort of thing may be seen on the northern side of the great Congo forests, particularly towards Wamba, Gemena, and in the Central African Republic.[2] On the other hand, forest which is no longer attacked by cultivators (or pastoralists) and which is simply exposed to bush fires, may extend at the expense of the savanna.[3]

It is important, however, not to be too positive about this. Despite long periods of fallow the forest sometimes does not regain possession of the cultivated areas; at B'Sar Deung, near to Dalat, in the mountains of South Vietnam, even though the fallow period is as long as thirty years, the villagers are faced with a dearth of forest to cut down. Forest has reoccupied only the valley bottoms and the hill-tops, and the slopes are now covered by savanna.[4]

How long should the fallow period be? We might express the opinion that it ought to last for at least twenty or thirty years in order that the soil may be completely restored. That indeed is what has been recorded amongst the Lalas of Zambia. But in this sort of thing there are no precise rules and no certain truth; one thing only is sure, that the fallow must be long to ensure fertility, for too short a fallow can have disastrous consequences for the next harvests. The inhabitants of the tropics always have a preference for forest soils, which can only exist after long fallows. In different areas, depending on the nature of the ground, on the density of population and on tradition, one finds fallows lasting only two or three years and others with a duration of thirty years; between eight and twelve years are necessary to get a good cover of woody vegetation.

1. I. Kelly and A. Palerm, *The Tajin Totonac, Part 1*, Washington, Smithsonian Institute, 1952; see also A. Kopp, 'La vanille dans l'assolement de la canne à sucre à la Réunion', *Rev. Botan. appliquée et d'agriculture tropicale*, 1932, pp. 32–47.
2. R. Sillans, '*Les savanes de l'Afrique central française, essai sur la physionomie, la structure et le dynamisme des formations végétales ligneuses de l'Oubangui-Chari*, Paris, 1956.
3. This is the case in the forest of Budongo, in Uganda; cf. W. J. Eggeling, 'Observations on the ecology of the Budongo rain forest, Uganda', *Jour. of Ecology*, 34, 1947, pp. 20–87.
4. R. Champsoloix, 'Le ray dans quelques villages des hauts plateaux du Viet Nam', *Rapports du sol et de la végétation*, ed. G. Viennot-Bourgin, Paris, 1960, pp. 216–62.

Certain agronomists in central Africa have noted the difference which existed between Sudanese and Bantu agricultural systems, and have regarded the latter as the more sensible. In the so-called Bantu agriculture of the lower Congo, the cleared land would be cultivated for only two years, and the people, after abandoning the area, would plant young trees so as to hasten the re-establishment of an artificial forest (*nkanku*). In the 'Sudanese' system, on the other hand, as practised in the north of the former equatorial province of Congo-Léopoldville, the cleared patch is hoe-cultivated to give as many harvests as possible; when the cultivator is forced to abandon the exploitation because of soil exhaustion, the forest has great difficulty in re-occupying the area.

This agriculture of axe and fire, sometimes supplemented by the hoe, is appropriate when there is plenty of land available, or when the cultivators are using soils that they have neither the desire nor the means to improve. Under the name of *essart* the ladang system has been practised also in temperate lands.[1]

The ubiquity of the ladang system in the tropics may well excite attention. Is it a case of diffusion or convergence? We may find much food for thought in the fact that the agricultural practices of the American tropical lands differ so slightly from those of the Asiatic and African tropics, even though the plants cultivated are (or were before the Columban discoveries) different.[2]

For five centuries a great mixing of plant species has been going on throughout the hot, wet lands. Of the basic foodstuffs the Americas have received few (only rice) but have contributed many (cassava, sweet potatoes, maize, beans and ground-nuts); likewise they have given many fruits (pawpaw, avocado, guava, naseberry) but have received few (only the mango).[3] Africa has made great haste to adopt new plants, particularly if their cultivation did not involve a departure from traditional methods; thus maize could be grown like sorghum, and sweet potatoes and cassava like yams. The success of American plants in Africa, linked with the simplicity of their culture, is such that today Africa would starve without cassava and maize.

1. Forest on poor soils was cut down; the trunks were sold and the branches burnt, and after two harvests the forest took possession again. This was a more careless and primitive type of agriculture than the permanent arable on better soils. *Essart* has disappeared only recently from the Ardennes, and it is still practised in Portugal, in Korea and in Japan. But in the temperate lands it was and is only found on soils incapable of supporting perennial agriculture.
2. The variations on the ladang theme are discussed by R. F. Watters, 'The nature of shifting cultivation, a review of recent research', *Pacific Viewpoint*, 1960, pp. 57–99.
3. The sweet potato is regarded as of American origin, even though it existed in Polynesia before the arrival of Europeans: the American origin of maize can hardly be doubted.

A definite example will give a better grasp of the characteristic agriculture of the tropics.[1] The Mayan village of Chan Kom[2] in Yucatan (see Fig. 7) has a population of 251 persons on an area of $9\frac{1}{2}$ square miles. The people feed mainly on maize grown on the *milpas*, i.e. on their ladangs. The land belonging to the village is reserved for the villagers, and they make their *milpas* where they will. A patch is owned by the man who clears it, so long as it is under cultivation, but reverts to communal ownership when it is fallow, though fruit trees remain the property of whoever planted them. As fruit trees are not planted in the *milpas*, this peculiarity involves no complications, but a combination of circumstances has given rise to a paradoxical situation in Chan Kom. At the time it was first built, the village had no plan, and each man sited his house where he pleased. When the village grew, the villagers wanted to give it a good appearance and drew up a plan with a central plaza and streets running at right angles to each other. As the houses were moved, some fruit trees found themselves on land no longer owned by the planters who, however, remained the owners of the trees and could sell them or pick the fruit.

The Mayan cultivator chooses the site of his *milpa* by the appearance of the soil and vegetation, and the ground must have been fallow for seven years at least. As a *milpa* is generally cultivated for two years, the cultivable land is used during two years in approximately ten. Of course, the land belonging to the village is far from being cultivable everywhere. The total area cultivated in a year (counting *milpas* used for one year and for two) is 300 acres out of a communal acreage of 6,000, i.e. 5 per cent of the total.

The jungle—there are no real forests in Yucatan—is cut down and burnt when dry. The choice of day for burning is a delicate one, for, if the fire is lit too early, there is risk of the wood being too green; and, if too late, rain may put out the fire. Holes are then dug with a dibble at intervals of a yard in all directions and in them are placed five or six grains of maize, some beans or pumpkin seeds. The grains of maize are taken from the largest ears of the previous crop, and the little grains at the upper end of the cob are thrown away. Sowing takes place in May and June, and not much attention is paid to the *milpa* until the crop reaches maturity in October or November.

A cultivator usually has two *milpas*, the one made in the current year and one made in the previous year, the latter giving a yield

1. For analyses of types of ladang see P. Gourou, 'Le pays de Belem', *Bull. Soc. Belge d'études geogr.*, 1949, pp. 21–36; 'Para, observaçoes geograficas na Amazonia', *Revista brasiliera de geografia*, 1950, pp. 171–250.

2. M. Redfield and Villa, *Chan Kom*, Carnegie Institution, Washington, publ. No. 448, 1934. See also some details about Yucatan, above, p. 10–11.

between 25 and 50 per cent lower than the former. Each family cultivates some five acres on the average every year and harvests about 39 or 40 cwt of maize. Reckoning the consumption in a family of five at 6½ lb a day, or 21 cwt a year, there remains a surplus for seed and for sale. The food situation is not bad, for there is no shortage; but the diet seems ill balanced, being deficient in proteins and especially in animal proteins.

Chan Kom lives on the *milpa* after having sprung from the *milpa*. The Mayas, hungry for good virgin land, often go far from their villages to clear a patch outside the village property, but on Federal Government land, the whole of Yucatan not yet being included in areas belonging to any one village. A man who thus clears a patch may make a permanent home, a *milperío*. If he is successful, relatives join him and make an offshoot hamlet, a *ranchería*. A new village, or *pueblo*, comes into being when the connection with the present village is broken. The parent of Chan Kom was Ebtun, and the original *milperío* dates from 1880.

The causes which gave rise to Chan Kom threaten it with desertion. By 1930 its villagers were clearing *milpas* six and even eighteen miles outside the village lands. Thus, with a density of twenty-six persons to the square mile the land attached to Chan Kom no longer suffices for the needs of the population. If numbers continue to grow, if new *pueblos* go on being formed, Federal land will end by becoming a patchwork of contiguous village properties. What will then be done by cultivators who are eager to make new *milpas* outside their own village boundaries?[1]

1. This need for fresh land has certainly played a part in the former history of the Mayas. See below, pp. 57–9.

BIBLIOGRAPHICAL NOTE

The immense bibliography relating to agriculture in the humid tropics cannot be given here. It must be handled with great care and with due regard for geography, for authors have a natural tendency to regard as original and unique the systems that they have studied in detail. Besides the works already cited in the footnotes, we may note the following: G. Sautter, 'A propos de quelques terroirs d'Afrique Occidentale', *Etudes rurales*, 1962, pp. 24–86; H. Nicolai, *Le Kwilu, étude géographique d'une région congolaise*, Brussels, 1963 (see pp. 227–68). See also various works of W. B. Morgan, particularly 'Agriculture in southern Nigeria', *Econ. Geog.*, 1959, pp. 138–50; F. J. Ormeling, *The Timor Problem. A geographical interpretation of an under-developed island*, Groningen, J. B. Wolters, 1955, H. S. Morris, *Report on a Melanau Sago-producing Community in Sarawak*, London, H.M.S.O. 1953, Colonial Research Series No. 9; O. H. K. Spate, *The Fijian people. Economic Problems and Prospects*, Legislative Council of Fiji, Council Paper No. 13 of 1959, Government Press, Suva, Fiji, M. R. Haswell, *Economics of Agriculture in a Savannah Village*, London, Colonial Office, 1953, P. M. Kaberry, *Women of the Grassfields*, London, H.M.S.O. 1952, Colonial Research Publication No. 14; *Problemas económicos y sociales de los Andes venezolanos*, Partes I y II, Caracas, Consejo de Bienestar rural, 1957,

CHAPTER 5

Consequences of the Characteristic Agriculture of the Tropics

THE agricultural system most widespread in the hot, wet lands has considerable human consequences; it is obvious that it must affect numbers and the density of population, the nature of rural settlement, and territorial organization, just as all these factors in turn have their influence on the agricultural system.

The ladang system is clearly adapted to communal rather than to private land ownership. It most often happens that the people of a village, or a large family group, are collective owners of an area of land. Whoever wishes to clear a patch of this land chooses his area in accordance with the usual customs and traditions, which are watched over by the elders or a patriarch. The cultivator does not lose all rights over a patch, however, when he has ceased to work it; he may still gather the fruits of the trees he has planted, and he often has a prior claim to the patch that he has cultivated and then abandoned. Quite often the clearings are not dispersed but adjoin each other so as eventually to cover all the communal cultivable area; such a plan of cultivation may take a circular form, with the successive clearings occupying sectors in clockwise rotation, as in New Guinea. It is also apparent that hereditary land rights will have greater precision around long-established permanent villages, whilst they will be more indeterminate on the periphery of the communal territory.[1]

The extent of the new clearings made each year depends on tradition; amongst the Bembas of Zambia, for a man to make too large a clearing would appear presumptuous and would expose him to a charge of witchcraft.[2] In areas in which the population density is very high, control over land use is of necessity more precise.[3] Since the village lands are collectively owned, and the lands of one village join those of its neighbours,[4] it is rare to find land with no owner, even in the sparsely peopled areas. Great care must thus be taken when laying out plantations or other enterprises of a colonizing character, for lands which appear unoccupied are nevertheless subject

---

1. Cf. G. Sautter, *op. cit.*, 1962.
2. A. I. Richards, *Land, Labour and Diet in Northern Rhodesia*, 1939, p. 272.
3. D. Forde, 'Land and labour in a Cross River village, Southern Nigeria', *Geog. Journ.* 90, 1937, pp. 24–51.
4. There are however, some vacant lands between the villages in Yucatan; and in the Koundou territory in the equatorial forests of Congo-Léopoldville there are 'no-mans-lands' called *ndelo*.

to native rights, which are by no means limited to the areas effectively cultivated, but extend also over the fallows and the lands held in reserve. Not to take account of this in schemes of land improvement would be plain robbery and a violation of the rights of the native peoples.

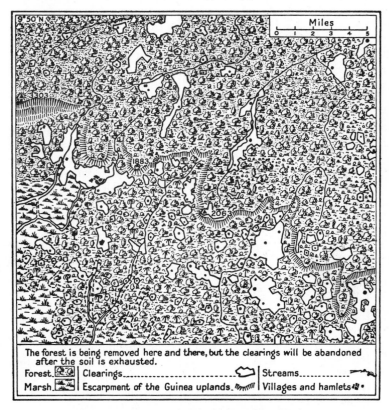

The forest is being removed here and there, but the clearings will be abandoned after the soil is exhausted.

Forest. | Clearings_____ | Streams_____
Marsh. | Escarpment of the Guinea uplands. | Villages and hamlets

Fig. 4.   Forest clearings in the Republic of Guinea

The ladang system leads to the concentration of population in hamlets and villages; the dispersal of the dwellings would be pointless, for the instability of the cultivated areas means that no house could remain for long attached to its plot. This does not mean that the villages are firmly fixed; it is sometimes necessary to move a village so as to be nearer to its cultivated patches which are too far from the original site;[1] and the construction of hamlets to be occupied only

1. As in the case of the Moi villages of South Vietnam, mentioned above.

during the cultivation season may postpone a complete shift. Many site changes, particularly over short distances, are for religious rather than agricultural reasons. Indeed, such a change of site is so frequent that there are regular rites for it.

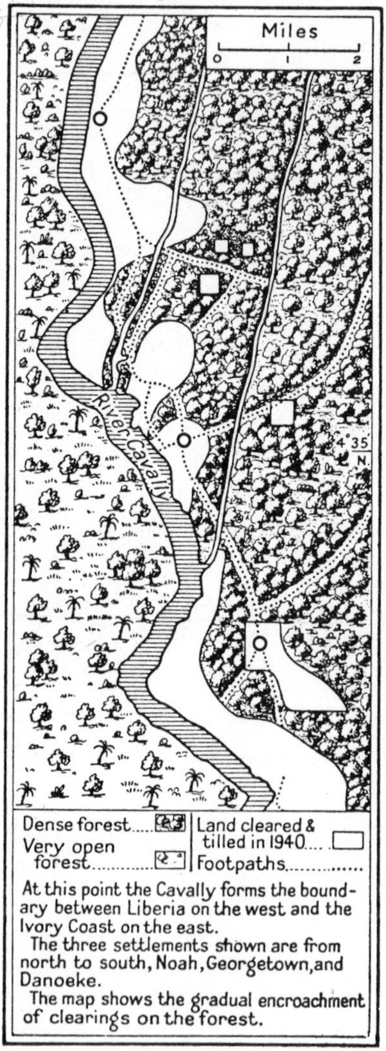

West African cultivators are much attached to their villages and the associated land, but readily accept the idea of a change of site. All that is asked is that the necessary formalities should be observed: viz. permission from the supernatural powers and the dead to leave the present site and settle on a new spot.[1] Among the Bembas, and certain Ibo tribes of Nigeria, each family keeps a preferential right to the spot which its house occupied in the deserted village, and the well manured soil yields heavy crops. It may also happen that the site of a village is changed, not because the neighbouring land is exhausted, but because the houses are falling to ruin; it is easier to build new ones on another spot than to try to repair the old ones.[2]

It must not be thought, however, that concentration of the rural population always takes place in a country where the ladang system is in force. Among the Mayas of Guatemala, who are cultivators

Dense forest...... Land cleared & tilled in 1940....
Very open forest.......... Footpaths..............

At this point the Cavally forms the boundary between Liberia on the west and the Ivory Coast on the east.
The three settlements shown are from north to south, Noah, Georgetown, and Danoeke.
The map shows the gradual encroachment of clearings on the forest.

FIG. 5. Forest clearings in the lower Cavally River valley

(After G. H. H. Tate, 'The Lower Cavally River', *Geog. Review*, 1942)

1. H. Labouret, *Paysans d'Afrique occidentale*, Paris, Gallimard, 1941, pp. 50–3.
2. Such a case is described by S. White in 'Notes on mixed farming as practised by some Shuwa Arabs in parts of Dikwa Emirate', *Farm and Forest*, June 1941, pp. 24–5.

using the *milpa* system, the population in certain districts is wholly concentrated in villages, whilst in other districts it is altogether dispersed. Thus, Nahualá, with a population of 16,000, has no other buildings in its life-centre than the church, a school, and the town hall. Nothing in the physical environment seems to explain the difference.[1]

Whilst in Central and West Africa the population is mostly concentrated in villages, East Africa provides many examples of dispersed settlement, as in the Ganda country, or partly dispersed, as in the Zandi territory of Ruanda.

The low density of population in hot, wet lands is due in great measure to the poor yields of the ladang system, in relation to the area occupied (see Figs. 4, 5, 6). The system cannot feed a dense population, because it uses only a small part of the cultivable land (see Fig. 15).

We may give precision to this statement by examining the effects of various ladang systems on a single square kilometre. In our first example, the cleared areas give a harvest in one year only, and then recuperate as forest fallow for twenty-four years; the rotation period is thus twenty-five years, or in other words the cultivated area represents only 4 per cent of the exploitable surface. But this exploitable surface is actually less than the total land surface, for inevitably a fair proportion of the surface cannot be cultivated, at least by the techniques of the ladang, by reason of steep slopes, rocky outcrops or lateritic crusts, river beds, or valley bottoms which are flooded during the rainy (i.e. the agricultural) season. True, different techniques, e.g. of paddy cultivation, could utilize these floodable areas, but to the ladang cultivator they remain useless, at least during the rainy season. If the exploitable surface is reckoned as 40 per cent of the total, it follows that the cultivated area, 4 per cent of this, is but 2·4 per cent of the total surface; in other words, our square kilometre yields to these 'slash-and-burn' cultivators a harvested area of no more than 2·4 hectares.

Since a family of five needs about one hectare cultivated land on which to live, one square kilometre could support twelve persons at a maximum under the conditions enumerated above. This is its potential population density in the physical and technical circumstances of our hypothesis. It may be expressed thus: if P is the potential density, A the number of cultivable hectares per square kilometre, B the length of the rotation (cultivation plus fallow), C the number of inhabitants per hectare cleared each year (in our example this was 5) then we can say the $P = \dfrac{A \times C}{B} = \dfrac{60 \times 5}{25} = 12.$

If there are only 4 persons living on this square kilometre we can say

TABLE 1

Total surface	Cultivable hectares per sq. km. (A)	Length of cultivation period (years)	Length of fallow (years)	Duration of rotation (B)	Average cleared area per year (hectares)	Persons per cleared area	Persons per hectare cleared each year	Potential population $\frac{A \times C}{B}$	Number of inhabitants	Difference from potential
1 km²	60	1	24	25	1	5	5	12	4	−8

TABLE 2

Total surface (Km²)	Cultivable hectares per sq. km. (A)	Length of cultivation period (years)	Length of fallow (years)	Duration of rotation (B)	Average cleared area per year (ha)	Persons per cleared area	Persons per hectare cleared each year (C)	Potential population $\frac{A \times C}{B}$
1	60	1	24	25	1	5	5	12
1	60	2	24	26	0·5	5	10	23
1	60	3	24	27	0·33	5	15	33
1	60	1	9	10	1	5	5	30
1	60	2	9	11	0·5	5	10	55
1	60	3	9	12	0·33	5	15	75

that the population is 8 per square kilometre below the potential. All this may be conveniently summarized in Table 1.

This table is useful since it enables us to appreciate the results of a change in one of the variables. Thus, in a second example, we may postulate a two-year cultivation period, with a rotation lasting twenty-six years; the area cleared each year on an average thus becomes 0·5 hectares (twice 0·5 hectares giving the 1 hectare needed for the family's subsistence), the number of persons per hectare cleared each year becomes 10, and the potential population $\dfrac{A \times C}{B} = \dfrac{60 \times 10}{26} = 23$.

These figures are contained in Table 2, to which are also added some further examples to show the great variety of possible human consequences of the ladang system.

This table is of course schematic, and is intentionally simple. In reality one would find many additional complexities. For example, in any given area account must be taken of possible variations in the length of the cultivation period, in the duration of the fallow and thus in the length of the rotation, and one would have to strike averages in order to calculate the population potential. There would also be found cultivators who do not make new clearances each year but only every other year; in this case the area cleared each year (column 6) would be obtained by dividing the area then cleared by 2. There are some cultivators who have a patch of perennial cultivation, e.g. a coffee plantation, as well as their ladang; but it would be very confusing to try to consider the complications that such situations create.

The area needed by a family to produce its food by means of crops grown on the ladang system has been measured in Sumatra for a family of about five persons and has been found to amount to 15 acres on fertile land and 50 on poor soil. This takes into account only the cultivable land. Assuming that 40 per cent of the soil is cultivable, 50 acres for a family of five would correspond to a potential population of 30 persons to the square mile. The *chitimene* system[1] practised in Rhodesia requires about 200 acres to the family, which means that the density falls to 7·7 persons to the square mile.

The ladang system is very dependent for its agricultural success on the incidence of the rainfall. As no tillage is carried out, the ground is very susceptible to abnormal drought (and the abnormal occurs quite frequently); no irrigation is provided. On the contrary, rains coming too early may compromise the burning-off process. The ladang cultivator cannot remain aloof from the rainfall; he must passively submit, whether he gets too much or too little.

1. See above, p. 32.

Human failings are heavily penalized: to be ill and slow down the agricultural work at the end of the dry season or at the beginning of the rains is a disaster. Any delay in sowing greatly reduces the yield, for the annual plants give very poor harvests indeed if they are not well advanced in their growth cycle by the end of the rainy season.

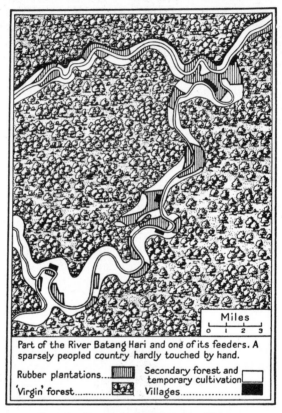

Part of the River Batang Hari and one of its feeders. A sparsely peopled country hardly touched by hand.

Rubber plantations... | Secondary forest and temporary cultivation
'Virgin' forest... | Villages...

FIG. 6. Forest clearings in eastern Sumatra
(After Herbert Lehmann, 'Die Bevölkerung der Insel Sumatra', in *Petermanns G. Mitteilungen*, 1938)

Irregularities of rainfall[1] aggravate the inadequacy of the yields. In hot, wet regions the lower the total mean precipitation, the more irregular is the rainfall. Districts with a heavy rainfall will always have water enough for the needs of their crops, whilst the badly

1. See for example E. Biel, 'Die Veränderlichkeit der Jahresumme des Niederschlags auf der Erde', *Geog. Jahresber. aus Österreich*, vols. 14 and 15, Vienna, 1929.

watered districts may suffer severely from drought.[1] The moment a tropical station falls below a mean precipitation of about 60 inches—which is of course a pretty high figure—the irregularity of the rainfall is far greater than in western or central Europe. The ratio of the driest to the wettest year usually falls below 30 per cent, whilst in western and central Europe it remains above 40 per cent. Many tropical countries are thus worse off than temperate lands. Lastly, years which were apparently satisfactory in respect of their total rainfall may have had their crops ruined by abnormally dry months. For instance, in western Bengal the famine in 1874 was due to drought in September and October, though the annual total was not deficient. A period of six days without rain can result in a most unfortunate lowering of the eventual crop yield.

One harmful effect of the ladang system is that it hinders the rational management of the agricultural land. The instability of the cultivated patches is not conducive to the construction of rural roads equipped with vehicular and foot bridges, or to the expenditure of capital with a view to increasing yields, such as marling or liming the soil (if it should need such treatment), or pipe drainage, irrigation, or works designed to combat soil erosion. In short, slash-and-burn agriculture invests nothing in the soil, and this inevitably results in low yields.

It is thus not surprising that the great weakness in the ladang system is its inability to keep pace with an increase in population. It works satisfactorily so long as a certain balance is maintained between the spontaneous possibilities of Nature and man's needs. If the balance is upset, natural fertility runs the risk of being quickly exhausted.

1.

Place	Country	Latitude	Mean annual rainfall inches	Driest Year inches	Wettest Year inches	Per cent of driest to wettest year
Freetown	Sierra Leone	8°29′N.	157	102	206	49
Tamatave	Madagascar	18°9′S.	119	93	158	62
Mangalore	India	12°52′N.	129	89	182	49
Val d'Emeraude	Cambodia	10°38′N.	210	169	246	68
Padang	Sumatra	0°56′S.	174	137	205	66
Accrá	Ghana	5°33′N.	27	13	35	29
Diego Suarez	Madagascar	12°10′S.	39	17	57	30
Allahabad	India	25°28′N.	39	19	76	24
Padaran	Vietnam	11°21′N.	30	16	46	34
Kupang	Timor	10°10′S.	57	30	87	34

In fact, if the population increases, man either adopts new agricultural methods which give greater yields without harming the soil—as in the case of the flooded ricefield—or else he keeps the *ladang*, but reduces the length of the fallow period. We noted above the great differences in population potential which arise from differences in the duration of the fallow. But if the natural vegetation is not given time enough to replace the thick forest covering, the soil will not be able to repair its fertility satisfactorily. Crops will be less good, and, to ensure his food supply, man will be led to extend his clearings still more. The forest replaces itself less and less well as the soil becomes progressively exhausted, and consequently the soil recovers less and less of its fertility during the fallow periods. Besides, the dangers of erosion and lateritization described above become more and more pressing.

For example, the Ibans of Sarawak grow unirrigated rice in their ladang system, and a single harvest followed by long fallow does not exhaust the soil. But if crops are harvested in successive years, or if the fallow is much reduced, then soil degradation soon occurs. The absolute minimum duration of fallow appears to be four years.[1]

The forest can no longer resume possession of certain clearings, which are then occupied by tall grasses springing from rhizomes, the most widespread being *Imperata cylindrica* ('*alang-alang*'). The great danger of these grasses is that they are reduced to the inflammable condition of straw at the end of the dry season and that fires lit to make a clearing are invariably communicated to the grassy areas. A real alliance is formed between the grass and the fire, for the latter may be spread by the grass which, thanks to its rhizomes, is not damaged by the fire. The grasses maintain their hold in this way, for if there were no fire, trees would grow again. The savanna landscape, with its fire-resistant trees, has only the appearance of equilibrium; if there were no more fires it would revert to forest.[2] The advantage derived from its rhizomes by *I. cylindrica* is clearly seen from an incident observed in Natal. *Passerina rigida*, another grass, had monopolized the surface of some coastal dunes. An invasion by *Imperata* was fatal to *Passerina*, for fires were promoted by the former (which will burn before it is quite dry) and thanks to its underground shoots this grass survived, whilst *Passerina* disappeared. A careful study of the *campos cerrados*[3] in a particularly well-known

1. J. D. Freeman, *Iban agriculture*. 1955
2. See below, p. 66.
3. F. Rawitscher; 'The water economy of the vegetation of the "campos cerrados" in Southern Brazil', *Journ. of Ecology* 36, 1948, pp. 237–68. There exist in these *campos cerrados* of São Paulo certain trees with large irregular leaves, which are not adapted to resist transpiration during the dry season and in consequence are able to combat the fire. The surprising appearance of these trees is

area of parkland landscape near Ribeirão Preto, in the state of São Paulo, has shown that this type of vegetation owes its origin mainly to the fires that sweep through the grasses during the dry season. The bush fires antedate the arrival of Europeans, and incendiarism was much practised by the Indians.

The damage done by fires is less serious in hot regions with weakly marked dry seasons. All the same, even in a climate as damp as that of Banka in Indonesia, where there is no dry month, bush fires have a baneful effect.[1] The secondary forest which springs up on the abandoned site of the ladang is called *belukar*. If it is left alone for several decades, it ends in a predominant growth of dipterocarps, which are not without economic value. These do not survive repeated fires, however, but give place to a worthless species, *Schima bankana*, whose clusters are easily distinguished by the red colour of their young leaves from the parts of the secondary forest which have not been burnt. If this new association is burnt annually, it may be displaced by savanna consisting of *I. cylindrica*. In the Philippines the *cogonales*, that is, areas covered with *cogón* (*I. cylindrica*) already occupy 40 per cent of the archipelago, which is certainly a forest environment.[2]

In short, the ladang system cannot support a numerous people or maintain the growth of an increasing population. The shortening of the fallow periods, which is an inevitable consequence of the increase

due to their very deep roots which can penetrate the mantle of decomposed rock to a depth of fifty or sixty feet and thus reach the permanent water table. This is conclusive proof that given protection from fire the forest would regenerate itself. Around the protected grave of the Danish naturalist P. W. Lund, at Lagoa Santa, there is a reconstituted forest of *Caryocas brasiliensis*, whilst on the burnt *campo cerrado* Caryocas is a tree whose main trunk is underground. See also L. Waibel, 'Vegetation and land use in the Planalto Central of Brazil', *Geog. Review*, 1948, pp. 529–54.

1. J. W. Gonggripp, 'Soil management and density of population', *Congr. Internat. de Géog. Amsterdam*, 1938, *Géographie coloniale*, p. 400.

2. It is also possible that the bamboo 'forest' of Lamao is the product of fire, with the bamboo taking the place of the *cogón*. See H. N. Whitford, 'The vegetation of the Lamao forest', *Philippine Jour. Sci.*, I, 1906, pp. 373–431. The notes made on this subject by Auguste Chevalier in respect of the forests on the Ivory Coast in *Revue Botanique appliquée et Agriculture tropicale*, 1937, p. 467, are of great interest, for they apply to a district in which the dry season is short enough (three to four months) and the vegetation is rain forest. If a section of the forest were felled without burning, no great harm would ensue, for a secondary forest would soon have replaced the primary. But in the burnt clearings made in the rain forest grow up 'pan-tropical' grasses which did not occur in the district before the destruction of the forest and which include *Imperata cylindrica, Sorghum guineense, Pennisetum purpureum, Hyparrhenia diplandra, Chasmopodium caudatum*, and *Andropogon tectorum*. These grasses dry up completely at the end of every dry season and burn every year, precluding the regrowth of trees and making the ground more and more favourable to grasses. It must be added, however, that if the cultivators did not insist on burning, the demise of the forest would be by no means certain.

in population, involves the ruin of the soil. It is true that different soils react differently. For example in Nigeria, the Benin sands, naturally very poor, require a thirty-year fallow in order to recover their agricultural capacity; in this wet region the savannas are the result of over-cropping.[1] By way of contrast the sandy soils of central Nigeria are capable of supporting regular if moderate harvests with quite short fallows.[2]

The ladang system is not an inevitable consequence of the tropical climate and soil; it merely represents a certain stage in agricultural technology. Other methods are possible, as we shall see. It must be recognized, however, that for a population that is small enough to permit a sufficiently lengthy fallow, ladang assures a return per man-hour higher than can be obtained from continuous cultivation by hand, unaided by animals or machines. True, the yield per acre from the latter method is higher, but only at the cost of a greater amount of labour. Fire is a remarkable economizer of energy. Numerous examples could be cited of African peoples who have taken refuge in mountain areas, where through lack of space they find themselves under the necessity of practising intensive agriculture by hand; as soon as they can without danger emerge from their mountain hideouts, they resume the slash-and-burn methods of the ladang on the neighbouring lowlands.

The ladang system is at the final analysis an inadequate economic basis on which a high civilization may achieve great political and intellectual attainments.

Nevertheless, the Mayan civilization—whose high standard is proved by the ruins it has left behind—was developed in the tropics. It was of necessity based on a dense population, and yet its only economic foundation was the *milpa* system. On the other hand, Mayan civilization was perhaps original and did not spring from germs imported from elsewhere. It was therefore very different from the high civilizations of tropical Asia, which are based on agricultural systems, such as the flooded ricefield, suitable for supporting a numerous population, and which owe much of their character to influence from outside the tropics. (See Figs. 7 and 8 and Plate 18.)

Certainly, a plentiful supply of labour was needed to build the temples whose ruins are scattered through now uninhabited forests

1. *Farm and Forest*, Ibadan, 1941, p. 119.
2. Cf. H. Vine, 'Is the lack of fertility of tropical African soils exaggerated?' *Deuxième conférence interafricaine des sols*, Léopoldville, 1954, vol. 1, pp. 389–412. Despite the interesting observations made in this paper, it is astonishing to read that the sandy soils of central Nigeria 'are perfectly adapted to mechanized agriculture'. For it is exactly on these soils that the experiment in mechanized cultivation at Mokwa came to grief.

10. A forest patch being cleared for cultivation at Yangambi in the Congo. At this stage the ground is covered with the bush and trees that have been cut down.

11. The second stage in clearing a forest patch for cultivation. The bush has now been burnt.

12. A forest patch being prepared for planting cassava near Belem in Brazil. In the oven in the foreground the bigger branches are being burnt for charcoal to be sold in Belem.

13. A crop of maize on a patch cleared near Bambesa in the Congo. Trunks and large branches still strew the ground. The oil palms have been purposely left standing, and the other trees which have survived the fire have the bare, straight appearance of forest growths.

on the borders of Mexico and Guatemala. An attempt has been made to calculate the density of population around Uaxactun. For this purpose the sites of houses have been counted within a radius of ten miles around the archaeological centre. These traces survive in the

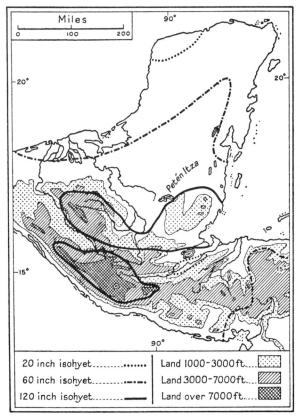

FIG. 7. The Mayan Countries

shape of low platforms, for Mayan houses were (and still are) placed on the ground on an artificially raised foundation of earth. If only 25 per cent of the houses are reckoned as having been occupied simultaneously, it may be concluded that 48,000 persons lived within this ten-mile radius. This gives a density of 470 persons to the square mile, a very high figure for agriculture based on the *milpa* system.[1]

1. O. G. Ricketson, Jr., 'Excavations at Uaxactun', *The Culture of the Maya*, Carnegie Institution, Washington, Supplementary publication No. 6, 1933, p. 3.

The Mayas had reached a high degree of culture, the highest in all pre-Columbian America. Everything points to this: the science and art of building, the beauty of their sculpture, the invention of a form of writing, the quality of their astronomical observations, the drawing

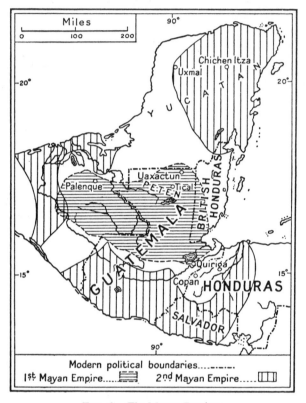

FIG. 8. The Mayan Empires

After H. J. Spinden, 'The Population of Ancient America', *Geog. Review*, 1928)

up of a remarkably accurate calendar and chronology, and, above all, the perfection of a system of notation including the discovery of nought and the determination of the value of figures according to their position. In short, a system only slightly inferior to our 'Arabic' notation and having no other equal in the world.[1]

1. S. G. Morley, *The Inscriptions at Copán*, Carnegie Institution, Washington, Publication No. 209, 1920, p. 643; Morley, *Guide-book to the Ruins of Quiriga*, *ibid.*, Supplementary publication No. 16, 1935, p. 203; and Morley, *The Inscriptions of Petén*, *ibid.*, No. 437, 1938, vols. 1 and 4.

Like all great civilizations, that of the Mayas came under the influence of others, and it may have owed much to the 'Olmeque' culture which arose about the fifteenth century B.C. in central Mexico. It is also possible that the original home of the Maya civilization was in the mountains of Guatemala, from which it descended to the plain of Petén.[1] There is no evidence however to show that the mountain environment was necessary for the birth of the civilization, or that it might not equally well have begun on the Petén plain. This sub-equatorial land,[2] typically hot and wet, ravaged by malaria, is made up of low plains studded with lakes, the largest of which is Petén Itza.

Most of this little territory is covered with forest, except on certain patches of savanna, where the hard red 'clay' may easily be lateritic. The district is almost uninhabited and is only passed through during the tapping season by the *chicleros*, who collect *chicle*[3] destined for the manufacture of American chewing gum. They are wretched folk riddled with fever and tortured by many diseases, not the least distressful of which is *chiclero* ulcer, a leishmaniasis which eats away the ears and the skin of the face and neck. These scattered and pitiful people have nothing in common with the strong, ingenious builders and sculptors of Quirigá, Uaxactun, Yaxchilan, and many other towns.[4] Today the administrative centre of the Guatemaltecan province of Petén is Flores, a wretched village with a population of 2,500 persons.

The 'old Mayan empire' made its appearance shortly before the Christian era and prospered until the sixth century A.D. But then it declined, and in 630 the last Mayan city became extinct. The decay of the towns seems to have happened suddenly, for the last date discovered in any of them is given in an inscription which in no way points to decadence, and after this the archaeological site offers no further inscriptions. But cities were founded in Yucatan between 120 and 180 miles farther north of the original Mayan area at about the

1. A. V. Kidder, 'Archaeological problems of the Highland Maya', *The Maya and their Neighbours*, New York and London, 1940, pp. 117–25.
2. The mean monthly figures for rainfall and temperature at El Paso Caballo, a point situated to the west of Uaxactun in lat. 17°23′N., are as follows:

	J.	F.	M.	A.	M.	J.	J.	A.	S.	O.	N.	D.	Year
Rainfall	1·8	1·6	1·2	1·9	6·6	9·1	7·7	7·4	11·7	10·7	4·7	3·8	68·2 in
Temperature	75	78	81	86	86	84	82	83	81	81	78	76	81°F
	24	25·5	27	30	30	29	28	28	27	27	25·5	24·5	27°C

(S. G. Morley, *The Inscriptions of Petén*, vol. 4, p. 350.)
3. *Chicle* is the latex of *Achras Zapota L.* and is called *chicozapote* by the natives.
4. The word 'town' should be understood in a special sense in the Mayan country, for it seems that the Mayas did not in fact build real towns. The buildings which have remained till our times marked rather the life-centres of rural communities. They were meeting-places and not towns, and only priests and officials lived in them permanently.

date when the earlier cities disappeared.[1] Though the chief centre of the 'new Mayan empire' was in Yucatan, Mayan settlements were formed farther north as far as the Isthmus of Tehuantepec and to the south of the old Mayan country in the Guatemala of today, which is now peopled by Mayas. It looks as if the Mayas left their original home in a body and settled to the north and south of it.

The Mayas experienced a brilliant revival in Yucatan shortly after the year 1000. The ruins of Chichen Itzá, Uxmal, and many other places bear witness to this. But Mayan civilization was in an advanced state of decay at the moment of the Spanish conquest, which dealt it its death-blow.[2]

What caused the great migration of the Mayas in the sixth and seventh centuries? If life had followed its normal course in the Petén district, inscriptions would have afforded evidence of it, for there are contemporary inscriptions in the territories newly colonized by the Mayas. The problem has roused the curiosity of scholars, and several solutions have been offered.[3] Did an earthquake devastate the district and drive away the people? But Mayan buildings bear no obvious trace of seismic action, and the dilapidations seen in them are easily explained as the work of vegetation. The same is true of the Khmer buildings, which are situated in identical circumstances. Besides, not one, but several, earthquakes must be imagined, for the abandonment of the old Mayan country took a hundred years. Moreover, this district is not specially afflicted with earthquakes. It is far less so than the mountainous part of Guatemala or Salvador, whose capital, San Salvador, though sixteen times destroyed by earthquakes, has never been abandoned. Man shows no anxiety to leave a district which is liable to earthquakes.

Must a change of climate be imagined? During the existence of the first Mayan empire the climate of the Petén district, we may suppose, was drier and healthier, and consequently the forest was less aggressive. As the climate became damper and hotter and the district more unhealthy, the Mayas presumably abandoned their native land in order to move into more propitious areas.[4] The proof of such a change in climate is said to be found in the growth-rings of Californian trees. During a period contemporary with Mayan splendour, the trees are said to show wide rings which reveal a high rainfall explained as due to the migration southward of the belt of high rainfall in the north-

1. Morley, *Copán*, p. 459.
2. Shattuck, *The Peninsula of Yucatan*, Carnegie Institution, Washington, No. 431, 1933, p. 29.
3. Morley, *Copán*, p. 442.
4. E. Huntington, *The Climatic Factor as Illustrated in Arid America*, Carnegie Institution, Washington, No. 192, 1914.

west of the United States. The climatic belts in Mexico are also pre-
sumed to have migrated southwards, so that a climate drier and
having greater ranges prevailed in the Mayan country. When, on the
other hand, the climatic belts moved back north again, the Mayan
country was, we may assume, occupied once more by a damp, hot,
climate—hence the flight of the Mayas.[1]

Ought the climatic explanation to continue to be held? No proof
of climatic change is found on the spot. The evidence of the rings
may perhaps be valid for California,[2] but does it indicate a general
displacement southwards of the American climatic belts at the beginning of the Christian era, followed by a retreat northwards in the
sixth century? Besides, the climatic changes to which such great
effects are attributed would not have been considerable. It would
have been but a shade of difference, not an upheaval. The climate of
Yucatan, whither the Mayas are supposed to have fled to escape the
heat and rain of their former country, is also tropical and is merely
less humid than that of the Petén district. Yucatan is not a very
healthy place, has few people, and seems unable to feed a large
population.[3] Lastly, and most important, the Mayas abandoned their
original country not only for territory situated farther north, but
also moved southwards, as is clearly shown by a map of the position
of the second Mayan empire;[4] and the southern settlements are very
far from being all situated on high ground. Could a climatic change
result in causing southward as well as northward migrations? The
fact must not be lost sight of that today about 300,000 Mayas live
in the lowlands, whilst 1,500,000 have settled in the mountains. The
Mayan area covers the whole of Guatemala, a part of Honduras,
Yucatan, and a large portion of the Mexican States of Tabasco and
Chiapas.[5]

The purely human explanations are scarcely more convincing than
the purely physical ones. The country is supposed to have been
ravaged by a Nahua invasion from the north. But nothing proves
that the Nahuas invaded Mayan territory,[6] and their advance seems
to have been limited to the shores of the Pacific. The final dates of
the various cities of the old Mayan empire are spread out over a

1. Karl Sapper is a supporter of the hypothesis of a change in climate; see
Gerlands Beiträge zur Geophysik, vol. 34, 1931, pp. 333–53.
2. *The Annual Rings of Trees*, Carnegie Institution, Washington, Supplementary
Publications, No. 9, 1937; W. S. Glock, *Principles and Methods of Tree-ring
Analysis*, *ibid.*, Publication No. 486, 1937, and critical review by E. Antevs,
Geog. Review, 1938, pp. 518–20.
3. See above, p. 10.
4. Spinden: *Geog. Review*, 1928, p. 651. Cp. Fig. 8 above.
5. G. and M. MacCutchen MacBride, 'Highland Guatemala and its Maya
Communities', *Geog. Review*, 1942, pp. 252–68.
6. Morley, *Copán*, p. 444.

hundred years, which is a very long time for the conquest of a little country. Would not the cities last abandoned bear witness to the invasion by means of fortifications or epigraphical allusions? But nothing of the kind is to be found. Was it civil war? But that this should lead to the abandonment of the whole country is not evident. Importance has been attached to an intellectual and political decadence which is manifest in the 'flamboyant' sculpture of the end of the first Mayan empire. But the technique of the sculpture shows no decadence; and why, assuming there was decadence, should wholesale migration be the consequence?[1]

There remain the explanations which are based on both physical and human factors and are associated with the interdependence of man and his environment. An epidemic might have frightened the people so much as to make them evacuate the district. Yellow fever might have been the cause,[2] but on the whole the specialists in tropical diseases think that yellow fever is of African provenance.[3] A delay of a hundred years is, moreover, very long for the evacuation of a country which has suddenly become unhealthy. A sudden increase in malaria might be imagined as a sequel, for example, of political troubles which might have impaired the cultivation of the country.[4] But this hypothesis does not square with a delay of a hundred years, and the factors it imagines should have caused a decadence which would have been perceptible in Mayan remains. Besides, if the explanation of the Mayan migration as caused by epidemic held good, it would emphasize the menace of parasitic and infectious diseases that constantly overhangs the people of the tropical world.

Exhaustion of the soil may well be the best explanation.[5] The pre-Columbian Mayas practised a system of agriculture identical with that of the Mayas now in Yucatan.[6] Since the former Mayan empire was densely peopled, the cultivation of maize on the *milpa*

1. Morley; *ibid.*, p. 447.
2. H. J. Spinden, one of the most learned scholars in Mayan matters, finally falls in with the yellow fever explanation in *Geog. Review*, 1928, p. 649.
3. See above, p. 12.
4. The Anuradhapura district in northern Ceylon was abandoned because it had become fever-ridden. It seems indeed that political troubles started the process of depopulation by disorganizing the network of irrigation and drainage canals necessary in this district of swamp rice cultivation. It was on this disorganization that the malarial complex which caused the depopulation of the country was based. Technical conditions were not by any means the same in the Maya country, where irrigation was not practised. And if it is true, as some American scholars think, that pre-Columbian America was free from that worst form of malaria, the so-called 'tropical fever', this disease can no longer be regarded as the explanation.
5. This hypothesis was first advanced by O. F. Cook, *Vegetation Affected by Agriculture in Central America*, U.S. Bureau of Plant Industry, Bull. 145, Washington, 1909. It is accepted by Morley in *Copán*, p. 447, and *Petén*, vol. 4, p. 334.
6. For this system of agriculture, see above, p. 40.

system without manure, working up the soil, or irrigation necessarily led to excessive shortening of the fallow period and therefore to the utter exhaustion of the land. *Milpas* had to be made at points more and more distant. We have seen above that the Mayas of Chan Kom are already obliged to do this, although they are not very numerous.[1] Still more striking is the case of the Indians now living in San Pedro Carcha in Guatemala. They have turned their district into an unproductive savanna and make their *milpas* fifty miles away in the district of Cajabón, whence they carry home the maize on their backs.[2] The former Mayan empire almost inevitably had the same difficulties. The cultivators were obliged to make their *milpas* farther and farther away, but clung to their homes in the old country to which with great trouble they carried part of the harvest. A moment came, however, when it must have seemed impossible to continue the practice. The authorities came to the drastic decision to move the life-centres near to the plantations. Hence, the emigration of the Mayas in all directions, because their *milpas* were situated all round the border of the old centre. To it was also due the sudden end, without any forewarning, which archaeology assigns to Mayan towns; and it explains the spacing out of the dates at which the towns were deserted, for the process of exhausting the soil was not completed at the same time everywhere. Lastly, the creation of new towns in Yucatan just when the old ones disappeared becomes intelligible.

The hypothesis is supported by a botanical argument. After a lapse of 1,400 years the forests of the old Mayan empire are still secondary growths, just as in Cambodia the site of Angkor is covered with secondary forest, though it was abandoned 500 years ago. And yet the insect life in the humus of the present forests in Péten is far from as abundant as in virgin forests, which is a further proof that the forests of this district have been entirely cleared away and have had great difficulty in recovering. Besides, some stretches of laterite are still savanna-clad. The clay which has filled various lakes in the old Mayan country must have come from soils eroded through deforestation.[3]

Outside the Maya territories, in central Mexico,[4] painstaking research has shown that the periods with dense population were

1. See above, p. 41.
2. Morley, *Copán*, p. 454.
3. A remark of C. Wythe Cooke, the geologist, in *The Culture of the Maya*, quoted by O. G. Ricketson, Jr., *Excavations at Uaxactun*, Carnegie Institution, Washington, Supplementary Publication No. 6, p. 2. S. G. Morley is of opinion that the filling up is much older than the end of the first Mayan empire. (*Petén*, vol. I, p. 5.)
4. S. F. Cook, *Soil Erosion and Population in Central Mexico*, Berkeley, California, 1949; idem, *The Historical Demography and Ecology of the Teotlalpan*, Berkeley, 1949; idem, *Santa Maria Ixcatlan*, Berkeley, 1949.

characterized by marked erosion of slopes and the accumulation of the eroded debris in valley bottoms; the debris often contains fragments of pottery which enable the date of the erosion and deposition to be ascertained. On the other hand, when the population was sparse, gullying of the slopes ceased with the reduction in forest clearance, whilst the rivers cut vertically downwards into the alluvial debris which had accumulated during the period of active erosion.

A recent study of British Honduras,[1] on the ground and from air photographs, has shown that there was a serious depopulation of this region in the ninth and tenth centuries A.D. The Mayas, of whom large members dwelt here, as evidenced by the ruins of many houses and much pottery, disappeared at this time, that is at roughly the same time as the first Mayan empire. The Mayas who inhabit the country at the present time are descended from those who arrived from Mexico and Guatemala in the thirteenth century. A second line of evidence is that traces of the ancient occupation are still visible in the abundance of the cohune palm (*Orbignya cohune*) the spread of which was encouraged by the burning. Finally, the old Mayas have left on the hill slopes many cultivation terraces consisting of accumulations of loose soil behind small dry-stone walls. It is clear however that these terraces were never irrigated (it would in any case be quite impossible on the permeable limestones of British Honduras); they were subjected to the *milpa* system like the rest of the unterraced areas. This study of ancient and modern Mayas (separated by a gap of a thousand years) in British Honduras does not indicate that the Mayas ever practised irrigation in this area; on the contrary it shows that the people preferred a less labour-exacting form of agriculture. For they were not ignorant of the type of hoe tillage known as *montones*.

It may be supposed that if the exhaustion of the soil contributed to the downfall of the first Maya empire, it may also have played a part in the decay of the second empire, which was apparent even before the Spanish conquest.[2]

1. D. H. Romney, ed., *Land in British Honduras*, London, H.M.S.O., 1959, Colonial Research Publ. No. 24.

2. H. J. Spinden, *Geog. Review*, 1928, p. 648, advances interesting arguments against the explanation based on the exhaustion of the soil, holding that there is no proof of the existing savannas of the Petén district ever having been cultivated. But how could such proof be given? Spinden also observes that all the Mayan towns were abandoned, whether placed on recent alluvium on the flood plain of the Usumacinta or on the thin soil of the Petén district. This objection is a weighty one. But when repeated, the *milpa* is able to ruin the most fertile soil; and we do not know if the areas which were regularly flooded could be cultivated, since the flooding coincided with the maize-growing season. It must be added that no proof has been found that the pre-Columbian Mayas knew the technique of irrigation.

The history of the Mayan people must have been repeated in other tropical lands, but such striking facts cannot be found elsewhere, because there is no other instance of a splendid civilization, which may have originated in a hot, wet climate and in any event reached its greatest brilliance in such a climate, suddenly moving away and then disappearing almost completely. The Marajo civilization, in the Amazon delta, has disappeared utterly, but perhaps it never attained the remarkable degree of civilization of the Mayas. The town of Surame in the Sokoto district of northern Nigeria lies in ruins in the middle of a desolate lateritic plain. It may be thought that the decay of the town, which was perhaps hastened by war and slave-raiding, was caused by excessive cultivation leading to the ruin of the soil. But this civilization was neither original nor splendid.[1] The case of Anuradhapura mentioned above is different from that of the Maya country, for the civilization to which Anuradhapura belonged survived after the fall of that city. Angkor has a similar history: after four centuries of splendour the magnificent city was overwhelmed by the forest, but the Khmer civilization survived both in Siam and in Cambodia.

At the close of this chapter it may be as well perhaps to suggest a thought or two on the effects of the characteristic agricultural system of the hot, wet regions. In this part of the world the soil is often poorer in soluble matter than it is in temperate regions. Its nitrogen content is weaker and less stable,[2] and it often contains less clay owing to the decomposition of the silicates and the removal of the silica. The clay which it contains (kaolinite) has less capacity for adsorption than the clays in temperate lands (montmorillonite) because of its far less favourable microcrystalline structure. It is often full of quartz of recent formation and even more so of fine lateritic gravel. In extreme cases a lateritic crust wholly deprives it of any agricultural value.[3]

In spite of all these defects, tropical soils can certainly give better yields than they usually do today. Of course this does not apply to crusts from which all soil has been eroded, but every type of soil which is physically fit for cultivation can yield better crops than it does at present. This is absolutely certain in the case of soil which can be flooded and used as ricefields. Elsewhere, the improvement of the soil, the use of fertilizers and irrigation could work wonders. If

1. J. H. Mackay, 'Perspective in Land Planning', *Farm and Forest*, Ibadan, 1944, June, I.15.
2. Cp. J. Meiklejohn, 'Nitrogen problems in tropical soils', *Soils and Fertilisers*, no. 6, Harpenden, 1955.
3. See, for instance, what is said of Haute Volta in *Geogr. J.*, vol. 122, Dec., 1956, p. 526.

these techniques have been consistently ignored, and if fruit cultivation shows such feeble development, in tropical Africa, this is not due to the poverty of the natural environment but to the state of civilization.

It must be recognized that a judicious blending of cultivation and stock-raising, the only means of agricultural progress before the coming of chemical fertilizers and motorized implements, was hardly realizable in pre-Colombian America because there were no cattle, or in tropical Africa because of cattle diseases. But it should also be noted that in tropical Africa there was a tendency—due simply to the nature of the civilizations—for the complete separation of agriculture and pastoralism.

CHAPTER 6

Stock-Rearing in Hot, Wet Lands

THE Mayas were not a pastoral people. Their only domestic creatures were turkeys, ducks, dogs, and bees, so they did not bother to make pasture out of the forest. The only purpose for which they destroyed the woods was to clear land for cultivation. The damage done to the forest, and consequently to the fertility of the soil, is far greater if pastoral requirements are added to agricultural needs, as they are in the Sudan, East Africa, Madagascar, India, and post-Columbian America.[1]

Hot, wet lands are not eminently favourable to cattle-rearing (see Fig. 9). First of all, because cattle are exposed to serious diseases there. Trypanosomiasis bars their approach to equatorial Africa, where the only cattle that can survive are small and of low value economically. Besides, the disease, including the terrible East African *nagana*, plays havoc with herds in tropical regions having a well-marked dry season. In Southern Rhodesia the tsetse (*Glossina morsitans*) disappeared after the cattle epidemic in 1896, but from 1918 onwards both insect and disease greatly increased. Energetic measures were necessary to stamp them out by killing all the big wild ruminants and clearing the bush away from strips of country in order to check the tsetse. Many other diseases, like cattle plague or pneumonia, may kill the animals. In East Africa attacks of piroplasmosis, heart water, and myiasis are also dreaded. The cattle may be so exhausted by the bites of various flies, such as *Stomoxes*, that stock-rearing would be impossible if the animals were not sheltered during the day in dark stables. This is what used to be done in some parts of Mengo in Uganda (where sleeping sickness was rife) and among the Shuwa Arabs of Bornu in Nigeria. The latter build large circular huts called *tum-tum*, the family sleeping in the middle of the *tum-tum* on a raised platform surrounded by about twenty oxen. The animals stay in this dark shelter from 11 a.m. to evening.[2]

The tropical climate is, moreover, unfavourable to the preservation of pastoral produce: meat, milk, butter, or cheese. But most impor-

1. Valuable information on the whole range of problems connected with stock-raising in the tropics is contained in G. Williamson and W. J. A. Payne, *An Introduction to Animal Husbandry in the Tropics*, Longmans, 1959.
2. S. White, 'Notes on mixed farming as practised by some Shuwa Arabs in parts of Dikwa Emirate', *Farm and Forest*, June 1941, pp. 24–5.

tant of all is the fact that tropical pasture of average quality has no great food value. The flora of tropical grassland is quite different from that of temperate pasture, for it consists almost wholly of grasses, whilst in temperate pastures it is the leguminous species that are important.[1] How could it be otherwise, since the soil in tropical savannas, being poor in humus, is not favourable to the bacteria indispensable if leguminous species are to flourish? There are some fairly good fodder grasses,[2] at least when they are young. Most grasses on tropical savannas quickly become hard and are very poor in phosphorus, which is necessary for the growth of cattle. This by no means surprising deficiency is due to the poverty of tropical soils.[3] Only during the few weeks just before seeding are savanna grasses comparatively rich in phosphorus. The most widespread species, found in every continent, are the least nourishing. Altitude makes little difference in the matter.[4]

The poverty of tropical grassland results first of all in the slow growth of the animals. A Malgash ox takes six or seven years to reach its full development. And the beasts need a vast amount of space. It is estimated that an acre of tropical pasture can feed only 48 lb of live weight, whilst the same area in Europe can feed 480 lb.[5] According to experts in the former Belgian Congo, it takes at least twice as many acres of grass as there are months in the dry season to feed one full grown ox in a tropical country. This of course does not take into account areas without pasture.[6] In fact, in Madagascar a zebu uses on the average some fifteen acres of pasture.[7] In the State of São Paulo in a modified tropical climate grassland which is 'natural', or at least is due to spontaneous growth after the destruction of the trees or shrubs, is of no great value as fodder. Poor pasture, that is, fields of *barba de bode* (a kind of *Aristida*) could only support eight head of cattle per 1,000 acres. Pasture of medium quality in the township of Cunha feeds one beast per *alqueire* (about 5 acres). Good pasture which has been modified by man and artificially planted with *capim*

1. B. Havard-Duclos, *Bulletin économique de l'Indochine*, 1940, p. 15.
2. E.g. in Africa *Panicum, Paspalum,* and *Pennisetum*; and in Eastern Indo-China *Digitaria, Paspalum, Setaria,* and *Phalaris.*
3. See above, p. 16.
4. Scaetta, 'Les pâturages de haute montagne en Afrique centrale', *Bull. Agr. Congo Belge*, 1936, pp. 323–78. See also *Revue de Botanique appliquée et d'Agriculture tropicale*, 1938, p. 783, and 1941, p. 239.
5. Cp. the article by Havard-Duclos referred to above. See also J. M. Joubert, 'Breeding for beef in tropical and sub-tropical climates, with special reference to the continent of Africa', *Colonial Plant and Animal Products*, 4, 1954, pp. 9–12.
6. It must be remembered that regions with an equatorial climate, and so without a dry season, do not suit cattle in Africa.
7. In the province of Guanacasta on the Pacific coast of Costa Rica at least ten and often twenty or more acres of pasture are needed for a full-grown ox. See *Geog. Review*, 1943, p. 79.

colonia, capim jaraguá, or *capim Kikuyu,* can support just one beast per 3 acres, provided that the animals are given some maize or cotton-seed cake at the end of the dry season in September–November.[1]

So hot, wet regions are not naturally adapted to pastoralism. Besides, man has generally taken the natural conditions into account and in these regions as a whole does not devote himself to stock-rearing. His food is mainly vegetable[2] and is perhaps too poor in animal proteins. On the other hand, agriculture depends only to a slight extent on animals either for manure or for work. The ladang system makes ploughing unnecessary. If the soil has to be turned over, this is done with the hoe. The plough was unknown, except to the rice cultivators in southern Asia; and its use was spread by Euro-peans in the other tropical continents. Animals were rarely used for transport. To put it briefly, the agricultural systems of the tropics function as if animals did not exist. There is no appreciable difference between the pre-Columbian *milpa* system, which was established by folk who had neither ox, nor horse, nor ass, and the African or Asiatic system of burning out forest clearings. In Africa and Asia it is as if the system had been perfected by men who knew nothing about stock-rearing and were introduced to it only after having established their agricultural system. In truth, the ladang system is in equilibrium and gets on very well without the help of working animals. It must be added that in the tropics most animals are too under-nourished to have great strength. Pliny the Elder noted that the inhabitants of what is now Ethiopia worked with swing-ploughs, whilst in the area to the south this implement was quite unknown. The situation has not changed since the first century A.D.

Taken by and large, tropical civilizations tend to be almost wholly agricultural, the reason being that the physical environment is not very favourable to pastoral work. However, there are regions in which, owing to the type of civilization and an inveterate liking for pastoralism, man has developed cattle-rearing. The Sudan and, even more so, East Africa, Madagascar, and India produce cattle. Thus, there is an area around the western Indian Ocean in which the same passionate interest in cattle is found underneath differences in race, tongue, religion, and standard of civilization. This area is strikingly different from the Chinese world, which, though not ignorant of the use of beasts of burden, considers them strictly as machines.

Obviously, cattle-rearing is an imported practice in tropical Africa. At the present time the chief pastoral tribes still look like com-paratively recent immigrants from the north-east, and people like the

1. Information from Messrs. Setzer and Borges-Schmidt, agriculturalists in the state of São Paulo.
2. See below, p. 76ff.

Peuhls (Fula or Fulani) of West Africa and the various Hamitic tribes of East Africa are quite distinct from the negro cultivators. The practice of stock-rearing has therefore been introduced from the arid regions of north-eastern Africa into the hot, wet parts in which it is not utterly precluded by cattle diseases.

The introduction was on the whole disastrous, for the damage done by pastoralism is incalculable, whilst the economic advantages are insignificant. In fact, the savannas that form the prevailing vegetation-type in the Sudan, East Africa, and Madagascar are mainly due to the need for making grazing grounds.[1] Shepherds are mainly responsible for the fires whose smoke darkens the horizon at the end of the dry season. The cultivator's clearings[2] and the desire to track down game easily when it has been frightened by fire, or to get honey and

1. The problem of the origin of tropical savannas cannot be dealt with here, but on the whole man seems to be the main cause of their existence. Forest is the climax of natural vegetation, even in regions with a very marked dry season. The Sahelian zone on the edge of the Sahara still carries a scrub of thorn-trees. In certain cases the savanna is possibly original. See, for instance, Pellegrin, 'La flore du Mayombé d'après les récoltes de M. G. Le Testu', *Mémoires Société linnéenne de Normandie*, Caen, 3 fol., 1934–8 (critical review by Auguste Chevalier, *Revue de Botanique appliquée et d'Agriculture tropicale*, 1939, pp. 276–297). See also W. Robyns, 'La forêt équatoriale est-elle discontinue?', *Journées d'agronomie coloniale*, Louvain, Etab. Ceuterik, 1938, p. 5. The *llanos* of Venezuela, which are immense savannas streaked with gallery forest, seem to have existed before the arrival of the Spaniards. However, the pre-Columbian Indians did not practise stock-rearing and had no interest in making large pasture lands. Had the Indians had time to destroy the forest by cultivating their *milpas* too often? Mounds, ramparts, watch towers, fragments of beautiful painted pottery have been found, which seem to point to a fairly advanced civilization among the Ashagua, Yagual, and Arichuma Indians who lived on the *llanos*. But the natives were in a state of utter decadence when the Spaniards arrived. (R. E. Crist has studied the influence of the geographical environment on man in 'Le Llanero', *Revue de Géog. Alpine*, 1935, pp. 97–114.) Today the Venezuelan *llanos* are burnt every year, for the *llaneros* claim that the fire gives them the best pastures and kills the ticks—a belief that remains to be proved. One wonders whether the *llaneros* are not merely subject to an irrational routine. The Kamarakoto Indians, who also live on the *llanos*, ingenuously admit that they like to watch the savanna burning. (H. Pittier, 'Consideraciones acerca de la destrucción de los bosques y del incendio de las sabanas', *Bol. Soc. Venezolana de Ciencias Naturales*, No. 26, vol. 3, 1936, pp. 1–12; G. G. Simpson, 'Los Indios Kamarakotos', *Revista de Fomento*, Ministerio de Fomento, Venezuela, nos. 22–5, vol. 3, pp. 201–660; and researches mentioned in *Geog. Review*, 1941, p. 429.) The problem of the origin of some of the tropical savannas cannot be solved except by exact floristic and pedological researches. But it seems to us that man's action must have been the predominant factor in creating the greater part of the savanna areas which are covered with common-place species found throughout the tropics. Thus it is noticed in East Africa (for example, in the national parks) that the protection of a portion of the savanna encourages the growth of trees and makes for the retreat of the grass owing to the stopping of fires. In that way the environment becomes less favourable to the big ruminants and their carnivorous followers, and the fauna is being modified. Ultimately, therefore, East African big game is largely dependent on the fires lit by man.

2. See above, pp. 32 and 50–1, for clearing by fire and complementary views about savannas.

wax, are far less effective causes of the burning. The savanna was necessarily made by fire, and afterwards shepherds who wished to feed their hungry beasts at the end of the dry season were forced to burn the tall grass, which at that time becomes too hard to be eaten by the animals and is reduced to hard filaments fully deserving of the name 'wire-grass' given to it in South Africa. The fire clears the soil of useless dry straw and at the first fall of rain favours the emission from the rhizomes of young shoots which pierce the sooty soil with pale green tips and give the animals a feast.

Once established in a tropical region, pastoralism is therefore driven logically to repeat its fires every year. The damage done by this is immense and out of proportion to the benefit obtained from the pastoral facilities it procures. It is ludicrous, says Mr Aubréville, to weigh the advantages of bush-fires against the disadvantages. 'The burning of a house may also have the happy effect of incidentally destroying some nests of termites and bugs.'[1]

In pastoral areas the annual burning of the grass has become a necessary and customary practice. Among the Biroms on the Bauchi plateau in Nigeria the kindling is a ceremony. Hence, it is very difficult to struggle against deeply ingrained customs and the immediate interests of the herdsmen. In East Africa the authorities try to compromise with the evil and do not attempt to suppress it. They recommend early fires to destroy the useless straw and to cause least harm to the trees, for at the beginning of the dry season the trees all have a vegetative rest, whilst at the end of the season they already have buds and little leaves and suffer great damage from fires then. Besides, it has been said that the complete suppression of fires would be imprudent, because if after three or four years' respite fires were to break out anew, the effects would be disastrous owing to the great quantity of combustible matter which would have collected. But the system of early burning may in the long run lead to the re-establishment of trees, thus diminishing the danger of fire by reducing the area covered by grass. Will the fanatical pastoralists of East Africa accept such a change?

It would appear that the soil in savannas does not keep its relative fertility in spite of burning; burning progressively ruins the soil and conduces to a succession of grasses each less exacting, but also less nourishing. In the Teso district of Uganda the first grass to appear after a burning is *Imperata cylindrica*. It is cropped by the cattle until it grows to about a foot high and blooms, after which it becomes too hard. The grasses which grow up a little later are eaten when young, but at the end of a few weeks the cattle avoid some of them

1. A. Aubréville, 'Les forêts du Dahomey et du Togo', *Bull. Comité Etudes historiques et scientifiques de l'Afrique occidentale française*, 1937, p. 24.

like *Trichopteryx*, *Sporobolus*, and *Urochloa*. When the rains come on, *Digitaria*, *Chloris*, and *Eragrostis* appear, but the cattle eat only *Eragrostis superba* and *E. Chalcantha*. On account of the unfortunate selection practised by the cattle and the progressive impoverishment of the soil owing to burning, the savanna is gradually changed to bare soil dotted at intervals with tufts of *Sporobolus pyramidalis*. In the Teso district this vegetation-type seems to be the final state of the savanna.[1] (See Plates 19–24).

The evolution is hastened by the tendency among tropical pastoralists to keep more cattle than the natural savannas allow, for the herdsmen take a pride in a large number of animals and care little about the return they get from the herds. Over-stocking brings on the usual consequences, viz. exhaustion of the grass and erosion of the soil. The first marks of erosion occur at the drinking pools, where the banks are worn by the feet of too many animals. The activities of certain termites may hasten the evolution. Termites of the genus *Hodotermes* pick green blades of grass in the East African savannas and may succeed in completely denuding the ground around the termitaries. In consequence, violent erosion occurs at the very next rain.

When the land is protected from the abuse of overstocking the state of the vegetation rapidly improves. For instance, between Timbuktu and Kabara the military authorities have since the conquest reserved an area of 10,000 or 12,000 acres to feed the herds intended for supplying the troops. Wandering tribes are excluded from the area. In about sixty years a 'Sahelian' forest has grown up, with trees 25 feet high. Though less vigorous, the protective measures taken in Gurma in the bend of the Niger have given good results.[2] But could such measures be extended to vast expanses without touching the immediate interests of the pastoralists?

In East Africa Hamitic tribes from the north are much given to cattle-rearing and have communicated their enthusiasm for pastoralism to many Bantu tribes (see Fig. 9). In their scale of values stock-rearing is a noble pursuit, and a man's dignity is largely measured by

1. See *Agriculture in Uganda*, 1904, p. 504, edited by J. D. Tothill. On exceptionally fertile soil like the black earth of central Uganda this evolution does not occur or else it takes place very slowly, and the mantle of tall grass (Elephant grass, *Pennisetum purpureum*) is permanent.

2. The facts seem to prove that the impoverishment of the vegetation observed on the northern borders of the Sudan is not due to present desiccation of the climate or the advance of the Sahara, but to bad treatment of the pastures and the damage done by fires.

dary forest in the Mayan
tains after a vegetable plot
een abandoned. The forest
urnt in May, 1945, and the
graph was taken in April,
The boles are those of Santa
trees (*Calophyllum brasili-*
var. *rekoi*). Putti palms have
ed the fire and at this eleva-
2,300 feet) a dense growth of
ferns has sprung up.

d watchman's platform in
showing the volcano Papan-
ayan in the background.

16.
A vegetable plot in a cleared patch in th
forest in Jamaica. It is more orderly tha
usually appears and contains yams, tanya
bananas, and sweet potatoes.

17.
Native huts and the vegetable garde
nearby. Yams are seen in the foregrou
and behind are sugarcane, bananas, a
other crops.

18.
An imposing Mayan ruin at Chichen Itz
The grandstand on the pitch where
dangerous ball-game known as *thax*
was played.

the number of oxen he has.[1] Certainly, the animals give meat, milk and even blood drawn off by skilful bleeding; but the herd is not only useful: it is held in honour. Usually, milking is forbidden to women and reserved to men. Among the proud Tutsi in Burundi the men alone have the privilege of milking.[2] They perform the task with great attention to cleanliness, for as a preliminary they carefully wash with fresh urine from the cow the wooden vessel in which the milk is to be caught. Yet they show great clumsiness in the operation, thus proving that, though enthusiastic pastoralists, they are not yet very expert at dairying. In fact, several men are needed for the milking: one or two to hold off the calf, one to quieten the cow, another to protect her from insects, and, lastly, one to do the milking. When two Tutsi chiefs meet, they greet each other with the words: 'I hope your cattle are well.' Stock-rearing is reserved to the chief tribe, the Tutsi, whilst the Hutu, a conquered tribe, are restricted to agriculture, though some of them may own a cow or two. Generally speaking, the more or less nomadic pastoralists have imposed their rule on the cultivators, and this has contributed no little to the excessive prestige of pastoralism. The same is true of many Peuhls in West Africa. If through poverty a Tutsi abandons stock-rearing for agriculture, he loses caste and even ceases to regard himself as a Tutsi.

The young Masai warriors in Kenya and Tanzania live exclusively on meat, milk, and blood. Among the Masai if an adjective is used without its noun, it is understood to refer to a cow. Among the Nilotic Dinka tribe a father gives a bull to his son on the latter's coming of age. The young man becomes fond of the animal and spends hours playing with it and singing songs to it. The death of a bull causes very great grief to its master.

Every head of a family makes a point of honour to add to his herd, if necessary by carrying off beasts from a hostile tribe. Being too numerous, the animals are underfed, ill-cared for, and in wretched condition. The Chaga, who live on the slopes of Kilimanjaro and keep their cattle indoors, feeding them with hay cut for the purpose, are exceptional; but they are cultivators, not herdsmen. It is not surprising that owing to peaceful conditions the number of cattle was doubled in the native reserves in Kenya between 1920 and 1933. In the latter year the Kamba reserve had 190,000 full-grown cattle

1. Some parts of East Africa are so high above sea level as to be no longer tropical. So the conditions are favourable to stock-rearing and afford especially interesting opportunities of transhumance. Owing to its altitude and the fertility of its soil the crater of Ngorongoro in Tanzania has pastures that are still green in the dry season and attract to its 60,000 acres some 80,000 head of game and 20,000 Masai cattle. In the rainy season the crater is deserted, and the vegetation can recover. Stock-rearing is not, however, confined to the high tableland, but is also found at low altitudes where *nagana* is rife.

2. H. L. Shantz, 'Urundi, territory and people', *Geog. Review*, 1922, p. 346.

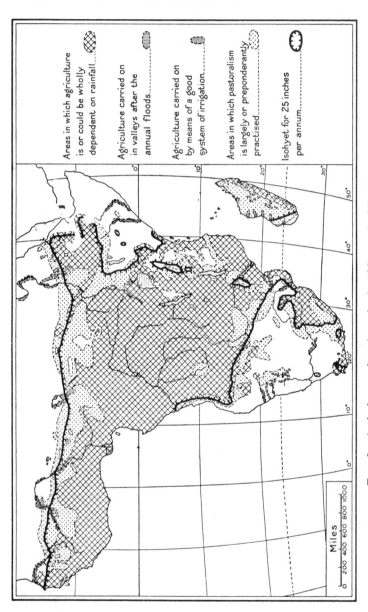

FIG. 9. Agriculture and stock-rearing in Africa south of the Sahara

(Mainly after F. R. Falkner, 'Die Trockengrenze des Regenfeldbaus in Africa,' *Petermanns G. Mitteilungen*, 1938)

Areas in which agriculture is or could be wholly dependent on rainfall

Agriculture carried on in valleys after the annual floods

Agriculture carried on by means of a good system of irrigation

Areas in which pastoralism is largely or preponderantly practised

Isohyet for 25 inches per annum

Miles
0   200   400   600   800   1000

and 57,000 calves, whilst its capacity did not exceed 60,000 head. And to the cattle must be added 260,000 goats and 150,000 sheep! So a good deal of the Kamba territory has been ruined, and the inhabitants, who can no longer migrate to other parts, are the victims of severe food-shortage. The situation is no better among the Sukumas south of Mwanza in Tanzania. It seems clear that ruin of the soil and pastures forced the Jabros to migrate from their original territory, which was situated to the east of Gondokoro in the Sudan, to their present position at Kavirondo to the east of Lake Victoria. The destruction of the soil through over-grazing is becoming a cause for worry in the Teso district of Uganda, where the number of cattle rose from 172,000 in 1921 to 386,000 in 1936.[1]

Cattle diseases, and especially trypanosomiasis (see Fig. 3), seem to be a bar to overstocking. Some people have seen in this a manifestation of nature's tendency to equilibrium, the rapid multiplication of one form of life being checked by the multiplication of another form. But optimism over the harmonies of nature seems misplaced, for in fact the fear of losses due to disease is one of the causes of overstocking. As cattle are the only form of wealth among the natives—or the only objects regarded as wealth—pastoralists guard against loss due to disease by keeping herds that are too big. It is difficult to ask them to reduce the number of their animals if at the same time the health of their beasts is not safeguarded. It should be noticed, furthermore, that disease leads to overstocking in another way. In Tanzania, for example, the pastoralists crowd their cattle into the dry, but healthy parts and avoid the damper, less healthy areas.

It would not be difficult to carry out the improvements which would make pastoralism in East Africa less harmful to the soil and give stock-rearing a greater economic value. The almost insurmountable difficulty today would be to persuade the people to put these improvements into practice. The first reform would be a reduction in the number of beasts. But how could this result be achieved if, as in India, cows have a sacred character or if, as in Urundi, cows continue to play an important part in the social organization? The pastoralists would have to change their outlook and regard their cattle as a purely commercial asset. But should this be achieved, cold calculators might be alarmed at the poverty of tropical pastures and their insignificant yields. Would not our business men regret the absurd period when they considered their beasts not as so many pounds sterling, but as living beings beloved for their gentle eyes and the colour of their coats?

1. Many other tropical lands suffer in the same way. An excessive number of goats has ruined the soil over vast areas of the State of Lara in northern Venezuela, where the bedrock now lies bare (*Geog. Review*, 1944, p. 66).

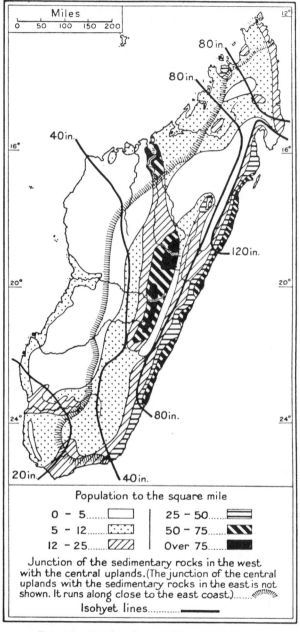

FIG. 10.   Density of population in Madagascar

Madagascar.(Fig. 10) with an area of 228,000 square miles and a population of 5,600,000, has 6 million head of cattle. The importance of the animals is of long standing and is not due to economic causes, for meat is not a usual element in the diet; indeed, many of the beasts die natural deaths and are buried, not eaten. Milk is not held in great esteem. Oxen were not used for transport, since the Malgash did not know of the wheel, but they were useful for treading down the flooded ricefields before the seedlings were planted out. This enormous number of cattle was indeed scarcely justified by economic reasons. But a large herd won for its owner the consideration of his neighbours, and the Malgash loves his oxen, regarding them as having a kind of soul not unlike that of man. Oxen are the objects of ceremonial washing of the same kind as that given to children and they are spoken of in the family with as much detail and affection as the sons and daughters. The Betsileo dialect has more than 120 names for describing oxen according to their coats. For instance, a *valaloaka* is a black or dark ox with white on all four feet, on the top of its hump, between the forelegs, on the thighs, and in the middle of the tail.[1]

But the animals are scarcely domesticated and are badly cared for. Malgash cows are not easy to milk. It is difficult to detach an animal from the herd, and when a zebu is to be sold all its companions must be taken to market with it. The oxen are tired out in immense journeys and are underfed. No trouble is taken to select, nor is there any effort made against the ticks which do great damage to the udders of the cows.

Of little economic value, this stock-rearing has had disastrous effects. Efforts to extend or improve the grazing temporarily have led the herdsmen to adopt the practice of regularly setting bush fires every year, which has ruined the forests and impoverished the savannas. Cultivation on patches cleared by fire and known as *tavy* has contributed to this result, but its ravages are very small compared with those perpetrated by herdsmen.

Before man's intervention the vegetation of Madagascar consisted of forest and bush of a very peculiar composition. Today the original Malgash flora occupies only 27,000 square miles out of the island's 228,000 square miles. The scrub in the south should also be subtracted from the area covered by the original forest. True forest covers scarcely more than 12,000 square miles. This tropical island, which is apparently well watered and has only 25 persons to the square mile on the average, is already without wood enough for its current needs and has to import timber from the north temperate regions. A town

1. R. P. Dubois, *Monographie des Betsileo*, Paris, Institut d'ethnologie, 1938, p. 488.

like Antananarivo, situated in a wet tropical climate, is without the least source of firewood within a radius of 60 miles.

A small portion of the country, about 16,000 square miles, is still under *savoka*, that is, secondary jungle growing on the *tavy*. But 180,000 square miles are under savanna. This savanna is perhaps not very old, possibly between 500 and 4,000 years.[1] Thus, in a very short space of time the vegetation-type in Madagascar has been radically changed by fire. The forests on the central mountains were very combustible. Those in the west were more resistant, but were gradually eaten away round the edges. The more fertile the soil the more violent the fires, for on rich earth the thicker grass formed better fuel for the flames. Hence, the forest has persisted only on the poorest soil and in lines along the watercourses.

The grassland is not uniform either in time or space. It varies according to the quality of the soil and the stage reached in evolution. The more advanced the stage, the greater the chance the savanna has of being poor. Three states can be defined: first, the savanna consists mainly of *Imperata arundinacea*, a tall grass which requires fairly rich soil and disappears as the soil becomes exhausted; this is followed by smaller grasses which are, however, more important from the pastoral point of view, viz. *vero* (*Cymbopogon rufus* and *Andropogon rufus*), *verobe* (*Cymbopogon cymbarius*), *tsimatiloha* (*Andropogon intermedius*), and *danga* (*Heteropogon contortus*); and, lastly, comes the *Aristida* grassland, in which tufts that cattle will not eat are dotted about at intervals, leaving much of the soil bare.

In respect of meat, milk, manure and work, tropical cattle do not make the contribution that their vast numbers would lead one to expect. In the whole of the tropical world in 1954, an area covering 16 million square miles and with a population of 1,100 millions, there were 475 million oxen and buffaloes, as against 450 million cattle in the temperate zones, which covered 22 million square miles and contained 1,600 million people. Such a comparison however, is of little significance for the figures are falsified by the huge areas of China and India. The latter has an immense stock of cattle, 200 million as against 460 million people, whereas the Chinese lands have but 50 million animals and 780 million people. If the Indian lands are excluded from the tropical world figures and China from those of the temperate zone, there are 35 oxen and buffaloes to every 100 persons in the tropics and 46 in the temperate zone. Is the difference worthy of attention? Most certainly, for the tropical animals yield but little meat, and under existing conditions their growth is very slow—the Peuhls of Macina sell cattle for slaughter which are sometimes ten

1. Perrier de la Bâthie, *La végétation de Madagascar*, 1921, p. 173, concludes that possibly man has not long existed in Madagascar.

years old. There is little milk yield either; an overall estimate of the average milk production per person per year gives 595 lb in the temperate zone (excluding China) and 48 lb in the tropical world (including India).

Pastoral activities in the tropics are thus not very productive, and they may be very destructive. But clearly, should cattle diseases allow (and at the moment they often do not) stock-raising, as an ancillary to agriculture, supplying it with manure and labour, would on the contrary offer great advantages. Great possibilities of economic progress are thus opened up for the tropical lands by the improvement of animal husbandry. For example, though cattle have so far been excluded from central Africa by diseases, goats do not seem to suffer, and they could be of much greater economic importance as well as providing meat, for at present they are only used to buy wives. The Jumna Pari variety of Indian goat yields 8 lb of milk a day if it is well fed; but since in Africa goats are not milked at all, there would be no point in introducing a good milking variety. Climate and unhealthiness are in no way responsible for this state of affairs, neither are they concerned with the all-too-frequent prohibition on the use of eggs which makes the consumption of this commodity even lower than the already very low production.

The weaknesses of tropical stock-raising arise in the main from inadequate techniques. For example, the Mvuazi region of the lower Congo can only carry 1 cow to 17 acres of grazing; controlled burning and rotation of grazing areas will enable this figure to be reduced to 7 acres, whilst the careful grubbing-up of shrubs, the mowing of the grass and the sowing of a leguminous crop can finally raise the stock to 1 animal per 2 acres.

If animals are not used for work it is the nature of the civilization that is responsible, not the natural conditions. The southern Tuareg and the Baggara Arabs have oxen as freight-carriers, the Hausa and Masai have pack-asses: the Hima and the Tutsi do not use their oxen as beasts of burden and they have no other pack animals either. The use of animals to tread out the harvested grain, common in northern Africa, does not extend beyond Ethiopia, though further south there are both cereals and oxen. Would it not appear that the technique of threshing by treading could have no part in a civilization that knew nothing of either harness or the plough?

CHAPTER 7

Problems of Food Supply

THE tropical world, as we have defined it (p. 1) is warm enough for crops to be harvested in every month of the year. The rainfall on the other hand exercises a restrictive influence; the true equatorial régime, which permits annual plants to grow at all times, occurs over only a small part of the hot, wet lands, and the bulk of the area falls under the tropical régime, which limits the agricultural season—at any rate for annual plants—to the rainy period and thus allows only one harvest a year. This being granted, however, the climatic conditions of the rainy tropics are remarkably favourable for agriculture, and at first sight it is surprising that almost all the population of the tropics suffers from food problems, either temporary or chronic shortages, or unbalanced diets that are deficient in protein and vitamins. In actual fact these food problems are the result not of the tropical climate but of the state of civilization; man himself is responsible for the shortages and the malnutrition, as a few simple examples will show. Irrigation is rarely practised, though it could eliminate agricultural unemployment in the dry season and overcome the irregularities in the rainfall régime—but irrigation is inseparable from permanent agriculture and incompatible with the ladang system. Manure is very little used in the traditional agricultural systems of Africa and tropical America; and food of animal origin plays a small part, a far too small part, in the diet, even of those people who have some cattle.

It is in the nature of things that non-pastoral people should have a vegetarian diet. The Mayas of Yucatan live almost entirely on maize and beans; meat (only venison) and eggs have but a small part in their diet, representing only 25 of the 125 pesos' worth of food consumed in 1932 by an average Chan Kom family.[1] But the Betsileo of Madagascar, in spite of their herds, live on rice eked out with cassava, sweet potatoes, maize, spinach, and fruit. Meat seldom forms part of their meals, and milk is unknown. Cockchafer larvae, caterpillars, grasshoppers, and small fish compose the main part of their animal food. The Fulas (Peuhls) of Futa Jallon, who consume more milk and meat than the average West African negro, feed chiefly on vegetables. Milk, melted butter, and (with all sorts of restrictions) meat figures in Hindu fare; and yet the main proportion of their food calories is

1. Shattuck, *The Peninsula of Yucatan*, p. 57.

derived from cereals and *dhal* (a mixture of chickpeas and beans). Even in the Punjab, where more animal food is eaten than in the rest of India, investigation carried out in Lyallpur has shown that 85 per cent of food-energy is derived from vegetable matter. The average daily ration of a Hindu rice eater[1] comprises 560 grammes of rice, 30 of peas and beans, 125 of fresh vegetables, 9 grammes of oil and vegetable fats, 14 grammes of fish, meat, and eggs, and a negligible quantity of milk. This ration is deficient in animal proteins and fats, in calcium, and vitamins. It is no exaggeration to say that in the tropics as a whole animal foods do not contribute to the diet more than 4 or 5 per cent of the total amount of calories. Attachment to ancient and traditional eating habits provides a better explanation than the restrictive effect of the natural environment. The Tarascan Indians of Mexico borrowed from the Spaniards the practice of ploughing with oxen, but they are poor stock-raisers; their beasts suffer during the dry season, meat and milk are consumed in only small quantities, and the Tarascans keep their cattle for reasons of prestige rather than as an economic resource.[2]

People living in hot, wet countries display great ingenuity in making use of the resources of the vegetable kingdom. They eat everything that is edible, and so far no reduction in the number of plants eaten as food is noticeable among them, though such a reduction is characteristic of modern European civilization. In Ghana there have been counted 114 kinds of edible fruit (which are in fact eaten), 46 kinds of leguminous seeds (groundnuts, beans, etc.), and 47 kinds of green leaves cooked like spinach.

The chief food throughout is a mess of carbohydrates (cereals, various tubers, and roots, bananas, breadfruit, and flour made from the ribs of *ensété* leaves). It is accompanied by boiled leaves, fat, oil, salt, and spices. For instance, in the Mossi district on the Ivory Coast a gruel is prepared with crushed groundnuts, pounded sesame, tomatoes, gumbo (*Abelmoschus esculentus*), hibiscus seeds and leaves, red pepper, leaves and butter from the butter-tree (*Butyrospermum Parkii*), *néré* fruit, baobab seeds and leaves, kapok tree leaves (Bombax), and many other ingredients. The quantity consumed in this way is at times considerable. For instance, in the Toma district on the lower Ivory Coast a man eats every day several hundred grammes of leaves boiled in water or oil.

As a whole, in making use of nature people in the hot, wet belt turn almost exclusively to the vegetable kingdom for their tools, clothes,

1. According to Aykroyd, quoted by Sir L. Rogers and Sir J. W. D. Megan, *Tropical Medicine*, London, 1944, p. 404.
2. R. L. Beals, *Chéran: a Sierra Tarascan Village*, Washington, Smithsonian Inst., 1946.

and dwellings. Like the people in the Far East,[1] they belong to a 'vegetable civilization'. They have evinced the highest degree of ingenuity in getting the best out of certain plants. The innumerable possibilities afforded by the bamboo are well known[2]; and in northern Ceylon the palmyra tree (*Borassus flabellifer*) has no fewer than 801 uses, whilst the oil palm (*Elaeis guineensis*) is quite as valuable to the people of the Guinea coast and is really the basis of daily life.[3] The fibrous husk of the nut yields oil which is used in the preparation of all kinds of food. The nut is eaten raw. Its oil, though less esteemed, is chiefly used for making cosmetics. After the extraction of the oil, the fibres are carefully kept, dried, and used for kindling fires. The ashes of the male flowers take the place of table salt. When the stalk which bears the bunch is teased out, it makes a good brush for whitewashing walls with lime or kaolin. A fibre used for mending broken calabashes is taken from the spathe covering the bunches. The leaves are made into roofing, screens to protect young plants from the sun, fish-fences, and baskets for carrying on the back or in the hand. The veins of the leaflets are used for making little fly-whisks which the chiefs carry in their hands. The spines of the fronds serve as rafters. When cut into thin laths, they make rat-traps or snares for birds, and when flattened, they give rough paddles. The juice from the spine is used for healing cuts. The fluff taken off the bases of the leaves catches fire easily and is used as tinder. The central leaf-buds are eaten raw or cooked as palm cabbage. Among the Fangs it is boiled with red pepper to form a remedy for bronchitis. The sap which flows from a hole cut in the central leaf buds is made into palm wine. The roots are chewed as an aphrodisiac. As soon as the tree is felled, the trunk is attacked by the larvae of a big beetle (*Rhynchophorus ferrugineus*), and these 'palm worms' are a popular dainty.

In New Guinea, whilst the inhabitants of the coastal areas live on sago and those of the neighbouring hills on taro, the mountain people of the high interior valleys, such as the Balim and the Tiom in Irian (western New Guinea), or those of the Chimbu country in eastern New Guinea, feed almost exclusively—to the extent of 90 per cent of their calorie intake—on sweet potatoes (*Ipomea*). The tiny alluvial plains are devoted exclusively to carefully maintained strips of sweet potatoes separated by water channels—a neolithic technology, but intensive, with good soil cultivation, use of manure, and careful irrigation. This is in great contrast to the ladang of the bordering

1. P. Gourou, *L'Utilisation du sol en Indochine française*, Paris, Centre d'études de politique étrangère, 1940, p. 192; P. Gourou, *La terre et l'homme en Extrême-Orient*, Paris, 1940, pp. 20 and 114.

2. See P. Gourou, *La terre et l'homme en Extrême-Orient*, p. 21

3. Abbé A. Walker, *Rév. de botanique appliquée et d'agriculture tropicale*, 1939, pp. 689–93.

hills and the exploitation of the sago palm (little more than mere collecting) in the coastal belt. It is remarkable and paradoxical that the most isolated people (and they are indeed remarkably cut off) should have the most intensive, skilful and productive agriculture (in terms of yield per acre), whilst those less isolated have much less careful techniques (though these may possibly yield more per man-hour).

This intensive agriculture in the high valleys is the result of their isolation; indeed one might almost regard these people as in a state of siege. It is practised by some 300,000 people in Irian and 400,000 in eastern New Guinea. The daily individual food intake comprises 1,500–2,000 grammes of tubers and 200–400 g of greenstuff; a special investigation carried out amongst the Dani people of the Tiam valley tried to estimate the effect on health of this vegetarian diet which contains such a high proportion of sweet potatoes.[1] Other than these potatoes the only items in the diet are green vegetables and sugar cane. The daily intake is extraordinarily deficient in protein—only 14 or 15 g of vegetable protein compared with the 30 g that are really necessary. Furthermore, the sweet potatoes contain very little fat, and the entire diet is very deficient in salt. These New Guinea mountain peoples get only 75 milligrammes of salt a day, and some nutrition experts say that the minimum intake should be 500 mg. But the food is rich in potassium, to the extent of three times the normal requirement, so that the sodium-potassium ratio in the urine of these people is 1 to 300, whereas the normal elsewhere is 2 to 1—even the most salt-lacking sick European never sinks quite so low! The diet is however rich in calcium and even more so in phosphorus. All in all, it is not surprising that people sustained by this sort of diet suffer from kwashiorkor (and cases of cirrhosis of the liver in children, due to lack of protein, are frequent); it is astonishing that they are as well as they are. In fact the general state of health is not bad and demographic progress is satisfactory.[2]

The same ill-balanced diets are to be found all over the tropical world, and the lack of animal protein, of fats, of vitamins or of

1. H. A. P. C. Oomen, et al, 'The sweet potato as the staff of life of the Highland Papuan', Tropical and Geographical Medicine, 1961, pp. 55–6.
2. It is not without interest that similar optimistic remarks could be made about certain East African pastoralists whose diet is the very antithesis of that of the Papuans. Most of the calorie intake of the Samburus is provided by milk; this milk is very rich in butterfat, and a warrior (moran) who drinks 12 pints of milk a day absorbs 340 g. of fat, making 60 per cent of his total calorie intake. We might note that this diet, so rich in animal products, does not seem to give the people any superiority over their vegetarian counterparts. The vegetarian Kikuyu would appear to have a greater future before them than the milk and blood-drinking Masai. See A. G. Shaper and P. Spencer, 'Physical activity and dietary patterns in the Samburu of Northern Kenya', Tropical and Geographic Medicine, 1961, pp. 273–80.

mineral elements is responsible for many deficiency diseases. It is true that animal protein can be replaced by vegetable protein in many not unpleasant ways; for example, polished rice is poor in lysine (an amino-acid) whilst peas lack another amino-acid, methionine, but the mixture of rice and peas may give an adequate ration of amino-acids. If combinations of this sort are not available the lack of protein, and especially of animal protein, can provoke serious trouble; kwashiorkor can lead to degeneration of the liver and even infantile cancer of the liver.

The consumption of animal protein may be reduced by unfortunate taboos;[1] the people of Grenada in the Antilles think that milk will give children worms, the Sinhalese regard milk as the cause of many diseases, the New Hebrideans look on it as a revolting food; in some parts of Tanzania women are forbidden to drink milk, whilst in parts of Uganda the same prohibition applies to men. Women are forbidden to eat eggs over the greater part of black Africa.

The spread of manioc (cassava) must be viewed with some disquiet, for the cassava flour is particularly poor in proteins, as indeed it is in fat and in mineral matter as well. When cassava is substituted for a cereal or for yams or taro, the greater richness of these foods in protein, fat and minerals is lost; famines may have been avoided, but deficiency diseases multiply rapidly.[2] However, the progress of cassava has also some advantages. The plant will grow on any soil, and accommodates itself to any tropical rainfall régime; the yield is enormous in favourable conditions and quite large even in poor conditions. Cassava requires less labour than cereals, yams or taro; its leaves are a useful vegetable, and the plant can be left in the ground, thus dispensing with the labour of building grain stores. It is easy to understand why cassava, which was introduced into Africa in the sixteenth century, has so appealed to the Africans. It is still spreading, and this equatorial plant has proved the salvation of many drier tropical areas. In Travancore, in southern India, rice is the main foodstuff, but the growth of the population can no longer be sustained by the paddy-fields which cannot be extended, and cassava cultivation

1. *Nutrition in the Colonial Empire*, London, H.M.S.O., 1939, *passim*; also F. J. Simoons, *Eat not this Flesh*, Madison, Wis., 1961.
2. The following data concerning amino-acids are interesting: cassava flour is very poor in methionine and cystine, the molecules of which contain sulphur; a kilogramme of cassava flour, which would supply a human being with 3000 calories, contains only 0·1 g. of sulphur, whereas an intake of only 1500 calories, made up of 400 g. of bread, 100 g. of meat and 500 cm³. of milk would contain 0·76 g. of sulphur. It may be noted also that the minimum ration of methionine for an adult man is 1·1 g. and the optimum 2·2 g., whereas a daily diet of cassava contains only 0·2 g. See E. L. Adrisens, 'Recherches sur la composition en acides aminés des protéins d'aliments végétaux du Congo Belge et du Ruanda Urundi', Brussels, *A.R.Sc. col. sect. Sc. nat. et méd.*, mem. 8, n.s. IV. 3, 1955.

has been developed on the poor lateritic soils of the high terraces. Similar developments have taken place in Java. It is the task of modern science and technology to enable the peoples of the tropics to continue to benefit from the immense advantages of cassava (for it is unthinkable that they should be deprived of it) whilst avoiding the unfortunate consequences of a cassava-based diet. The well-fed specialist dietician should not just advise half-starved people not to eat an imperfect product; he should discover simple means of correcting the imperfections.[1]

The lack of vitamins is as serious as the deficiency in proteins. To this cause, plus the lack of lime, has been attributed the low fertility of Hausa women; and it is probably one of the causes of phagedenic (i.e. spreading) ulcers. The negroes of West Africa are very wise in eating large quantities of baobab leaves, which are rich in lime and vitamins. If, as is the local custom, the leaves are dried in the shade before being crushed to powder, the vitamins are not destroyed and stores of pulverized leaves can be laid up for the dry season. The lack of vitamins is perhaps surprising in a climate in which fruits can ripen all the year round; but in most parts of the tropics the culture of tree fruits is but poorly developed. Diseases of the digestive system also exercise a baneful influence, and these too may be due to lack of vitamins. The Moba people in northern Togoland have a vitamin A deficiency which could easily be counteracted by eating ripe mangoes (they eat them green, before the vitamin content has developed) or better still by consuming butter. The Moba mix with the Fulas who produce more butter than they need, but the Moba refuse to eat it. In order to use up their surplus the Fulas make it into soap, which they sell in the markets—and the Moba, who do not eat butter, wash their clothes in vitaminized soap![2]

After all due consideration has been given to these qualitative deficiencies in tropical diets, it remains further a matter of regret that the food intake of the people is also all too often deficient in quantity. A careful study (which has, however, missed certain details) of the Bembas of Zambia[3] has shown that the average ration of a grown man does not exceed 1,700 calories a day, although, according to calculations made by League of Nations experts, the ration of an unemployed man should be 2,400 calories a day, and the miners in the Copper

1. The poisonous prussic acid that cassava always contains is easily removed by soaking, and in spite of this the preparation of cassava before cooking does not take up more time than that required for cereals. Furthermore, it is an error to think that cassava ruins the soil; on the contrary, it is a soil-conserving plant.
2. J. Périsse, *L'alimentation des populations rurales du Togo*, Paris, ORSOM, 1959 (duplicated).
3. A. I. Richards, *Land, Labour and Diet in Northern Rhodesia*, London 1939, p. 35.

Belt are provided with a ration containing 4,300 calories. In northern Nigeria, an adult in yam-eating districts should consume every day 40 oz of yam, between 0·2 and 0·4 oz of meat, between 1 and 2 pints of whey, and 0·4 oz of large millet. Now, though the Tivs eat more or less that quantity of vegetable food, they have neither meat nor milk.[1] How could a wage-earner in Ceylon earning no more than 40 cents a day (1939) feed his family properly, seeing that a man's food (the usual food and not the optimum) costs 15 cents?

The inadequacy of the diet is especially marked at the end of the agricultural year, when stocks are running out. Most tropical peoples go short at that time. Efforts are made to eke out the insufficient rations by collecting on the savanna or in the forest seeds of wild grass, tubers, wild fruit, mushrooms, and caterpillars. It is a common sight in the African bush to see parties of women in search of these supplementary foods.

Food shortage is rife even among good cultivators like the Dans and Wobës around Man on the Ivory coast. These people live on the borderline between forest and savanna park, where they attain a density of 20 to 25 persons to the square mile. They cultivate upland rice and have been able to distinguish thirty-seven varieties with different properties; e.g. early and late rice. These they sow deliberately according to the qualities of the soil and the calls of the diet, and they have devised five different kinds of rotation which they apply to fields of different qualities. They even attempt commercial agriculture, for they cultivate the kola-nut tree. All the same, they suffer from a considerable shortage in July and the beginning of August and have to eke out their fare by collecting various things, especially the little tubers of a very poisonous wild yam (*Dioscorea latifolia*, var. *sylvestris*), which are not edible until they have been soaked for a long time in water.[2] Food is very short from July to September among the yam-eating Baulës on the savanna of the Ivory Coast. The Melanesian people of Dobu island in the Entrecasteaux group (New Guinea), who are yam-eaters, suffer shortages every year before the commencement of the harvest; but at least they have the sense not to eat the yams which have been laid up as seed for next year's crop—if they did eat these they would just starve. The Dogons of Bandiagara in the Niger bend try to protect themselves against famine by building barns big enough to hold two or three crops, but even so they do not always avoid a shortage of food. Though Futa Jallon has the reputation of not being one of the poorest districts and though its population reaches a density of 50 to the square mile, dearth reigns there every year. When their barns are empty, the Fulas fall back on

1. *Farm and Forest* (Ibadan), 1944, June, p. 22.
2. H. Labouret, *Ann. de Géog.*, 1937, p. 604.

oranges.[1] Among the Bembas of Zambia dearth of food occurs from January to March, when the stocks of eleusine are exhausted and nothing remains except gourds, a little maize, and whatever can be collected.

By an unfortunate but inevitable coincidence the busiest period in agriculture occurs just when the cultivators are worst off for food. The end of the dry season and the beginning of the wet is in fact the time when the fields must be hoed and the ridges and mounds made, and it is just then that the barns become empty. Thus the area prepared for sowing is too small because the workers are hungry and lack energy, and for the same reason the work may be delayed, so that planting takes place sometime after the beginning of the rains and the resulting harvest is much reduced. In this way the physical exhaustion of the cultivators at sowing time aggravates the next year's shortages. The spirited Bamenda women have nothing to sustain them, at hoeing time, but a bowl of soup made from ground leaves, which they consume in the evening.[2] One reason for the success of cassava is, as we have seen, that it can overcome this annual food shortage. The success of maize is in part due to the same thing, for maize can be harvested early if necessary, since the unripe cobs are quite edible.[3]

The belt of equatorial rains with no marked dry season has as a rule an advantage over regions with a tropical rainfall régime. First, the vegetation, both spontaneous and cultivated, benefits from the continuous rains. It has been observed in Congo-Léopoldville that soil poor in chemicals, but enjoying a uniform rainfall system, is equivalent to soil relatively rich in chemicals, but having a dry season lasting four or five months.[4] Besides, the rainfall systems are more irregular when there is a marked dry season. Even the provident Dogons, who eat millet, were subjected to famine by the drought of 1914; and the ravages of locusts, which commonly occur during a dry period following several wet years, are often quite catastrophic on the borders of the arid zones. On the contrary the inhabitants of the equatorial zone, who consume tubers and yams, are much less affected by annual shortages. Climate alone, however, is not directly

1. Ch. Robequain, *Revue de Géog. alpine*, 1937, p. 575.

2. P. M. Kaberry, *Women of the Grass fields*, Colonial Research Publ. No. 14. London. H.M.S.O. 1952.

3. Sometimes the annual shortage of the customary food crop can be relieved by eating another variety of food which would normally not be touched. Thus from the beginning of May to the middle of August the Kuranko and the Ture of the Ivory Coast, having exhausted their stocks of rice, consume taro, sweet potatoes and cassava; they do not like this, for they much prefer rice, but it keeps them alive.

4. J. Baeyens, *Les sols de l'Afrique centrale*, 1938, p. 22; see above, p. 16, n. 4. The author adds on p. 139 that a rainfall of 55 in is critical, and less than this causes a water deficiency in the lower Congo region.

responsible for the lack of adequate food supplies in the tropics. It is a case of inadequate techniques, which produce harvests that are only just sufficient to feed the producers; there are no surpluses to create a margin of safety over and above current consumption. This situation cannot be explained simply in terms of the natural conditions; it also involves human responsibility in two directions, first, for the sowing of too small an area per person, which results in too small a harvest, and secondly, for the low yield per acre. The inadequacy of the sown area may be linked with the excess of rural population (as in parts of Java) but this is rather unusual, for in the tropical lands as a whole, even allowing for the ladang system, there is no lack of space, as our population studies have shown. The smallness of the sown area is due far more to the complete absence of animal or mechanical aids, and to the concentration of agricultural work into too short a period (for in the dry season the soil is too hard to be hoed, and the sowing must be done as soon as the rains begin). Weeding and soil cleaning are very time-taking and difficult operations in fields with mixed crops, so much so that there is no point in extending the cultivated area unless the ability to keep it clean can be assured either by an increased labour force or by the use of machinery (which would mean abandoning the mixed polyculture). In such circumstances the attractions of cassava are easily understood, for this crop enables famine and even food shortage to be avoided with but a small cultivated area and a minimum of labour. In the Banda country of the Central African Republic, where it is true the population density is low (13 per square mile), each cultivator grows more cassava than he needs, so that much remains unharvested, to be uprooted by wart-hogs.

The time devoted to agricultural operations is often far too short. In the village of Madomale, in the Central African Republic,[1] the men devote only 9·8 per cent of their time to agriculture and the women 13·5 per cent; these percentages are all the more significant since the number of men taking part in the agricultural work is only 72 per cent of the number of women. Amongst the Nsaw tribe of the Bamenda,[2] the aversion of the men to agricultural work is such that they devote only six days' labour to the fields, which cover about one and a half acres, whilst the women and girls give 190 days of labour in six months. A study of the Zande area in the Wele region of Congo-Léopoldville in 1959–61 showed that the menfolk devoted 19 per cent of their working time to agriculture and the women 27 per

1. République centrafricaine. Mission socio-économique Centre-Oubangui (Bureau pour le développement de la production agricole), *L'emploi du temps du paysan dans une zone de l'Oubangui central* (1959–60), Paris, Ministère de la Coopération; 1961.
2. Cf. P. M. Kaberry, *Women of the Grass fields*, London. H.M.S.O. 1952.

19. Grassland in Kenya resulting from overstocking. Note the scattered Kikuyu village.

20. Masai women moving their village across scrub on the Nyeri plains. They belong to a tribe of nomadic cattlemen.

21. An abandoned vegetable plot covered with *Imperata cylindrica* in the Katanga district in the Congo.

22. The Bateke plateau twelve miles north of Brazzaville in the Congo. The plateau top is sandy, and the dry valley has incised meanders and convex sides. The vegetation consists of tufts of grass. This is burnt every year to facilitate the hunting of game. Popula tion density does not exceed five persons to the square mile.

23. Cultivation of the savana near Thysville in the Congo. The top soil has been heaped into little mounds called Mafuka. Nothing grows between the heaps. The grass on the heaps is burnt off and cassava, beans, etc., planted. Note the Leopoldville–Matadi railway in the background.

24.
Grassland near Kigali Ruanda. The animals a protected from the tset fly by the elevation of t land. These cattle a valued according to the si and beauty of their horn

cent.[1] These diverse observations are in a way encouraging, because they confirm not only that if the men worked as hard as the women the food situation would be much improved, but also that the men's state of health would not hinder them from supplementing the labour force, for the women, who work much harder, are in no better (or worse) health than the men.

Another factor to be borne in mind is that female labour may be slowed down for purely social reasons. A curious but significant example, which to be appreciated must be quoted in detail, comes from the Lélé tribe in the north of the Kasai district of Congo-Léopoldville.[2] These people are underfed and badly nourished, but not for want of space, for the density of population is no more than four to the square kilometre, nor because of soil poverty. The real reasons are: first, that the men take no interest in agriculture or animal-rearing, but only in hunting, which yields almost nothing; and secondly, that the women, who do all the agricultural work, are very conservative in their methods, and are rigidly bound by customs that restrict their activity. Amongst these are the observance by the Lélé of a three-day week, with every third day being one of rest; and whether Christian or not, they rest on Sundays; and they always take a holiday after the visit of any important person. The following sequence, which occurred during a week in September at the time of planting, is perhaps somewhat exceptional, but it illustrates the possibilities:

Sunday: (fortunate—or unfortunate?—coincidence of the Christian Sunday with the day of rest in the three-day week).

Monday: women work in fields.

Tuesday: day of rest to mark departure the day before of an important visitor.

Wednesday: day of rest in the three-day week (unfortunately on this day a European agricultural expert came to inspect the progress being made with the cultivation prescribed by the government; the women willingly agreed to accompany him into the fields, carrying a token basket of ground nuts—but they did not sow any).

Thursday: there was too much rain for working.

Friday: a holiday in honour of the agronomist who left the day before.

Saturday: rest day in the three-day week; and then,

Sunday again!

1. Documents collected by the Centre d'études scientifiques et médicales de l'Université libre de Bruxelles au Congo.
2. Mary Douglas, *The environment of the Lélé*, Zaire, 1955, pp. 801–20; *Social and religious symbolism of the Lélé of the Kasai*, Zaire, 1955, pp. 385–402; 'The Lélé of the Kasai', *African Worlds*, Internat. African Inst., 1954, pp. 1–26; also *The Lélé of the Kasai*, London, 1963.

The poor yields per acre, which are both cause and consequence of the low productivity per hour of work, are only in part due to the general poverty of the soils, and much more to the almost complete lack of manure, the ignorance of irrigation, and the absence of careful selection of the plants cultivated. Account must also be taken of the very low technical achievements in transport and in food preparation.

The harvest is effected by very primitive and slow methods, often using a knife rather than a sickle, and sometimes plucking the grain ear by ear; and since the ears do not all ripen at the same time the harvester must select the ripe ones only, so that in any case the use of the scythe is impossible. Food crops are subjected to much waste of time between harvesting and consumption; they are usually transported from the field to the house on men's backs or more likely on the women's heads; the garnering is slow and uncertain, and rats and insects probably consume one-fifth of the entire African harvest. One of the reasons for the success of maize in Africa is that the unshelled grain keeps well, and can even be left in the fields if the precaution is taken of breaking the stalk so that the cob bends downwards. Some accurate records made in the north-east of Congo-Léopoldville showed that of the total time taken in the preparation of a meal of gruel, only 28 per cent was represented by the agricultural preliminaries (forest clearance, hoe-cultivation, sowing and weeding), 34 per cent by harvesting, transport and garnering, and 38 per cent by the preparation and cooking of the actual food.[1] The last of these items is a very slow process; the hulling and pounding of the grain to make flour for the gruel is done in a mortar, or between two stones. Such primitive tools are found in all the continents, even amongst peoples who are in contact with more advanced civilizations; thus the Mois in the Annamese mountains still use the hand pestle and mortar, whilst the Vietnamese on the neighbouring plains have far better implements, such as a hand-mill for husking and a pestle worked by a foot pedal.

The preparation of meals by the methods usual among tropical peoples is a long process. Among the Bembas[2] the woman whose task it is to cook, husks millet (eleusine) every day. This takes an hour to complete and consists of beating the grain with a pestle, winnowing it, beating it with the pestle a second, though shorter, time, then after another winnowing the grinding of the grain with a stone on a fixed millstone. But every day the cook has also to go and fetch firewood (which takes nearly an hour) and get water (which sometimes takes an hour when it has to be fetched from a distance). She must also

1. P. de Schlippe, *Bull. agric. Congo belge*, 1949, pp. 361–402.
2. A. I. Richards, *Land, Labour, and Diet in Northern Rhodesia*, 1939, p. 91.

pick in the allotment or the forest the ingredients needed for preparing the sauce which goes with a kind of porridge made of millet, and this may take an hour too. Lastly, water must be boiled to make the porridge, and the sauce must be put to simmer. So the preparation of a meal requires at least three hours. Hence, it is not surprising that there is only one meal a day. Although the Bembas are apt to swallow enormous quantities of millet porridge, the one meal, as may well be imagined, does not give food enough. The mealtime is extremely irregular. It varies between noon and 5 p.m. according to the agricultural activities of the women, and the Bembas, who are quite accustomed to this practice, are not upset either by the irregularity or by the insufficiency of the meals. Sometimes it happens that the housewife is too tired to undertake the three hours' hard work needed to prepare a meal, so she sits down and does nothing. On such occasions the members of her family assuage their hunger by eating whatsoever comes to hand, an ear of maize or a potato roasted in the ashes. (See Plates 25–8).

The practice among the Lobis on the Ivory Coast is less laborious, but no better. They live on a mess of sorghum (large millet) and on soup made from fresh baobab leaves and butter from the butter-tree. They do not even use a mortar, and grain has to be crushed whole on the fixed grindstone. This hard task is done by the women, who prepare the sorghum gruel every fifth day. Not surprisingly, the gruel turns sour on the third day. By the fourth it can only be eaten by being mixed with water. When they go to work in the fields, the Lobis take calabashes containing a little of the gruel mixed with water. That is to be their food during the day's work.

It is surprising, at first sight, that people practising subsistence agriculture in areas which are sparsely populated and which could easily support more, should suffer shortages every year; and one is tempted to charge them with lack of forethought. But forethought is difficult when every extension of the clearings may hasten the exhaustion of the soil to such a degree as to endanger future supplies. Forethought is difficult when disease saps one's enthusiasm for work; difficult when the social system does not leave the individual the control of his harvest. Why should one reap more grain than one's neighbours since, when they have exhausted their stocks, the more economical man cannot avoid sharing out what remains in his store? It is difficult to be far-sighted within the framework of a subsistence economy in which surpluses, should they occur, would have no commercial value. Lack of forethought is more clearly seen when the Mois make alcohol from large quantities of maize which will be needed in time of shortage, or when Africans devote too much millet to making beer. But alcohol and beer play such a great part in the social life that forethought would appear in these cases to smack of the antisocial.

The food problems of the tropical lands fall into two types: in regions with a very dense rural population (as we shall see later on) the food shortage arises from too many people trying to subsist on what the land can yield; in regions with sparse population the shortages are due to the small areas cultivated and the very low yields per acre. The immediate remedies that can be brought to bear differ in the two cases. In the first, the urgency is to increase the yield by more intensive and scientific methods: in the second, the measures that can be taken are more varied and subtle. Education, for example, to eliminate taboos, can best be done by teachers coming from the populations themselves, whilst a free economy offers the best possibility of increasing production by assuring a profitable market for any surplus. Shortages will disappear from the sparsely peopled parts of the tropical world as soon as the natives are encouraged to produce marketable surpluses. There are two pitfalls to avoid, however, which come with a rising standard of life. The first is a rural exodus, which would be disastrous because it would lower agricultural production; the second is a tendency for the people, through a kind of snobbery or merely for the sake of convenience, to turn to imported foodstuffs, such as wheat flour and canned meat. The dietetic benefit of the rise in the standard of living would be but small if these things happened.

CHAPTER 8

Industrial Possibilities in Hot, Wet Lands

THE hot, wet lands have but a feeble development of industry; the production of coal and of steel are quite small. Great industrial districts are very few and far between; the most noteworthy are the Calcutta–Jamshedpur district of India, and the neighbourhood of Rio de Janeiro, São Paulo and Volta Redonda in Brazil. Apart from these localities there is little to describe. And the industries are merely transplanted copies of the industrial techniques of the temperate lands. The explanation lies not in any particular hostility of the tropical climate towards industrial activity, nor in the lack of raw materials, nor in the inability of the inhabitants to master existing industrial techniques and invent new ones, but simply in the general technical backwardness of the tropical world as a whole, which has discouraged modern industry, with its scientific backing and heavy capitalization, from developing. The difficulty of catching up is almost insuperable, for every year sees the temperate world advancing still further ahead; it is the fable of the hare and the tortoise, but the temperate hare runs straight to the winning post.

The state of civilization, or more precisely the technical backwardness, is thus responsible for the present level of industrial development in the tropics. It may be true of course that the poor resources of coking coal are responsible for the weak development of steel-making. It is true that within the tropics vast areas are occupied by ancient eroded crystalline platforms; coal is not found in these areas, any more than it is in the Laurentian Shield or the Scandinavian Shield. But lack of metallurgical coke is not the main reason for the feeble development of the steel industry; lack of technical skill, lack of financial resources and lack of markets are far more cogent reasons. The iron ore resources are in fact immense, and large quantities are exported by Liberia, Sierra Leone, Angola, Venezuela, Brazil, India and Malaya; so too are the resources of manganese, chrome and tungsten.

The energy sources are also immense, whether in terms of oil— from Venezuela, Mexico, Nigeria, Indonesia—or of hydroelectric power. Petroleum is found in the sedimentary rocks that fringe the pre-Cambrian massifs—as in Angola, Gabon, Nigeria and Bahia— or in the sedimentary folded ranges that give occasional variety to the tropical scene—as in Burma, Indonesia and the Andean countries.

The hydroelectric potentialities are enormous, thanks to the nature of the relief; the pre-Cambrian massifs frequently have edges upturned towards the ocean, and down those slopes the rivers cascade in a series of rapids. The Congo is the finest example of all: below Stanley Pool the river, which has a flow of 706,000 cubic feet a second, falls 1,000 feet, thus providing a simply colossal power potential. A dam at Inga could easily furnish 25 million kW and produce 200 thousand million kWh a year, or nearly twice the entire output of Great Britain, which in 1958 was 118 thousand million kWh. The great gorge of the Zambesi at Cahorabassa in Mocambique is another example of the possibilities for hydroelectricity.

The steep oceanic slopes and gentle inland slopes so frequently found in the ancient massifs also provide another rather different possibility for hydroelectricity, for streams flowing inland can be diverted to the coastal slope, thus producing a very high fall though with but a modest volume of water. Such artificial river capture can be effected by comparatively inexpensive dams, and examples of this type are to be found near São Paulo, where the hydroelectric installations at the foot of the Sierra do Mar use waters which have been diverted from the Parana basin; at the foot of the Western Ghats in India, and near Antananarivo in Madagascar.

If these enormous hydroelectric potentialities of tropical rivers—especially those which, like the Congo, reach the sea only after having crossed considerable relief obstacles—were fully developed, an economic asset of far greater value would be created than can be provided by the accessibility which a navigable river like the Amazon has to offer. It is true, of course, that in the Brazilian part of the Amazon basin low falls with high volume could be harnessed at the first upstream rapids of the northern and southern tributaries, but these localities would be several hundred miles from the main east–west navigable river.

An interesting industrial problem is presented by the forests, which in the tropical world are of vast extent and little value. It is surely surprising that these tropical and equatorial forests should have an economic value so much inferior to that of the temperate forests. But a study of the forests reveals quite simply the economic and technical backwardness of the tropics. The technology of wood, and more particularly of paper (and the manufacture of paper and of cellulose for man-made textile fibres is the principal outlet for the temperate forests) have been developed in the temperate world in relation to the characteristics of the temperate forests. It is important to realize, however, that paper-making techniques were first developed to utilize the resinous timbers of the great boreal forest belt, and that much later it became necessary to adapt the processes to the non-resinous woods of the temperate belt. The first exploitations led to the belief that the pine forests held a monopoly of pulp-wood production; but the technical difficulty of using 'deal' woods has now been overcome. There is, on the contrary, much to be done before a tropical paper industry can develop, for tropical woods do not yet appear to provide good raw materials for paper-making. After many failures, some progress has at last been made, but complete success is not yet assured. It may well be, however, that in course of time—with-in the next century—the tropical world might be able to make paper under economic conditions approaching those of the temperate belt.[1]

A comparison of the temperate and tropical regions in respect of their forests and pulpwood production brings out clearly the significance of the differences. The technology of paper manufacture has been developed particularly in Europe and North America, where it has depended on the vast demand for newsprint and on progress in chemistry and engineering, both of which factors are absent from the tropics. When this technology was applied in the tropics it encountered very different forest conditions, and few efforts were made to create a new technology, for tropical needs were but small and the temperate world already produced an abundance of cheap paper. In attempting to evaluate the relative economic advantages of the tropical and temperate forests, it is as well to realize that the technical progress that has been achieved in the temperate zone could not be transplanted into the tropical world without careful and delicate adaptations that would require a state of civilization equivalent to that of the temperate zone, with its large markets for paper and its associated scientific and technical progress.

There are some 15 million square miles of forests in the world, of which about half are in the tropics (2·9 mn square miles in America, 3·0 in Africa, 1·2 in Asia, 0·3 in Melanesia and 0·03 in Australia). The tropical forests grow in a climate in which no month has a mean temperature of less than 65° F (18° C) and which has adequate rainfall to support trees; all-the-year rainfall produces the evergreen forest of the equatorial zone, a marked dry season the deciduous tropical forest.

In order to compare the economic value of the tropical and temperate forests we may quote Paterson's estimates of the 'productive' forest area.[2] The productive tropical forests cover an area of

1. M. de Roover, 'Etudes et projets pour la fabrication de pâtes de cellulose au Congo', Brussels, *Ac. roy. Sc. Coloniales. Bull. Séances*, 1957, 1231–45.
2. M. S. S. Paterson, *The Forest Area of the World and its Productivity*, Göteborg, 1956.

4·6 million square miles, as against 5·4 million for the productive temperate forests. From these areas, the tropical forest produces 12·5 cubic metres of timber per hectare, the temperate forest 2·8 cubic metres. The tropical forests increase by 15,000 million cubic metres of timber a year, and the temperate forests by 4,000 million m³. However, the quantity of timber cut and used by man amounts to 1,200 million m³ from the temperate forest and only 250 million from the tropical forest. These figures include timber used locally by the people who dwell in the forests. The quantities entering trade channels make the tropical forests appear even less important. In 1938 a square kilometre of temperate forest exported 1·6 cubic metres of timber and 290 kg of wood-pulp, whilst a similar area of tropical forest exported only 0·22 cubic metres of timber and no wood pulp at all. There has been little change in the situation since that time, for in 1953 the world output of industrial timber (excluding firewood) was 764 million cubic metres, of which 685 million at least came from temperate forests (the 'at least' being due to Brazilian output, which is classed as tropical, being in fact partly temperate). In 1961, of a world output of 330 million cubic metres of sawn timber, only 10 million came from the tropical world (including Brazil). In 1962, out of a world total export of forest products amounting in value to 2,800 thousand million U.S. dollars the tropical world contributed only 200 million dollars. The entire world output of wood-pulp in 1961, amounting to 62 million tons, was of temperate origin. Under present conditions the greater part of the natural increase of tropical forests rots on the ground or goes up in the smoke of the agriculturalists' fires, which in fact are the chief consumers of the forest.[1] An actual example, from a particularly well-exploited part of the forest, will underline the feebleness of production in the equatorial belt: in the district of Lake Leopold II in Congo-Léopoldville, in 1951, a forested area of 50,000 km² produced 50,000 cubic metres of timber and 482,000 cubic metres of firewood. True, these figures only relate to the quantities actually measured, but the total output can hardly have been much greater; and the extent of the forest within the district may in fact have been underestimated. Thus in this case a square kilometre (247 acres) of forest produced but one cubic metre of timber a year,[2] a figure far below the annual growth of the forest; and in 1951 the demand for forest products did not seem to warrant the investment of capital to augment production.

1. See also *A World Geography of Forest Resources*, American Geogr. Soc. New York, 1956.
2. J. L. Robert, 'Monographie agricole du lac Léopold II', *Bull. agric. du Congo Belge*, 1952, pp. 617–95.

The forests of the intertropical belt differ according to the nature of the soil,[1] and to the amount and seasonal distribution of the rainfall. It is unnecessary to go into detail regarding these differences, and we need only remark those characteristics which help to explain the small industrial significance of the intertropical forests, at least in the present stage of technological development.

The first drawback to the forests is their heterogeneous character. This is in itself an obstacle to exploitation, for the desirable trees are interspersed with many species which are of no value.[2] In the forests of Madagascar, amongst 100 trees growing side by side there will be 30 or 40 different species; a detailed study of 100 square metres revealed 239 individual plants (not all of them trees), belonging to 102 different species.[3] In the Ivory Coast there are at least 500 species of trees belonging to 248 genera and 55 families. On Mt Makiling, a little volcano in the island of Luzon (Philippines), only some 3,600 feet high, there are more species of woody plants than in the whole of the United States.[4] A census taken on 10 acres of forest in Cochin-China recorded 1,080 trees with trunks more than 4 inches in diameter, belonging to 58 species; but of these 814 were of no value (*Malvaceae, Steruliaceae, Cupuliferae*), and there were only 266 belonging to useful species—of which only 9 had a diameter large enough to be worth cutting. Most of the useless species were of soft wood of no value for either firewood or paper-making.

The heterogeneity of the tropical forest is thus a considerable obstacle to exploitation. Considerable preliminary prospecting would be necessary, together with the construction of a series of trackways; these could only serve for one extractive operation, because once the marketable trees were taken out it would be necessary to wait several decades before the forest would be worth a second exploitation (always assuming, rather optimistically, that the desired species renewed themselves). The removal of the boles from the forest is also very expensive because the most sought-after trees are heavy and cannot be floated down rivers.

The forest of Maniéma in Congo-Léopoldville looked very fine to the prospectors, but when it came to be exploited, it yielded only 360 cubic feet of marketable logs to the acre, and these mostly *Chlorophora excelsa* (African teak). Since the extraction of single trees of commercial value could hardly be repeated for a century the

1. G. Mangerot, 'Etude sur les forêts des plaines et plateaux de la Côte d'Ivoire', *IFAN Etudes éburnéennes*, IV, 1955.

2. For an excellent study of the forest see P. W. Richards, *The Tropical Rain Forest*, London, 1952.

3. P. de la Bâthie, *La végétation de Madagascar*, 1921, p. 94.

4. R. L. Pendleton, 'Land utilization and agriculture of Mindanao', *Geog. Review*, 1947, pp. 180–210.

annual marketable output works out at no more than 4 cubic feet per acre. This is all the more remarkable since a well-developed secondary forest contains about 160 tons of dry matter to the acre (measurements made in an old secondary forest at Kade in Ghana, where the rainfall is 65 inches a year, gave 150 tons of dry matter). A very revealing example is provided by the Ford enterprise in the Amazon region of Brazil. Here, in the Tapajos region above Santarem, rubber plantations achieved but limited success; at the same time the company proposed to use the timber from the deforested area, and a large saw mill was constructed, identical with those used in the forests of the United States. But they were disillusioned; the timber passing through the sawmill was of no commercial value, for it had not been carefully selected; it rapidly wore out the saws, and the mill simply functioned as a closed circuit, producing logs that were burnt to provide the steam to drive the machines. The whole enterprise was abandoned. The ungraded products of tropical deforestation cannot, in the present state of technology, be commercially exploited; the cultivators do well to burn it on the spot. The peasants in the vicinity of Belém use part of the cut timber to make charcoal which they sell in the city, but this is hardly compatible with a modern standard of living, and the charcoal sold by these *roças* of Belém cannot compete with gas and electricity.

There are, however, some homogeneous tropical forests. One that has been the subject of speculative exploitation is the pine forest (*Pinus caribaca*) of the Miskitos coast in Honduras and Nicaragua,[1] but others present difficult problems.

The most widespread primary forests of the central Congo are heterogeneous; the botanists' habit of classifying forest types by a single species (e.g. the *Scorodophlocus zenkeri* forest) is misleading, since the species is not dominant. But there are homogeneous forests of notable extent, characterized by *Gilbertiodendron dewevrei*; these are magnificent evergreen equatorial forests.[2] Bambesa, in latitude 3° 26′ N at 1,625 feet above sea level and close to the *Gilbertiodendron* forest of the Wele, has a mean temperature of 74° F (23·5° C) in the coolest month and 78° F (25·3° C) in the warmest month, with 75 inches of rain a year; the dry season lasts for about two months, centred on January (average 1·5 inches). The forest is very dense, with a closed canopy, and the trees are very large (thirty-eight of more than 6 feet circumference per hectare, and reaching heights of 100 to 130

1. J. J. Paisons, 'The Miskito pine savanna of Nicaragua and Honduras', *Ann. Assoc. Amer. Geog.*, XLV, 1955, pp. 36–63.
2. See the excellent study by Ph. Gerard, *Etude écologique de la forêt à Gilbertiodendron dewevrei dans la région de l'Uélé*, Inst. Nat. Et. Agr. Congo belge, série scientifique no. 87, 1960.

feet); the amount of light reaching the ground is very small, for the tree-crowns which form the canopy are thick, and on a clear day in the dry season the light value at 3 feet from the ground is only 35 per cent of that above the canopy. In other words, this forest resembles the popular conception of 'equatorial forest'; the boles are straight and without buttresses, and when the soil allows the tap-roots penetrate deeply.[1]

The branches come off from the trunk about 60 feet from the ground, and the forest thus looks rather like a gothic cathedral. Penetration is easy since there is very little undergrowth and few lianes; in the dry season a thick litter of leaves and large seed-pods of *Gilbertiodendron* crackles under foot. Silence reigns. Such a forest regenerates itself easily, and young *Gilbertiodendron* saplings in large numbers await the demise of their elders in order to reach the sunlight. The development of wood is considerable, for a large *Gilbertiodendron* grows about 7 inches a year. The cutting of all trees which have a circumference of 6 feet at 6 feet above ground level would yield between 120 and 160 tons of merchantable timber per acre; but it would be between 50 and 100 years before the operation could be repeated. There is therefore, in the 3,800 square miles of *Gilbertiodendron* forest lying south of Bambesa (in Congo-Léopoldville) an enormous potential wealth of timber. The wood has both good and bad qualities: it is solid, resistant to termites and free from decay; but it is hard, heavy, brittle and of dull appearance. It is used locally for timber framework and fencing, and it would be excellent for railway sleepers, but there is no large market for these. This is one more proof that technical progress has not yet caught up with the availability of resources, for there is no local need for the timber and no local progress in science or technology.

This fine forest, which possesses the economic advantage of homogeneity, is being nibbled at around its edges. Deforestation

1. The existence of these vast homogeneous forests poses many problems May we believe that they are the end-product of an evolution in which *Gilbertiodendron* slowly overcame the rivalry of other species? And if so, that they represent a later stage than the heterogeneous forests that are generally regarded as primary? Or is it that they became established by reason of a more humid climate on areas that in a previous period of dry climate had temporarily lost all their forest species —even as the boreal forests of the northern hemisphere occupied territories scoured by the ice-sheets? Such an explanation, undoubtedly true for the boreal forests, is merely hypothetical in the case of the *Gilbertiodendron* forest; there have indeed been drier climatic episodes than the present in central Africa, but it would be presumptuous to claim that a homogeneous forest is due to the replacement of a dry climate by a more humid one. These forests are ancient, and they show that in these areas of central Africa man has never been numerous or addicted to tree-felling. See, on the subject of the effects on soil of alternations of forest and deforestation, H. Ehrart, *La genèse des sols en tant que phénomène géologique*, Paris, 1956.

that is quickly followed by the abandonment of the land allows the *Gilbertiodendron* forest to regain possession, albeit after a long interval with secondary forest. But if the clearing is persistently cultivated for several successive years, or if cultivation is resumed after only a few years of fallow, then the *Gilbertiodendron* forest loses its power of recovery, for the seed-bearing trees will be too far away, owing to the regular incursions of the agricultural fringe.[1] Such forests are thus condemned to disappear without ever having been properly used. And yet one must recognize the fact that the secondary forest, with its oil palms and its raphia palms, and its many tree species of which some may be useful, may perhaps be of more practical value than the *Gilbertiodendron* forest.[2]

The high quality timbers which enter international trade (for example mahogany, gaboon, and afara) are derived from hetero-geneous tropical forests that produce them in small quantities. In the lower Ivory Coast there is an average of only one mahogany tree in 25 acres. The trees usually come from old secondary forest rather than from the primary jungle; gaboon and afara flourish in areas that were cleared for villages that have long since disappeared. The mahogany of British Honduras is also found in forests that have replaced ancient clearings.

The question may now be asked, whether it would not be more advantageous to practice silviculture rather than rely on the chance distribution of trees in the natural forest? It is by this means that the fine forests of western Europe have been created, none of which is really spontaneous. It is certain that the tropical world, if it wishes to produce considerable, reliable and increasing quantities of cheap timber of the quality required for joinery, cabinet-making, veneers and paper, will have to manage its forests systematically or else create actual plantations of forest trees. Such a programme would require careful preliminary studies and a strong administration that would have respect for the plans made, and would provide for the expense incurred in protecting the plantations from disease and from insects, by chemicals sprayed from helicopters. The teak forests of Burma and Java, and the studies made at the Stanleyville arboretum, suggest that tropical silviculture might have a brilliant future. *Terminalia*

1. Another weakness of these forests is that the litter, composed of dry leaves and seed-pods as big as shoes, burns very easily in the dry season (January). Fire which rages through the forest does not destroy the large trees but is fatal to the seedlings, so that if there is a blaze every year the forest cannot regenerate itself and must inevitably perish. The fire is generally man-made, so everything depends on whether the people practice incendiarism every year or not.
2. The stages in the destruction of the forest are studied by R. Sillans, *Les savanes de l'Afrique centrale française*, Paris, 1956, he emphasizes the major role of the cultivator in the wooded savannas of the Central African Republic.

superba (afara), cultivated in pure stands, has yielded 250 cubic feet of wood per acre after only seven years. *Cleistopholis grandifolia,* which has yielded 325 cubic feet in seven years, may be an excellent paper-making species.[1]

Silviculture would enable much larger quantities of timber to be obtained than can be got by 'skimming the cream' from the natural forest, and from much smaller areas of land. In this way it would be possible to reconcile the retreat of the forest, which is inevitable owing to the expansion of the agricultural population, with an increased production of timber. Thus an afforestation project could yield without difficulty 2,850 cubic feet of timber per acre in fifty years; in other words an annual output of 2,850 cubic feet needs 50 acres, and 1 acre would produce an average of 57 cubic feet of marketable timber a year. The 400,000 square miles of forest in the former Belgian Congo yielded, in the years before 1960, some 10·6 million cubic feet of timber, the equivalent of 290 square miles (or 185,000 acres) of silviculture.

1. P. Liégeois and L. Petit, 'L'Arboretum de Stanleyville', *B. Agric. Congo belge,* 1950, pp. 3–36; see also P. Maurand, 'L'Indochine forestière', *Bull. econ. de l'Indochine,* 1938, pp. 801–29; L. Haguet, 'Pour une colonisation rationelle des terres vierges de la Guadeloupe', *Rev. forestière française,* 1951, p. 16; L. Huguet and E. Marié, 'Les plantations d'acajou d'Amerique des Antilles françaises', *Bois et Forêts des Tropiques,* 1951, pp. 12–25.

CHAPTER 9

Some exceptional regions of dense population in the humid tropics of Africa and America

THE improvement of living conditions in areas of low population density encounters many difficulties. It is expensive and hardly worth while to invest large capital resources if there are only a few people to the square mile. Even the construction of a road system to open up the countryside and permit commercial agriculture is a costly business, and adequate returns in the shape of increased economic activity may be long delayed. In sparsely populated areas the maintenance of roads which are subject to frequent damage by heavy rainstorms is an impossible task for the inhabitants, whose living conditions may even be worsened rather than improved by the creation of roads. For the road-builders of the colonial powers, and also their successors employed by the new national governments, have a habit of choosing routes that are easy to construct and to maintain, notably across smooth plateaux and ravineless interfluves; and in general these are not the routes that the native population would have sought, so the roads pass through areas where there are no people. As a result many governments have been unable to resist the temptation to uproot the people and re-establish them along the roads.

It is also difficult to improve sanitation and health in sparsely peopled areas; anti-malarial campaigns stand but small chance of lasting success, whilst the tsetse fly finds such areas very much to its liking, for it is impossible for a population of ten or a dozen persons to the square mile to keep down the vegetation to a level unfavourable to this insect. Health services are difficult to maintain, and doctors and hospitals are inevitably far removed from patients; whilst education is almost impossible.

The problems of development are so closely linked with the density of population that we may well ask whether the resources of capital and personnel necessary to effect an improvement in sparsely peopled areas would not be better employed in areas of denser population. Indeed, the question arises whether, in areas of sparse population that are to receive economic aid, the best interests of the people would not be served by concentrating the population into one part of the territory, which would then have a sufficient density to make the provision of equipment and the promotion of economic progress worthwhile. The evacuated areas could then be systematically re-occupied as the population expanded, care being taken to see that the new 'colonists' were sufficient in numbers and in skill to make the best use of the equipment and facilities provided.

With this in mind it will be useful now to examine some of the geographical problems of certain tropical areas in Africa and America that have unusually dense populations. The case of tropical Asia will be examined in a later chapter.

The most important countries of tropical America with high density of population are to be found in the West Indies, where densities range from 140 persons to the square mile in Cuba (1955), 142 in the Dominican Republic (1955), 337 in Haiti, 362 in Jamaica (1958), 570 in Martinique (1955) and 699 in Puerto Rico (1958), to 1,373 in Barbados.[1] These figures result from the peculiar history of the islands, which though but moderately peopled by Caribs or Arawaks in the pre-Columbian era, appeared to the Europeans as ideal for the establishment of sugar plantations. The rainy tropical climate, the generally fertile soils, the easy access for shipping, and the character of the islands as natural maritime prisons in which slaves could easily be kept in captivity, all helped to encourage a large sugar production to serve the European market; and the African slaves began to multiply as soon as births began to exceed deaths.

The high density of population in these islands owes much to the sale of tropical produce, the income from which permits a broadening of the diet by the purchase of food from abroad. Commercial agriculture is however only partly responsible for the density, for one must also take account of the fact that the small islands are like cages, from which the expanding population has great difficulty in escaping.[2]

Guatemala (Fig. 7) may be taken as typical of the human geography of Central America. It contained 3,500,000 people in 1958, i.e. a density of 83 per square mile. This figure, however, conceals the great contrasts within the territory, for the mountainous parts, mostly above 5,000 feet, are densely peopled; thus the province of Sacatepequez, lying almost entirely between 5,000 and 10,000 feet, has a

1. The very high density in Barbados is even more striking when we note that this tiny island, with 228,000 inhabitants on 166 square miles in 1956, has only 62,000 acres of cultivated land; the density in relation to arable land thus rises to 2,362 per square mile, a remarkable figure for an essentially rural population. For the background to this situation see O. P. Starkey, *The Economic Geography of Barbados*, New York, 1939.

2. This 'cage' effect is particularly well marked in the case of a poorly endowed island like Fogo, in the Cape Verde group, where a large population, some 16,000 on 184 square miles, struggles painfully against the difficult conditions provided by an active volcano, immature soils, a dry climate and poor water resources. See the excellent book by Orlando Ribeiro, *A ilha do Fogo e as suas erupcoes*, Lisbon, 1954; and a résumé by P. Gourou, *Les Cahiers d'Outre-mer*, Bordeaux, 1959, pp. 9–24. The peopling of this island was not by free movement, but mainly by African slaves.

density of 334 per square mile, the highest in Guatemala and remarkable for a mountainous area. On the contrary the lowlands are but sparsely peopled, especially in the north, where in the province of Petén the density falls to 1 person per square mile, and in Izabal province to 15. Malaria has been largely responsible for this difference: thus while Sacatepequez recorded twelve deaths from malaria per 10,000 inhabitants, about 1937, Petén had 145.[1] The high density of the main part of the country is thus due to its relative healthiness, but it is only a relative salubrity, for malaria is prevalent at least up to 5,000 feet and often higher. *Anopheles* larvae flourish in the high lakes (Atitlan, Amatitlan), and malaria was endemic on the shores of Atitlan at 5,100 feet, though the occasional epidemics might be due to new stocks of haematozoa brought by labourers returning from the Pacific coast plantations. The Mayas who inhabit these mountains are keen and skilful cultivators working entirely by hand and without any animals at all.[2] On the rare alluvial plains, as at Panajachel, on the river of the same name which flows into Lake Atitlan, they obtain high yields of maize and vegetables.[3] The population of the township of Panajachel is 1,200, on an area of 2 square miles of which 1·2 square miles are cultivated; this represents a general density of 600 persons per square mile, or 1,000 with relation to the cultivated area only. The steepness of the slopes is sometimes so great that the peasant cultivator can hardly stand upright on them; to combat soil erosion little piles of earth (*monton*) are heaped up around each maize plant; and to the same end maize haulms are laid along the contours. Elsewhere erosion is slowed by infiltration, as on very friable volcanic soils.[4]

The reasons for the dense population of the Guatemalan mountains are thus their relative healthiness, their fertile friable soils and their abundant rainfall. In addition, there is a long tradition of careful peasant agriculture, albeit low in productivity per hour of labour, an attachment to the soil and a frugal way of life. The habit of trade is an indication of a superior civilization; the peasants are not content with the mere cultivation of the land to ensure their livelihood, but devote part of their time to crafts and to peddling the articles they

1. G. C. Shattuck, *A Medical survey of the Republic of Guatemala*, Washington, Carnegie Inst. publ. 499, 1938.
2. This is not quite true, for though the mountain people are not stock-raisers and use neither the milk nor the labour of animals, they do rear pigs, under peculiar circumstances resembling transhumance. Herds of pigs, with their herdsmen, spend the wet season on the eastern lowlands and the dry season in the mountains, and since pigs are not naturally fitted for walking long distances, they are provided with leather shoes to prevent their trotters from getting worn out.
3. Sol Tax, *Penny capitalism, a Guatemalan Indian economy*, Washington, Smithsonian Institution, Inst. of Soc. Anthropology, publ. 16, 1953.
4. G. and M. McCutchen McBride, 'Highland Guatemala and its Maya communities', *Geog. Rev.*, 1942, pp. 252–68.

...gware woman hoeing the soil with a ...ed stick at Mahagi in the Congo. ...h such a poor implement a vast deal of time and effort is wasted.

26.
The use of the mortar and pestle makes for slowness in the preparation of food. The photograph was taken in the outskirts of Elisabethville in the Congo.

...ore laborious preparation of food. The ...oman is opening palm nuts one by one.

28. Another photograph illustrating the waste of time in preparing food. This woman is kneading cassava farine, which will be wrapped in leaves and baked into *chikwangue*.

29.
A primitive cassava pre[...]
near Ubatura on the [...]
the State of Sao Paulo[...]

30.
Waste of time through poor metho[...]
one of the causes of poverty and u[...]
nourishment in the tropics. The m[...]
husking beans at Aminbhavi [...]
Dharwar, India.

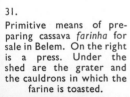

31.
Primitive means of pre-
paring cassava *farinha* for
sale in Belem. On the right
is a press. Under the
shed are the grater and
the cauldrons in which the
farine is toasted.

have made during the slack periods in the agricultural year. Carrying on their backs a bulky load of pots, baskets, hats, or cloths, these hardy peasants trudge the rough paths that lead from one market centre to another. Sometimes, too, they may earn wages in the coffee plantations of the Pacific slope.[1]

Madagascar (Fig. 10) also shows the importance of altitude in the distribution of population. The centre of the island is occupied by highlands mostly rising to between 3,000 and 6,000 feet; this pre-Cambrian massif is bordered on the east by narrow alluvial plains and on the west by a large basin of sedimentary rocks through which broad alluvial valleys run to end in large deltas. The mean density of population (18 persons to the square mile) is normal for a tropical country. But at first sight the distribution of population is surprising,[2] for the most densely peopled parts are the cantons in the central high-lands which consist of the districts inhabited by the Betsileo and Merina tribes. Over an area of 20,000 square miles the density is over 65 persons to the square mile, and in some districts it is over 250. The alluvial plains on the east are moderately populous, with between 25 and 50 persons to the square mile, though in certain parts the density rises to 250. Most of the interior highlands and much of western Madagascar are almost uninhabited, the Kandreho district having the lowest mean density, with 1·3 persons to the square mile.

Such a distribution is not explained by the climate, which is no-where hostile to man. South Madagascar, comprising the Mahafaly and Antandroy districts, is semi-desert, but is not the least densely peopled part of the island, for it contains more people than the Kandreho district, where the annual rainfall is at least 40 inches. Nor is the distribution of population to be explained simply by the soil; within the populated parts of the interior highlands there are large expanses of rock outcrops, of lateritized *tampoketsa* and of slopes ravined by *lavakas*, whilst the alluvial plains on the western side of the island are hardly occupied at all. Perhaps altitude has been a decisive factor, people having sought the comparative coolness of the highlands—but this is an unproven hypothesis; though it is true that the most densely peopled parts of Madagascar lie between 4,000 and 6,000 feet above sea level.

Is the cause to be sought in malaria? The matter is not so clear here as in Guatemala. Malaria is indeed rife today in the populous

1. See below, p. 172.
2. Decary and Castel, *Modalités et conséquences des émigrations intérieures récentes des populations malgaches*, Tananarive, Imprimerie officielle, 1941; Ch. Robequain, *Madagascar et les bases dispersées de l'Union française*, Paris, 1958.

parts of the interior highlands as well as on the east coast lowlands and the deserted areas in the west. There is reason to think, however, that this was not so until the end of the nineteenth century, before the mixture of peoples which has taken place from that date onwards. Formerly, indeed, the people in the interior highlands kept to themselves. Possibly they had become immune to the local stock of haematozoa, the virulence of which had perhaps been diminished by the relatively low temperature of the highlands. It is probable that malaria had been less severe in the highlands for centuries. But it has ravaged them whenever new plasmodium stocks have been introduced by Merinas returning to their home district after having visited the plains; and these Merinas of the interior highlands appear peculiarly susceptible to malaria when they go down to the coast.

One circumstance in Madagascar has no equivalent in Guatemala. The Merinas, who form the most numerous and densest group of people, are distinct from the other Malgashes, though they speak the same language of Indonesian origin. They are more advanced both in terms of production techniques—for they have a carefully maintained system of flooded ricefields—and of political organization, with a monarchy and a complex system of institutions. They have thus naturally developed higher densities of settlement, made possible by their higher level of agricultural output and fostered by the strength and stability of their political régime.

It may be, therefore, that the level of civilization is the main reason for the peculiar distribution of population in Madagascar.

The hot, wet parts of Africa south of the Sahara include a few areas which present an exceptionally high density of population for the tropics. Contrary to a too widespread belief, these blocks of population are not found especially on the highlands. Indeed, the most important centres of dense population in West Africa do not correspond at all with the uplands. Other causal factors must therefore be sought.

Central Africa[1] is sparsely populated throughout, and a map of population density shows much less variation than in East or West

1. Including the following countries: Congo-Léopoldville, Congo-Brazzaville, Gabon, Central African Republic, with a total area of 1,390,000 square miles and 16,800,000 inhabitants, giving a mean density of 11·9 per square mile. Central Africa is characterized by an equatorial or sub-equatorial climate, by the importance of forest and by sparse population; it is differentiated from West Africa through lacking the influence of the ocean and the Sahara. The distribution of population in Congo-Léopoldville may be studied in the following maps: P. Gourou, *Carte de la densité de la population au Congo-Belge*, 1/500,000, Brussels, Institut Royal Colonial, 1961; P. Gourou, *Carte de la densité de la population dans la Province de l'Equateur au* 1,000,000e, Brussels, Acad. Roy. des sciences d'Outre-Mer, 1960; R. de Simet, *Carte de la densité de la population dans la Province Orientale*, Brussels, Univ. libre de Bruxelles, 1962; P. Gourou, *La densité de la population au Congo belge*, Brussels, Ac. roy. sc. col., 1955.

Africa. The least densely peopled parts are found both in the forest (where the Oshwe territory in Congo-Léopoldville has only 2·3 per square mile) and in the savanna (where the territory known as 'East of Feshi' in Congo-Léopoldville has only 1·5). Some parts are not quite so poorly populated, such as part of Lower Congo, particularly the Mayumbe country, a belt roughly along 5° S. latitude (Kwila, Kwango, Kasai and the middle Lulua), and the Ngbaka territory north of the great forest. These last two examples show that the zone of contact between savanna and forest may give rise to greater densities, probably by reason of the greater fertility of the clearings newly made on the edge of the forest; but this should not be taken as a rule of general application, for there are indeed areas of very low density in such contact zones, such as the Lélé country south of the forest in Congo-Léopoldville, or the northern forest-savanna border in southern Cameroon.

East and West Africa present a more varied picture, in which areas of dense population stand out from the general background of low density. In East Africa there are vast areas of sparse population in which the rainfall is often marginal for human settlement; but at the same time the well-developed peasantries of the Sahel and the West African Sudan exist with a rainfall that is certainly not abundant. The Masai steppes are no worse than the Dogon plateau. Areas of high density show up in great contrast to the general low level; they coincide with certain physical and human conditions that have enabled the potentialities of African native civilization to be developed. An example is provided by the island of Ukara, in the Tanzanian section of Lake Victoria, on whose 28 square miles dwell 17,500 people, at a density of 610 per square mile; but only 13·5 square miles are cultivated, so that the density in relation to the agricultural area is 1,300 per square mile. These extraordinary figures are certainly not due to either urbanism or industry, and the natural environment would not appear to be exceptionally favourable; the climate is good, but no better than in other areas that are but sparsely peopled.

The island of Ukara is a fragment of the East African crystalline plateau; the *inselbergs* that dominate the relief are incapable of use, and the soils on the flatter areas are but mediocre. Nor has the population any particular qualities. It is but a mixture of various East African Bantu peoples and has not developed any advanced form of organization. There were not even any chiefs before the arrival of the Germans. The human quality of Ukara would seem to be due to two factors: first, that the island has been a refuge, and secondly, that in order to survive the refugees have simply had to practise an intensive form of agriculture, getting at least one harvest a year from every field. Such agricultural techniques are certainly not the monopoly of the Ukarians, for they are found in other parts of East Africa. The Ukarians cultivate carefully and give the land plenty of manure, obtained from stable-fed cattle. They gather forage and take it to the cattle, which are allowed out, for health reasons, for only a short period each day. All the cultivated land is devoted to subsistence cropping, and the people are fed just as well (or as badly) as the Bantu cultivators of the sparsely-peopled districts. Have these Ukarian techniques any future in Africa? Possibly, but it is significant that when the Ukarians leave their over-populated island and occupy clearings on the sparsely-populated eastern shores of Lake Victoria they forget their intensive techniques and go in for ordinary ladang—clearance by burning, sowing and harvesting, with no cultivation and no manure. One cannot help thinking that the Ukarian does this deliberately, for experience has taught him that though the yield per acre is greater with intensive cultivation, productivity per work-day is greater with ladang.

The Chaga are also a mixture of Bantu peoples, who have found a refuge in a well-watered area on the southern slopes of Kilimanjaro. They also practice an intensive form of agriculture, based on manure obtained by more or less the same methods as those of Ukara. They have developed a system of irrigation by tapping the streams which come from the snow-capped volcano. Such techniques, with a food supply largely based on the banana, give a population density over 210 square miles of 725 per square mile. The Chaga have a more advanced system of territorial organization than the Ukarians, and they have also developed profitable coffee plantations.

The Kikuyu occupy the southern slopes of Mt Kenya; in the heart of their district the population density is over 400 to the square mile. Other examples could also be found in East Africa of nodes of dense population in the mountainous areas, as in the Kamba and Teita regions of Kenya. But they do not add up to the generalization that all such mountain areas are densely peopled, for neither the Ngorongoro nor the Hanang areas of Tanzania carry a dense settlement, and these areas are indeed the grazing grounds of transhumant pastoralists, such as the Masai and the Barabaig.[1]

The case of Rwanda and Burundi is a complex one. In order to understand it we must first look at the Kigezi area of south-western Uganda. Here forbidding mountains of pre-Cambrian rocks carry a large population of hard-working peasants whose carefully cultivated

1. It is true that this has not always been the case; on the eastern side of Ngorongoro, at a place called Engaruka, there is a vast number of ruined stone houses. These, as in the similar case in the Inyanga mountains of Rhodesia, may be the relics of a large agricultural settlement of refugees, in a defensible position. The Agoro people, a Nilotic tribe in the Acholi district of northern Uganda, still build stone houses in villages perched up on slopes.

fields on the steep slopes permit a density of between 500 and 1,000 per square mile. These Bantu cultivators have no cattle, and their system of land management is simple; their territory is of small extent, amounting to no more than 1,000 square miles. But the protection afforded by this difficult mountain terrain has favoured the growth of a dense population, whilst the abundant rain allows careful cultivation to yield two harvests a year. The superiority of Rwanda and Burundi rests not in a higher density of population but in the much larger area—15,000 square miles in the two territories—over which the density is maintained. The difference is explained by the more ambitious political organization of the Tutsi pastoralists in Rwanda and Burundi; these people, with a constitutional monarch and an aristocracy, were capable of controlling a much greater territory.[1]

Above the sandy plains of eastern Sudan, the Nuba Mountains have provided a refuge for African peoples against the fierce slave-raids of the Arabs. Here we find similar features to those already noted elsewhere—so long as lack of security forces the people to remain in the mountains, they practise intensive cultivation, but as soon as peaceful conditions obtain, they descend to the plains and resume more extensive methods.

Certain areas of East Africa other than the mountains also have high population densities. Such areas are to be found on the Indian Ocean coast, where Swahili-speaking peoples cultivate swamp-rice. In the islands of Zanzibar and Pemba, despite the poverty of the soil, the general density rises to 300 per square mile. This is due to the clove plantations, for the local food crops are but meagre. Some parts of the shorelands of Lake Nyasa and the Shiré valley also have a high density; in Malawi[2] the 800 square miles of lowland that have at least 250 persons per square mile contrast with the 1,900 square miles of mountain and plateau that have a density of under 10. Certain parts of the shores of Lake Victoria are also densely peopled; we have noted the case of Ukara island, and some parts of Bukoba district (in Tanzania, west of the lake) have densities of as much as 1,300 per square mile, as on the six square miles of Kitobo.

Some parts of the Nyanza region of Kenya, around the Gulf of Kavirondo, are also densely peopled; and in the Ganda region of Uganda, to the north-west of Lake Victoria, there are 1,500,000 people on 7,700 square miles (the political territory of Buganda had a population of 1,834,000 on 23,000 square miles in 1962); some

1. P. Gourou, *La Densité de la population au Ruanda-Urundi*, Brussels, Inst. roy. colonial, 1953.
2. F. Dixey, 'The distribution of population in Nyasaland', *Geog. Rev.* 1928, pp. 274–90.

administrative divisions have a density of over 500. The main reason for this is the existence in former times of a strong monarchical organization with an efficient administration which enabled the population resources to be capitalized. A second factor is the banana, which was the essential element in the food supply; this tree gives a very high yield per acre, and fruits all the year round for many years; it regenerates itself naturally, and provided the dead leaves are allowed to cover the soil, suffers little from soil erosion and needs no manure. Commercial cultivation of cotton and coffee has been very successful; this is a tribute to the enterprise of the Baganda, but it has also attracted numerous non-Baganda workers who have helped to increase the population density.

West Africa, though less mountainous, also contains a number of 'refugee' peoples in its upland areas, such as the Dogon of the Bandiagara plateau in Mali, the Tura of the Ivory Coast, the Dagamba in Ghana, the Kabre and Bassari in Togo, the Somba in Dahomey, the Birom of the Bauchi plateau, the peoples of the Adamawa area of Nigeria, the Bamileke and the people of Mandara in Cameroon, the Hadjera of the Central African Republic, and others. There are also people who have found refuge not in the mountains but in the coastal swamps, where they have developed the technique of the flooded rice-field. Such are the Sévères in southern Senegal, the Diola of the lower Casamance in Senegal, the Balantes in Portuguese Guinea, the Baga in Guinea Republic, and the Temué and Mendé in Sierra Leone; further east the coastal marshes cease to exist. All these 'refugee' peoples have in common the practice of intensive agriculture to support dense populations in small areas; but their techniques of land-use are primitive. The Biroms of the Bauchi plateau[1] make terraces on which a poor and thin soil overlies the lateritic crust; the fields, carefully hoed and enriched by village waste and the droppings of the Fulani herds, grow the traditional millet (*Digitaria*), but of late the Biroms have begun to cultivate and to sell potatoes. On the Adamawa plateau of Nigeria, several small tribal groups (Wakara, Hidkala, Azgavana, Kuvoko, Matakum, Chikkide, Glebda) total 52,000 people, living on 290 square miles, giving an average density of 180 per square mile, which is greatly exceeded in a few localities. These high densities are due to the intensive and prudent cultivation of relatively poor soils; parts of the area are covered with piles of crystalline rock-debris, and are quite useless, and the rest, though of poor fertility, is worked in terraces supported by dry stone walls. These terraces, which sometimes rise in staircases for hundreds of

1. T. L. Suffil, 'The Biroms, a pagan tribe of the plateau', *Farm and Forest*, 1943, pp. 179–82.

feet, are quite old, perhaps before the time of the present tribes. They are never more than 10 feet wide, and some are so narrow that they take only a single row of millet. The need for fallow is almost eliminated (it lasts only two years in fifteen), by reason of the use of manure from stable-fed cattle, sheep and goats. Trees are planted to provide timber for building, firewood and leaves for forage.[1] The same sort of thing recurs in the Mandara mountains of northern Cameroon—isolated mountains, 'refugee' peoples, intensive terrace agriculture.

In West as in East Africa, peace empties the mountain refuges. The people disperse into the neighbouring plains and adopt extensive methods of agriculture. The 'Hadjerai' formerly dwelt in and cultivated the isolated hills that interrupt the otherwise low relief of the Mongo region of the Central African Republic; there they found an easily-defensible refuge from the raids of the Arab slave-traders. Since the establishment of more peaceful conditions they have come down from the hills, which are now abandoned, and have spread their houses and their cultivated fields over the lower ground. The old terraces on the deserted slopes are a prey to soil erosion, and the hillsides are becoming denuded. The same thing has happened in the case of the Azgavana and the Matakum in the Adamawa region.

West Africa also contains pockets of coastal 'refugees'; these people have found in the mangrove swamps and the network of tidal channels a protection against the military superiority of more highly organized tribes. Confined within a very narrow coastal strip, they have used intensive methods of agriculture, including the construction of polders protected by dykes from the brackish water, and drained at low tide, when the need arises, by ingenious sluices. Here are the flooded ricefields, a form of agriculture which certainly seems more certain and more civilized than the slash-and-burn of the ladang. However, with the coming of peace and of trade, the Diola of the lower Casamance have emerged from their seclusion and, abandoning their polders and their ricefields, have adopted the extensive technique of the Mandingas.

As in East Africa, the interest of the intensive agricultural systems of the many 'refugee' peoples is in demonstrating that such methods are just as possible as extensive methods. But the latter are more productive, in the sense of being less expensive in human labour. The intensive practices of the 'refugees' are last-resort techniques, induced by population pressure. It is impossible to say that such intensive methods are more ancient than the extensive methods. The two types coexist amongst many peoples, as in the Gambia where the

1. S. White, 'Agricultural economy of the Hill Pagans of Dikwa Emirate, Cameroons (British Mandate)', *Farm and Forest*, 1944. pp. 130–4.

men use extensive methods for millet and groundnut cultivation, whilst the women grow swamp rice.[1]

In general, the women use techniques which are very labour-consuming but which enable them to get heavy yields of vegetables from tiny plots situated close to their houses. The 'refugee' peoples are subject to circumstances which force them to specialize and intensify. It is clear that agricultural progress in Africa will be directed towards methods which preserve the advantage of intensive cultivation (high yields and greater reliability) whilst overcoming its disadvantages (low productivity per man-day). Mechanization to lessen human labour, irrigation and the use of fertilizers—these are some of the means of increasing productivity.

Outside the clusters of 'refugee' people, the population distribution map of West Africa shows some interesting features.[2] Two discontinous belts of relatively dense population, one in the north and one in the south, are separated by a sparsely peopled zone. The northern belt comprises (from west to east) the San region, the Futa Jalon towards Labé, the extreme north-east of Ghana and the Mossi country, the Baoulé country of the Ivory Coast, the northern part of Togo continuing into the Lama-Kara area of Dahomey, the Hausa territories around Sokoto, Katsina, Kano and part of the Bornu county of Nigeria, and the Sara region of Chad Republic. The southern belt extends through Sénégal, Gambia, the lower Casamance, the coastal strip of Portugese Guinea and Guinea Republic, the Sierra Leone coastlands, southern Ghana (including the Ashanti region), the coastal belt of Togo and Dahomey, and the Yoruba and Ibo territories of southern Nigeria. The densely peopled parts of these two belts have 100 to 130 persons per square mile, with the highest figures being reached in Nigeria. The intermediate zone of sparser population is particularly well marked in Nigeria, along the Niger-Benue axis.

The northern or Sudanese belt coincides with the existence of relatively advanced and stable political organizations that have shown themselves capable of controlling large territories;[3] there is a long political tradition here that gave strength in the past to the empire of Ghana, which flourished in the first millenium A.D. within what is now the Republic of Mali, and to the Mossi kingdom; it was fostered

1. M. R. Haswell, *The Changing Pattern of Economic Activity in a Gambia Village*, London, H.M.S.O., 1963.
2. Ch. Robequain, *Carte de la densité de la population en Afrique occidentale et centrale au 5,000,000e*, Paris, Bureau d'études humaines de l'Office de la recherche scientifique coloniale, 1944.
3. Y. Urvoy, *Petit atlas démographique du Soudan entre Sénégal et Tchad*, Paris, 1942, p. 14.

at a later period by the political inspiration of Muslim peoples who possessed the art of writing—as in the Mali, Souray, Hausa and Fulani kingdoms. The southern belt got its dense population without any Muslim influence, as in the states of Ashanti, Dahomey, and Yoruba; the case of the Ibo will be dealt with later. The intermediate zone of sparse population cannot be explained by the physical circumstances; the rainfall is heavier than further north, and though the extent of lateritic crusts is noteworthy it is not more so than in the north. A lack of security owing to the raiding habits of the northern peoples has undoubtedly had an effect in the Niger-Benue lowland, for here the incursions of the Fulani and Hausa have virtually depopulated the country, except for the 'refuges' already mentioned. Proof of this is given by the events which have followed the establishment of peace and security, for the Tiv people, from the uplands to the south-east, are actively engaged in colonizing these vacant lands of the Benue valley, which are thus shown not to owe their lack of population to some physical disability.

Nigeria offers the best field for the examination of population distribution in West Africa (see Figs. 11 and 12). The characteristics of this distribution are being emphasized by the demographic growth, which has made Nigeria, with 36 million people on 356,000 square miles, by far the most populous state in the whole of Black Africa. The population is very unevenly distributed.[1] The coastal zone of dense population is broken into two widely separated nodes. On the west, in the Yoruba district, the density often exceeds 260 to the square mile. Although the population is mainly agricultural, it tends to cluster into large towns, which is a symptom of fairly advanced social and political development.[2]

As long ago as 1925 there were eighty-four towns with between 10,000 and 20,000 people, and nineteen with 20,000 to 50,000. In 1960, the chief towns were Ibadan (460,000), Ogbomosho (140,000), Oshogbo (130,000), Ife (110,000), Iwo (100,000), Abeokuta (85,000), Oyo (75,000), Ilesha (72,000), Iseyin (50,000) and Ede (45,000). Apart from the towns there are huge villages inhabited by cultivators

1. Niven's map of 1935 has been retained as Fig. 11 since it shows the distribution clearly. For a more refined version see K. M. Buchanan and J. C. Pugh, *Land and People in Nigeria*, London, 1955.
2. On the human geography of the Yoruba country see R. Galletti, K. D. S. Baldwin, and J. O. Dina, *Nigerian Cocoa Farmers, an Economic Survey of Yoruba Cocoa-Farming Families*, Nigeria Cocoa Marketing Board, Oxford Univ. Press, 1956; P. Gourou, 'Les plantations de cacaoyers en pays yoruba', *Ann. Econ. Soc. Civilisations*, 1960, p. 6082; N. C. Mitchel, *Some Comments on the Growth and Character of Ibadan's Population*, Ibadan, Univ. Coll. Dept. of Geography, Research notes no. 4, 1953, and *The Nigerian Town, Distribution and Definition*, *ibid*, no. 7, 1955, pp. 3–13.

who spend part of their time on their land, which may be several dozen miles away. The establishment of peace has encouraged these people to go further and further afield to exploit the cocoa plantations that are the Yorubas' main source of wealth. Though cocoa is less important in Nigeria than in Ghana, these Yoruba plantations still have a substantial yield, of the order of 100,000 tons as against 300,000 tons from Ghana. This enterprise on the part of the Yorubas is not

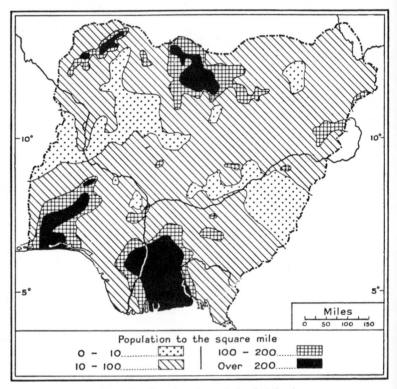

Population to the square mile

0 - 10........   100 - 200......⊞⊞

10 - 100......⧄⧄   Over 200......■

FIG. 11.   Density of population in Nigeria

After C. R. Niven, 'Some Nigerian population problems', *Geog. Journ.*, 85, 1935, pp. 54–8)

surprising in view of their long history of political maturity and artistic development. The 'Benin civilization' was developed by the Yoruba and the Fons of Dahomey as well as by the Bini themselves; though it lacked the art of writing and had not developed any very advanced agricultural techniques, it had progressed quite a long way in other directions, and the cast bronze work is evidence of aesthetic sense, technical competence and a considerable trade in the necessary metals. Expert opinion is still divided as to whether this bronze-founding technique was imported from Egypt via the Sudan, or brought from Mediterranean Europe, or invented on the spot.

The Benin area proper, which lies to the south-east of Yorubaland, also merits our attention. The town and kingdom of Benin surprised the first Portuguese visitors by their high degree of organization. But the prosperity of the sixteenth century was succeeded by a rapid decay.

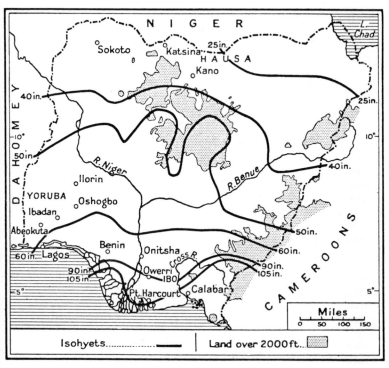

FIG. 12.   Relief and rainfall in Nigeria

The cultivated area declined; forests that were thought to be primeval revealed on closer examination traces of agricultural clearings, with fragments of pottery and charcoal in the soil, whilst the presence of the commercially valuable iroko tree (*Chlorophora*) is a certain proof of ancient deforestation, for it only flourishes by colonizing the fallow. Was the depopulation of Benin due to soil exhaustion, to over-exploitation, without an adequate restoration of fertility, of the very poor 'Benin sands'? Or was it the result of political events and the ravages of war? The decline in the export of slaves from the Benin coast, and the prosperity of Lagos, point in this direction. It is however worthy of note that at the present time the Yoruba cocoa trees succeed on soils derived from the decomposition of the crystalline rocks of the African massif but give poor results on the Benin sands, where rubber is the main tree crop (not that *Hevea* dislikes good soils, but it can survive on poor soils which cause the cacao tree to die prematurely).

To the east of the densely peopled Yoruba country, the Niger delta is but sparsely populated. This tropical delta, covering 7,700 square miles, with a wet climate and a powerful river, is no better and no worse than other tropical deltas that teem with humanity, like the Godavari and the Red River. The distinguishing feature of the Niger delta is that it has not been adapted by man: the people of the Ijaw tribe have built neither dyke nor drainage ditch; they live by fishing (sales of dried fish assuring them of the means of exchange) and by subsistence cultivation along the natural levées where they build their villages.

Beyond the Niger there is another abrupt change in the cultural landscape, and we are in the Ibo country. This is the most densely populated part of Nigeria: over 5,800 square miles the mean density is 310, whilst in the Okigwi division of Owerri province, covering 1,100 square miles, the density is everywhere more than 675 and in some parts more than 1,000. South of this main area of high density the population tails off towards the almost uninhabited coastal swamps that the Ibo people have so far not occupied.[1] The forest has been banished completely from the main populated area, and resumes its importance only in the south. Ibo agriculture has accommodated itself to a rising population by decreasing the length of the fallow.[2] A fallow lasting three years (after one year's cropping) corresponds to a population density of 770 to the square mile, a fallow of five years to a density of 500 to 250, and a fallow of seven years to a density of 300 to 150. The critical density, above which the length of the fallow would be too short to allow the soil to recuperate, is about 500 per square mile.[3] Demographic pressure has forced the Ibo to adopt certain techniques of intensification, but their agriculture is not distinguished for its progress in yields and productivity; the most densely peopled areas have to import foodstuffs (yams, cassava

1. G. I. Jones, 'The human factor in land planning', *Farm and Forest* (Ibadan), 1943, pp. 161–6.
2. L. D. Stamp, 'Land utilization and soil erosion in Nigeria', *Geog. Review*, 1938, pp. 32–45. See also M. J. S. Harris, 'Papers on the economic aspect of life among the Ibo', *Africa*, 1943, p. 20.
3. W. B. Morgan, 'Farming practice, settlement pattern and population density in south-eastern Nigeria', *Geog. Journ.* 121, 1955, pp. 320–33. See also A. T. Grove, 'Soil erosion in Nigeria', *Geographical Essays on British tropical lands*, London, 1956, pp. 79–111.

and taro) from the areas with fewer people, and these purchases are made with the profits from the sale of palm oil and with the wages earned by Ibo men in the Enugu coal-mines or in other parts of Nigeria. But the Ibos have shown a great enthusiasm for education and modern technology; they are to be found as office employees, nurses, doctors, chauffeurs and engineers all over Nigeria, and some Ibo villages have as many as 30 per cent of their youngest men absent.

What is the explanation of these high densities amongst the Ibos? The climate is favourable, with a high all-the-year rainfall (Owerri 93 inches); the soils are but mediocre, but they are easily worked and the low relief means that there are no unusable areas. The Ibo people, who came probably from the north, have no long political history behind them; they had neither chiefs nor monarch; yet they have a well-developed sense of nationhood. Their country lay beyond the limit of slave-raiding from the north, for the forest and the tsetse fly prevented the incursion of horsemen, and they came to terms with the slave-traders of Forcados and Bonny, to whom they sold as slaves persons condemned to death. Undoubtedly the main reason for the high density is the very high birth-rate that has been allowed, under the peaceful conditions that have prevailed since the end of the nineteenth century, to develop into a very great increase in numbers.

So the population situation of the Ibo results from a well-developed spirit of enterprise, a passion for work, and demographic expansion. It is not due either to the fertility of the land or to a particularly healthy environment (for endemic tropical diseases are present in force, and water-borne ailments are particularly widespread, most so-called potable water supplies being in fact polluted); nor does it result from high-yielding agriculture, nor from profitable commercial production, nor from an elaborate system of land management. The example of the Ibibio tribe brings this out clearly.[1] The Ibibio are closely related to the Ibo, and resemble them in all respects; their population density exceeds 650 per square mile in some parts. It is surprising that these people, who live but poorly within a small territory and rely on money sent back by emigrés for part of their income, have done almost nothing to improve the yield of their oil palms. These palms are all self-sown, and many are very old; no care is bestowed upon them; they are not pruned, nor manured, nor cleared of weeds. It is not surprising that the yields are small, an average of no more than 28 lb of nuts per tree, giving 4 lb of oil and an equal quantity of kernels. In terms of yield per acre, this amounts to the miserable total of 320 lb from eighty trees.

Towards the east the density of Ibo (and Ibibio) settlement decreases. The Cross River area presents a problem, for its sparse

1. Anne Martin, *The Oil Palm Economy of the Ibibio Farmer*, Ibadan, 1956.

population is no more a result of physical circumstances than is the density of the Ibo country. It is a great forest, but the environment is not particularly hostile, and the abundance of oil palms in the Calabar region shows that this area at least has been cleared in the past, for the *elaeis* is a tree which grows on deforested land. The area must have been depopulated at some time—perhaps due to its proximity to the great slave market of Calabar.[1]

Central Nigeria interposes its wide open spaces—only 3 million people on 115,000 square miles—between the densely peopled north and south. But this central area is better watered than the north, with a mean annual rainfall of between 30 and 40 inches, and it forms a broad depression crossed by the navigable rivers Niger and Benue. Although the confluence of these two rivers would seem to present a geographical site of remarkable centrality, there is nothing there but a modest village of quite recent origin, Lokodja. The territorial capitals are peripheral, and so is the federal capital, Lagos. The low population density has often been ascribed to the incidence of sleeping sickness. It seems however that the tsetse fly simply finished off an operation that was begun by the raiding Fulani from the north. In the dry season, when the tsetse is less in evidence, the horsemen ravaged the plains of central Nigeria, massacring or carrying off the inhabitants as slaves. These raids increased in intensity during the eighteenth century; the Ilorin Yorubas and the Nupes were plundered, weakened and made to submit to Fulani authority, whilst the Benue plains were even more fiercely devastated; the Jukun kingdom was not even converted into a vassal state, but was ruthlessly destroyed; its inhabitants were dispersed and the area became a dry-season grazing ground for Fulani herds.

Northern Nigeria covers 115,000 square miles and supports 10 million people; the greatest densities are reached in the western provinces (Sokoto, Katsina and Kano) which have 8 million people on 34,000 square miles. This is not due to exceptional physical advantages but is a matter of history. For over a thousand years the Hausa kingdoms maintained a relatively stable and efficient control, whilst elements of a superior civilization were brought in by Muslims. The association and the fusion of the Hausa cultivators and the Fulani pastoralists succeeded in firmly implanting Islam, at the same time solving the thorny problem of the relations between the two ways of life. Over the greater part of the territory the Hausa continue

1. On the western edge of the Cross River forest there are some important river-bank villages inhabited by the Yako people; one of these, Umor, has been studied by C. Daryll Forde, 'Land and labour in a Cross River village', *Geog. Journ.* 1937, pp. 24–51; see also C. D. Forde, *Marriage and Family among the Yako in South-eastern Nigeria*, London School of Economics, 1941.

their traditional agricultural practices: sorghum is grown on hand-cleared plots, carefully hoed to get rid of the savanna grass roots. After several years of cropping the plot is left fallow; the period varies, but seven years' fallow is considered adequate. The plot may be manured by the folding of Fulani flocks and herds, and this may modify the length of the cultivation and fallow periods. The Hausa cultivator is not indifferent to stock-raising; he has his cattle, which he keeps at home or rents to a Fulani herdsman. Groundnut cultivation has achieved considerable success, and it has brought an income in addition to that derived from the sale of goat skins, which were formerly the only export. The most interesting feature, however, is the existence of centres of intensive agriculture, for they may point the way to possible developments in the modernization of African farming.

The Hausa have achieved their most remarkable control of rural land in the vicinity of Kano. Here, within a radius of a dozen miles, the rural population density exceeds 1,000 to the square mile; the land surface is completely utilized all the year round, with no fallow, by the use of irrigation. The natural conditions allow this kind of development but did not determine it, for the rainfall is only 30 inches a year and the climate is very hot, with a long and blistering dry season. The skilful and hard working countryfolk grow sorghum, maize, sugar cane, wet rice and vegetables, with the aid of very careful techniques, irrigation water provided by *shadufs* almost as numerous as in Egypt or Madras, and human excreta transported every morning from the town by a malodorous procession of donkeys. So the town fertilizes the fields that provide its food, and the flat *fadamas* that form the environs of Kano are one vast market garden studded with fruit trees. Town and country are closely linked in an economy which proves profitable to both, a situation which is very rare in Africa, and one which betokens an advanced form of civilization. Further away from Kano, the physical conditions remain almost unaltered, but the human circumstances are different, and horticulture gives way to a less intensive form of cultivation. Nevertheless the commercial orientation remains, and the Hausa peasant is strongly devoted to his groundnut cultivation.

The type of agriculture that may be regarded as typical of the hot, wet lands, namely slash-and-burn, with long fallows (which become longer with every increase in the length of the cultivation period), is a theme on which it is possible to compose many variations. The shortening of the fallow and the use of the hoe—or in Melanesia, for example, of an implement to raise up mounds of earth—are means of introducing variety. There remains a dominant note, which is the poor yield per acre of this type of agriculture, a yield which becomes minute if one takes into account not only the surface actually harvested but also the whole area subjected to the rotation of cultivation and fallow.

In certain circumstances tropical cultivators do practise an intensive form of agriculture, with no fallow and with the use of manure. Such techniques, however, appear to be expensive in terms of labour, and the people thus prefer the ladang system, to which they return when the circumstances which led to the intensification no longer apply.

Neither ladang nor the 'last resort' intensive agriculture offer much scope for the future, for they are unsatisfactory both in yield and in productivity. The flooded ricefield, as in Madagascar and in several localities in tropical Africa, is an advanced technique that assures high and above all reliable yields, absolving the population from dependence on a seasonal and uncertain rainfall; but there is much to be done before the output of the flooded ricefields is markedly superior to that of the ladang. Wider areas must be cultivated and commercial markets must be opened up so as to provide the incentive for a greatly increased productivity.

The main spur to progress in tropical agriculture is undoubtedly the possibility of commercial cropping. The cultivator must work to sell his products and not merely to feed himself. Subsistence agriculture condemns him to a poverty-stricken rut. The means of progress clearly include the following: (1) the improvement of means of communication, for no development is possible with isolation; (2) the creation of market-garden zones around the towns, which are ready to give a good price for foodstuffs; Kano points the way, for many large tropical towns have no such food supplies on their doorstep and have to import from abroad; (3) the production by the native populations of tropical crops which are articles of world commerce—following the example of the cocoa producers of Ghana and Nigeria and the coffee growers of Kilimanjaro. Once commercial agriculture is established, it is necessary to perfect the techniques which will give high yields both in terms of area and of labour. The object is to get more from the soil with less human toil, without damaging the soil's fertility, and without unduly lowering the price of the commodity, and this demands a high degree of technical skill. Fertilizers must be used to prevent soil exhaustion,[1] plant varieties must be carefully selected, animal-drawn or motorized implements must be used to give the soil more careful tillage for the expenditure

1. A better use of animal manure is essential. First, those people who are exclusively cultivators must develop stock-raising as well; secondly, it must be realized that feeding animals on an area is not the best way of getting it manured, for in a tropical climate much of the dung is lost; the sun dries it up, the wind disperses it, ants eat it and heavy rains wash it away.

rich ricefields at the bottom of the
y are in strong contrast with the
soil on the slopes. The latter have
denuded by thoughtless cultivation
ell as by erosion. Notice that the
e in the foreground is cut by a gully
covered with lateritic gravel. The
ograph was taken near Trivandrum
in Travancore.

efields to the south-west of Calcutta.
fields are flooded from canals. Note
fish-fence, the fisherman's shelter,
the canoe made by hollowing out
the trunk of a palm tree.

34. Ploughing flooded ricefields near Pondicherry, India.

35. Rice cultivation on the Tongking delta near Hanoi. The woman is scooping water from a ditch into a ricefield. On the left is a pond containing water for household purposes. In the background are a water buffalo and a clump of bamboos. The district contains 1,300 persons to the square mile.

of less human labour, and irrigation must be introduced to guard against irregularity in the rainfall and to permit the all-the-year-round production that the hot tropical climate allows, and that alone can cover the expense of land improvement.

Ladang is not the inevitable product of a hot, wet climate. It is an archaic form of agriculture which has survived through the isolation of individual groups of subsistence-cultivators, through the isolation of the various parts of the tropics,[1] and through the prolonged isolation of the tropical world from the rapidly developing world of European civilization. This isolation at several levels has been emphasized by certain physical circumstances, such as the lack of overland communication between the various parts of the hot, wet lands, and the difficulty of applying in the tropical world modern techniques of agriculture and medicine that were developed in the temperate lands. Fundamentally, however, the isolation is a product of history and civilization.

It is obvious, therefore, that ladang, the product of antiquity and isolation, must give way to better techniques. This chapter has shown that we should be chary of believing that such intensive techniques as are to be found in parts of the tropics have any future; their low productivity rules them out of court. Progress must be made in other directions, and above all, as we have seen, in the commercial orientation of tropical agriculture. But we must not forget that the production of commercial crops simply by an imprudent extension of ladang will obstruct future progress. Along certain African railways, for example, can be seen large clearings, hurriedly burned and sown with maize; this is a squandering of soil resources and a distortion of the beneficial effect that the encouragement of commercial agriculture ought to have. The careless use of the mechanical plough can also have disastrous effects; the possession of one of these implements often leads to the cultivation, year after year, of large areas that ought really, in the absence of manure, to be allowed to revert to forest fallow.

Tropical Asia has long perfected a more judicious and high-yielding type of agriculture. But even this is an example that should not be copied without some reservations, as the next chapter will show.

1. See below, p. 163.

CHAPTER 10

Hot, Wet Asia

THE densely populated parts of tropical Africa, America and
Melanesia occupy but tiny areas and support a small total number of
inhabitants. India, south-east Asia and the East Indies, on the other
hand, cover more than three million square miles and contain 850
million people. In tropical Asia the average population density is
280 to the square mile; over the rest of the hot, wet lands it is eighteen
to the square mile. It is as if mankind in the tropics can only go to the
two extremes of sparse population on the one hand and excessive
density on the other!

The contrast between these two types of human landscapes in the
tropics is not due to differing physical conditions: there are deltas that
are densely populated, as in Bengal and Tongking, and those that
have but few people, like the Niger and Amazon; there are tropical
mountains teeming with people, as in Java and Rwanda, and others
that are almost uninhabited, as in central Annam, in Cambodia, and
in the Kundelunga highlands of Katanga; there are equatorial
forests still more or less in their primeval state, like the selvas of the
Amazon and the Congo jungles, and formerly forested regions that
have long since been cleared, as in Java. All these contrasts are the
results of civilization; they result from the differing response of various
civilizations to a natural environment that did not itself offer wide
variations.

The contrast in cultural landscapes is very striking in the eastern
part of the Indochinese peninsula. This area, comprising Burma,
Malaya, Siam, Laos, Cambodia and Vietnam, lies between India and
China, and has been subjected in varying degrees to the cultural
influence of these two civilizations. Our first example is a very
revealing one; it is Vietnam. The country is hot and wet; true, the
northern part is on the edge of the tropical world, for the coldest
month at Hanoi has a mean temperature of 61° F (16° C), and our
definition (p. 1) of tropical conditions has stipulated 64° F (18° C)
as the thermal limit; however, the Hanoi region has no frost (the
absolute minimum is 41° F (5° C)), and has a growing season of 365
days with a landscape that is obviously tropical in character. Besides,
the temperate-tropical climatic boundary is a particularly difficult
one to define in the Far East, and the climate of southern China, to
the north of Indochina, is still transitional in character. Vietnam

118

occupies the eastern face of the Indochinese peninsula, with a latitudinal extent of 870 miles. Most of the population lives in the alluvial coastal plains, in a discontinuous belt from the Red River delta in the north to that of Mekong in the south. These plains, covering some 29,000 square miles, support 22 million inhabitants, whereas in the rest of Vietnam there are scarcely 5 million spread over 100,000 square miles. The mountain backbone that forms a large part of Vietnam is very sparsely peopled, particularly the parts occupied by the Moi. These people of Indonesian origin, who have a language and a civilization quite different from the Vietnamese, practise traditional subsistence agriculture called *ray*, the equivalent of ladang, consisting of forest burning followed by maize and dry rice cultivation. These 'forest-eaters', as they have been called, have converted large areas of forest into savanna, despite their low density of less than ten persons to the square mile. They live in poverty and their methods of occupying the land are very primitive. The plains, teeming with people, are an astonishing contrast to these lonely mountains.

It is as well to begin a study of the Vietnamese plains with the Red River or Tongking delta, which exhibits the most interesting geographical characteristics and has the densest population. On its 5,800 square miles the density is at least 1,300 to the square mile, and in some parts the rural density exceeds 3,800 to the square mile.[1] There can be few geographical 'fronts' sharper than that between the delta and the neighbouring hills; within a few hundred yards the population density changes from many hundreds to the square mile to less than thirty—a phenomenon typical of the Asiatic tropics. The causes of such a contrast can be stated very precisely, and they help us to understand the geographical peculiarity of the tropical environment. The delta is completely occupied by intensive cultivation; the hills in which it is framed are only utilized to the extent of about one or two per cent of their surface, and that by extensive methods. The delta is inhabited by the Vietnamese, who during the past two thousand years have perfected the occupation of the land surface, on the Chinese model; the hills were occupied by non-Vietnamese people, with no tradition of political organization. Finally, the delta has no malaria, whilst the hills may be counted amongst the most malarial of territories.

The soils of the delta are not always very fertile, for they are often lacking in soluble bases. However they are always in good physical condition, without any lateritic tendencies, and are easily worked, responding well to the prodigious labour that is expended upon them. If the delta were exploited by the cultivation of unirrigated food

1. P. Gourou, *Les paysans du Delta tonkinois*, Paris and Hanoi, 1936.

crops, with fallow, it could certainly not support 1,300 people to the square mile; but its actual land use follows a very different pattern, with flooded ricefields, harvested year after year, and actually giving two crops a year over rather more than half the area. The fields are very carefully manured and the entire agricultural operation demands an enormous expenditure of human labour, amounting to 250 work days a year per acre on the two-crop land.

The flooded ricefield, through the regularity and abundance of its harvests, favours a high population density and the progress of civilization. It will give regular harvests even without manure—and despite the care of the cultivators it sometimes does not get any. Beneath the flood water the soil does not deteriorate, nor is it eroded. The planting-out process means that the growing season in the flooded field can be shortened, for one generation of rice plants can be growing in the seedbed whilst the preceding crop is coming to maturity; and scarcely has the latter—the first or 'sixth month' crop—been harvested in June but the ground is made ready to receive the plants from the seedbed, which will give the second or 'tenth month' harvest in October–November.

The cultivators must thus have their fields available all the year round, and must have access to the water necessary for irrigation. The climate is relatively favourable, for there is no interruption of the growing season through cold; the summer monsoon rains are in general sufficient to keep the ricefields flooded, provided that the individual fields are of small extent and are separated by carefully maintained bunds. The dry season is alleviated from time to time by damp mists that prevent evaporation and keep the soil moist. Nevertheless, the cultivation of swamp rice is possible at this season only in the lowest parts of the delta. At all times the cultivators correct any deficiencies in the natural water supply by very energetic means involving the use of simple devices such as basket-scoops, scoops suspended from tripods, and pedal-norias. The greatest enemy of the cultivators is in fact the Red River itself, which derives its name from the red alluvium which it has carried from the hills of Yunnan, and which floods extensively in summer. In its natural state the river would inundate a large part of the delta, leaving a trail of alluvium behind, but this would mean the loss of some of the most profitable agricultural land, that which can make the best use of the rain and heat of summer. An untamed delta would support but few inhabitants. The Red River has been for a very long time confined by embankments, maintained and improved during the centuries in order to give the cultivators the maximum possible security. At first no doubt these dykes were fragile, but little by little they have been reinforced so that they are now virtually unbreachable.

The first dykes were of purely local concern, but very soon they were constructed and controlled by the state, thus showing that the techniques of land management had reached a sufficiently high level to have a specialized administration. The Vietnamese methods were inspired by those of China, for the Chinese occupied and colonized northern Vietnam for six hundred years, and contributed to the foundation of the Vietnamese nation, which is separate from the Chinese but owes to them its writing and many of the techniques of production and organization.

Agriculture in the delta is remarkably perfect, though in its traditional way and with an enormous expenditure of manpower. The ground is very carefully prepared by repeated ploughing and harvesting. In some parts of the delta, ploughing is followed by the spade-digging of the subsoil, and the clods are piled up in low walls to aerate them; then the heaps are dismantled, the clods broken with a mallet and the earth spread out over the field. The preparation of the seedbed is conducted with infinite attention to detail; the soil is reduced to an impalpable mud, and is manured with the greatest care. The ricefield itself receives little farm manure or human excreta, for these are reserved for the seedbeds, but it is enriched by mud dredged from the pools, and by green leaves, especially of *Azolla*, a floating fern that makes an excellent green manure when it is killed off by the heat just before its vegetative development would have interfered with the growth of the rice plants. The conservation of layers of *azolla* during the hot season is a subtle and clever art. Altogether, this is an agriculture practised by hard-working and knowledgeable people, in complete opposition to the extensive and careless ladang.

The most densely peopled parts of the delta are in the south, towards Nam Dinh and Thai Binh. The explanation lies in the higher yields that are obtainable in this area, resulting partly from the greater inherent fertility of the soils which are of recent alluvium, but in large measure from the favourable hydrological régime. Neither excess nor shortage of water is here to be feared, and two rice harvests a year can be regularly obtained. The proximity of the sea helps to lower the level of the floods and modify their torrential character; the tide plays an important part, for the Gulf of Tongking has a peculiar tidal régime with but a single high and low during the twenty-four hours, and this facilitates drainage at low tide and fills all the small river channels with ponded-up fresh water at high tide. The lower delta, with a minimum of human intervention, is thus endowed with a better water situation than the upper delta. Nevertheless it has needed a civilization equipped with the necessary technical skill and powers of organization to take full advantage of this.

There is little malaria in the Red River delta, though the surrounding hill country is very unhealthy. The countryfolk know this well, and are afraid of moving off the plain. Agricultural labourers working on plantations situated in the unhealthy area which fringes the delta do not hesitate to commute several miles, night and morning, between their village and the plantation, so as not to spend the night away from the plain, exposed to the bite of the *anopheles*. During the military operations in the Red River delta in 1954, the French troops were free from malaria; but those who left the delta for the campaign around Hoa Binh suffered severely. The healthiness of the delta (as far as malaria is concerned) is surprising at first sight, since the country is covered with flooded ricefields and ponds, so much so that in summer there is more water than land. Mosquitoes certainly swarm in these waters, but the dangerous *anopheles* are absent or very rare, for their larvae do not like the muddy, stagnant water of the ricefields and ponds. The care taken by the cultivators to manure the ricefields with leaves, plants and street sweepings affords an excellent protection against mosquito larvae. The main arms of the Red River and its distributaries are not dangerous during the season of high water since they are scoured by the floods, but they may become so in the dry season through the formation of pools of clear water. The peasants, however, are so greedy for land that the whole of the main river bed, between the major and minor dykes, is cultivated, and there is no opportunity for pools to remain in which the anopheles larvae might survive. There have been occasional exceptions to the general malaria-free character of the delta; small localized epidemics may occur owing to an exceptional swarm of *Anopheles sinensis*, a mosquito that normally feeds on animals; or they may perhaps be due to the import of new strains of malaria plasmodium by people returning from a visit to the highlands. In the coastal parts of the delta, as on the banks of the Thanh Hoa, Nghé An and Ha Tinh, occasional severe outbreaks of malaria occur during the winter season, when the northeast monsoon is blowing. They are produced by *Anopheles ludlowi*, the larvae of which flourish near the shore in pools of fresh water to which the north-easterly winds add salt spray which gives the pool exactly the right degree of salinity for this particular mosquito larva; the wind then blows the insects inland. Such exceptions as these, however, only serve to emphasize the generally healthy character of the great Tongking delta.

Only a few hundred yards from the edge of the healthy delta lie the malarial hills. Here there are clear, running streams, subject to much sunlight since the slopes have been completely deforested; in other words the ideal breeding ground for the most virulent of the mosquitoes, particularly *Anopheles minimus*. The healthiness of the delta is not the gift of nature. Man has achieved it by utilizing the whole area and controlling the water, that is, by substituting a completely tamed landscape for a wild one. Healthiness is but the by-product of the complete control of land use, and man has brought it about unintentionally. More healthy conditions have followed on civilization, and have fostered a dense population. When it had but few people the delta must have been malarial, for there would have been no lack of limpid pools and streams of fresh water to encourage the *anopheles* larvae. Nature has merely assembled the physical conditions which, when exploited by civilized man with suitable agricultural techniques and an adequate system of organized control have led to the complete utilization of the area and so to the dis-appearance of malaria. The same civilized men were unable to use the mountain areas completely, because it was impossible to cultivate regularly every square yard of the slopes and impossible to eliminate malaria from areas incompletely occupied. Nowadays it would be possible to make the thinly-peopled mountain areas healthy—but only within a technological environment that combines the scientific understanding of malaria with rational methods of combating it, including a battery of insecticides and antimalarial medicines. For people who did not possess this technical mastery, and who felt the need to extend their territory, there was an irresistible urge to occupy the alluvial plains where the known agricultural methods of the delta could be applied, with a resultant improvement in health conditions of which the nature was not understood but the reality was easily appreciated. The Vietnamese civilization was very slow in assimilating the mountainous areas behind the delta, and these were left to non-Vietnamese people; but they spread southwards, first to the plains north of the Porte d'Annam (Thanh Hoa, Vinh, Ha Tinh), then the plains between the Porte d' Annam and the Col des Nuages (Quang Binh, Quang Tri, Thua Tien), the plains between the Col des Nuages and the Massif of Padaran (Quang Nan, Quang Ngai, Binh Dinh, Nha Trang, Phan Rang) and finally reached the approaches to the Mekong delta (Phan Ri, Phan Thiet) and the Mekong itself. In their southward expansion the Vietnamese almost annihilated the Cham people (of Malayan affinities), and broke the resistance of the Cambodians, the former occupants of the Mekong delta. This move-ment from the twentieth parallel of latitude to the eighth, effected along the coast by a non-maritime people, resulted in the constitution of a peculiar national territory, for the Vietnamese plains are often only a few miles wide between the sea and the mountains. When the mountains come right to the coast the ethnic continuity of the Vietna-mese is almost broken, as around Cape Padaran and Cape Varella, where the fires of the Moi blaze on the hillsides overlooking the sea.

The superior organization of the Vietnamese enabled them to conquer and subjugate the Cham and the Cambodians (Khmer) However, the Vietnamese themselves, who had reached the Mekong only in the seventeenth century, have had some difficulty in maintaining their national cohesion, and the north and the south (beginning at the Porte d'Annam) have been but rarely united during the course of history. This is a consequence of the configuration of the country, which resulted from the particular ideas of the Vietnamese on the relation between man and the soil.

The reasons for the complete exploitation of the Tongking delta, and for its dense population, are clear enough. But they are insufficient to explain why the rural density should average 1,300 to the square mile and attain 2,600 in some parts. In north-west Europe rural densities of 130 to the square mile are regarded as indicative of overpopulation, whilst in the United States the rural density is only 12 to 25 per square mile even in areas entirely occupied. Why should the number of agriculturalists per square mile of cultivation in the Tongking delta be ten times greater than in Europe and a hundred times greater than in the United States? The productivity of the soil is not a sufficient answer, for the yield of cereals is very far from being greater than in Europe. Even if two good rice harvests are reaped in the lower delta, the amount of paddy obtained in twelve months is no greater than 1·1 tons per acre, which is substantially less than the yield of rice on the Valencia *huerta* or the plain of Emilia, or the yield of wheat on the loamy plains of Valois and Brabant.[1] It is true that the very high yields of the temperate lands are quite recent, and that part of the land was formerly left fallow, whilst in Tongking the soil is never idle. And one must admit that Asiatic yields were formerly greater than those of Europe. This advantage, however, which has in any case now vanished, could never have been great enough to explain the enormous difference in the density of population between the Red River delta and north-west Europe or North America. The very high densities in the delta result from the nature of the civilization, not merely from the intensiveness of the agriculture but mainly because of the nature and very modest level of consumption. The peasants are content with very little; they consume what they produce, and although they are very abstemious their food represents about 80 per cent of the monetary value of their entire cost of living. Even without the occasional bad harvest they live at almost starvation level, for their diet is almost exclusively vegetarian (to the extent of 98 per cent of the calorie intake). Foodstuffs of animal origin are costly to produce, because the intermediary animal will absorb into

1. The communist authorities of North Vietnam claim to have greatly increased rice yields. If this is so, as may be hoped, North Vietnam will have no food problems.

its own system a large part of the calories that it consumes. A vegetarian diet enables many more people to be supported on an acre of cultivated land than could be nourished on a mixed diet.

The peasants keep just sufficient oxen and buffaloes for ploughing and harrowing; but since there is no grazing land, the animals have to be fed, especially during the periods of heavy ploughing, on the cereals that could equally well feed the people. No other work than ploughing and harrowing is demanded of the oxen and buffaloes, and all transport is effected by men with yokes or by boat. Cow's milk is not used, and beef is eaten only on rare occasions; pork, dog-meat, poultry and eggs, though more common, are certainly not eaten every day. Pigs, which are efficient consumers of waste, scavenge among the village refuse, and are fed on minced banana stalks and aquatic plants, and on rice-bran, all substances that humans cannot eat. The peasants are very interested in fish but actually consume relatively little; the fresh waters of the delta are exploited to the full, thanks to the careful pisciculture. Sea-fishing is but poorly developed, despite the Vietnamese liking for a kind of pickled fish, called 'nuoc-mam', which they purchase in spite of their poverty.[1] The high population density, though associated with a vegetarian diet, is not the cause of it. It is not because the people are so numerous that they adopt this kind of diet, for in the more sparsely populated parts of Indochina it is equally vegetarian. The Meo people, who live in the mountains with large animal herds, do not bother to milk their buffaloes any more than the delta-dwellers do. Vegetarianism is a characteristic of the civilization, which is an important factor in the high population density but is not the cause of it.

Despite their poverty, and despite the small part of their total income that is available for spending on anything else but food, the delta-dwellers belong to an advanced civilization; such manufactured articles as they are able to buy are made in villages which specialize in one particular type of product and sell it to other villages that are equally specialized in some other direction. An active trade in such articles as cloth, pottery, ironwork, basketwork etc., thus develops in the market towns of the delta. Most peasants can devote much time to such crafts, for agriculture, despite its intensive character, does not demand of the peasant more than 125 days' labour a year.

The delta-dwellers, whose diet is so completely vegetarian, dress in cotton cloth, and pad their winter garments with cottonwool; they protect themselves from the rain with coats made of straw, and cover their heads with banana leaves. Their equipment is almost entirely

1. For greater detail see P. Gourou, *L'utilisation du sol en Indochine française*, Paris, Centre d'études de politique étrangère, 1940, especially pp. 192–6; and P. Gourou, *La terre et l'homme en Extrême-Orient*, Paris, 1941, especially pp. 114–25.

of vegetable origin; containers are made of laquered basketwork, houses are built of timber and bamboo, with thatched roofs and walls that are often made of leaves. So much so that this might indeed be called a 'vegetable civilization'. In such circumstances the vegetarian diet is more readily understandable.

The more southerly plains of Vietnam are less densely peopled than those of the north. In the Mekong delta, especially its south-western projection which ends in the Pointe de Camau (or Cape Cambodia) there are large expanses with less than 100 people to the square mile. The difference is not fundamentally due to physical factors, but to the more recent (seventeenth-century) arrival of the Vietnamese in the area, in which demographical development has not progressed as far as in the north. Sheer necessity has not yet forced the people in this area west of the Mekong river to develop all the hydrological works necessary for the complete utilization of the soil. The Khmer or Cambodians, who occupied the area when the Vietnamese arrived, and who still form an important minority, had not tamed the landscape of the south-west at all, and in any case they had not the same propensity as the Vietnamese for clustering in large rural masses; their agriculture was less intensive and their organization nothing like so effective.

Some general features may be discerned in this Vietnamese example which are to be found throughout tropical Monsoon Asia. In the first place, there is the juxtaposition of areas of dense and sparse population; secondly, the areas of low density have physical and human characteristics resembling those of the greater part of the tropical world, namely, unhealthiness, poor and easily exhausted soils, unirrigated food crops grown on the ladang system, and a sparse and backward population. The peculiarity of Monsoon Asia is its possession of very densely peopled plains, in which the superabundant population is closely associated with fertile soils,[1] advanced social and political organization, intensive cultivation (especially of swamp rice) and sound agricultural methods, or, in a word, with an advanced

1. The question arises: are the alluvial plains built up by the rivers of Monsoon Asia more fertile than those at the mouths of African and American rivers? The deltas of the Red River, Mekong, Irrawaddy, Brahmaputra and Ganges get a great deal of their alluvium from mountains of sedimentary rocks, which yield quantities of fertilizing elements. The Niger delta has been constructed by a river that carries little, either in suspension or in solution, and it has poor soils. A comparative study of deltas is very much needed, for it alone could give a worthwhile solution to this problem. The answer is unlikely to be a simple one, for there are also Asiatic deltas at the mouths of silt-free rivers that traverse areas of pre-Cambrian crystalline rocks and yet have high population densities, like the Mahanadi, the Godavari, the Kistna, and indeed almost all the alluvial plains on the Coromandel and Malabar coasts of India.

stage of civilization. These teeming plains are much less malarial than the rest of the tropical world, and the enormous rural population can be sustained only at a low standard of living and on an almost exclusively vegetarian diet. In the case of Vietnam, it is clear that its superior civilization was brought from the north by the Chinese.

Siam and Burma are far less interesting than Vietnam, from the point of view of human geography, because their plains do not carry the high population densities that are found in Tongking. The reasons are primarily historical, for the deltas of the Menam and the Irrawaddy are areas of relatively recent settlement and have not yet had time to become overcrowded. As in the case of the Vietnamese, the southward movement of the Siamese and Burmese was effected only in the last few centuries; indeed the Burmese colonization of the Irrawaddy delta dates only from the nineteenth century. It is to their excellent physical conditions and their relatively light population that the deltas of the Mekong, Menam and Irrawaddy owe their importance as sources of rice exports.

India and Pakistan contained 530 million inhabitants in 1961, of whom 80 per cent were rural and agricultural. The greatest concentrations are round the edges of the Deccan on fertile areas of recent alluvium that either have a good rainfall or are easily irrigated (Fig. 13), and the densest areas are devoted entirely to rice cultivation. The density of population on the Ganges plain increases from west to east with the rainfall and with the relative importance of irrigated rice. The Bengal delta, now partitioned between India and Pakistan, is the largest area of dense population in the whole sub-continent. The Pakistan section had in 1951 a density of 885 per square mile over the whole area of 46,000 square miles, but the group of villages in the 'Rampal Union', south of Dacca, had 16,334 people living on only 3·4 square miles, that is a density of 4,790 to the square mile. This exceptionally high rural density is related to the importance of horticulture, especially the cultivation of the betel tree (the leaves and nuts of which are chewed with a pinch of lime). The district of Tippera has a density of 3,885 to the square mile, and the *thana* of Lohonjang are of 4,140.[1] East Pakistan has but a small urban population, only 6 per cent of the total.

The coastal plain on the eastern side of the Deccan, from Bengal to Cape Comorin, is a continuous ribbon of dense population; in

1. N. Ahmad, *Land Use in Rampal Union*, East Pakistan Geographical Society, monograph no. 1, 1961; N. Ahmad and F. K. Khan, *Land Use in Fayadabad Area*, monograph no. 2, 1963. See also B. L. C. Johnson, 'Rural population densities in East Pakistan', *Pacific Viewpoint*, 1962, pp. 51–62, in which the author indicates that the *thana* of Dokar, in Dacca District, has a density of 6,268 per square mile— though perhaps this is partly due to the proximity of the city of Dacca.

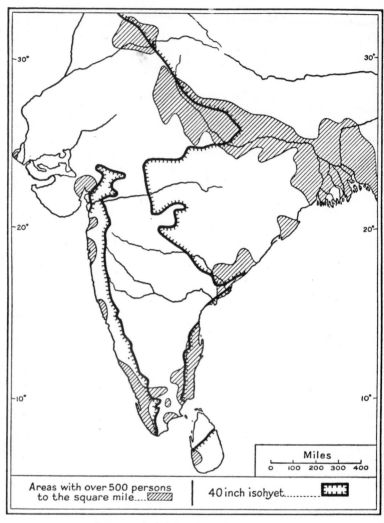

FIG. 13. Rainfall and population in India

Orissa, the Mahanadi delta has a general density of over 670, with over 1,300 downstream from Cuttack; the Tamil areas, in Madras, are even more densely peopled. The western coastal strip in Travancore and Cochin is teeming with people; in the village lands of Elankunnapurzha, in Cochin, the density in 1941 was 4,900 per square mile, and over the whole of Cochin it was 1,900.

The mountain areas are much less densely peopled, and often by backward tribes who are not yet Indianized. Instances of this are seen in the Vindhya mountains, the Mahadeo hills, Chota Nagpur plateau, and Nilgiri and Cardamom Hills. The contrast between the areas of dense and sparse population is generally very abrupt, and nowhere is this better seen than in the Terai, at the foot of the Himalayas, which used to be so malarial as to be almost uninhabitable.

The regions that are densely populated and completely cultivated are less malarial than the rest. Thus it comes about that the southern and eastern parts of the Bengal delta are both more populated and less malarial than the western part, where the great increase in malaria towards the end of the nineteenth century provoked an appreciable decrease in the population. This western part is on the edge of the delta; side by side in Burdwan there are valleys full of recent alluvium part of the delta, and old alluvial terraces through which run fresh, clear and sunlit streams (for the area was long ago deforested) that are ideal for the larvae of the most dangerous species of anopheles. These borderlands are also exposed to invasions of mosquitoes from outside the delta; thus, in the Mahanadi delta the northern and southern ends, liable to be visited by anopheles from the neighbouring hill country, are much more malarial than the central part. In Burdwan the situation is aggravated within the terrace lands by the irrigation tanks, which are less well maintained than in times past, changes in agricultural system having led the peasants to neglect the maintenance of the dams. The tanks, which were constructed by throwing earth dams across small valleys, are not dangerous if they are deep and if their banks are kept clean; but if through want of care, they become silted up, whilst the banks are eroded by the treading of buffaloes, the anopheles larvae find conditions which suit them. The decline of agriculture and the increase of malaria go hand in hand, each acting on the other. And underfed humans are an easy prey to the most severe forms of malaria.[1]

The western fringe of Bengal formed an excellent starting place for the spread of malaria just at the time when conditions favourable to the progress of the disease were developing on the western delta itself. In the sixteenth century the waters of the Ganges almost stopped flowing through the western arm (the Bhagirathi, whose mouth is the Hooghly), to run into the Brahmaputra through the Padma. The results were disastrous. There was not enough water for flooding the ricefields, and the deposition of fertilizing mud ceased; the main channels of the streams, no longer scoured by the floods, became ideal breeding grounds for the anopheles. The same kind of

1. A. Geddes, *La civilisation du Bengale occidental et ses facteurs géographiques*, Montpellier, 1927.

thing was observed in Ceylon in 1933, when the streams ceased to sweep their channels because the prolonged drought weakened the current. Lastly, the attraction of Calcutta has given rise to a network of railway lines and embanked roads; and owing to lack of care the drainage system has been disorganized and irrigation impaired. The causes of an increase in the incidence of malaria are thus many, but all of them, whether physical or human in origin, indicate a falling-off in the area under cultivation.[1]

The people of India use intensive agricultural methods, though they show less care than the Vietnamese in making use of manure; most cow dung is used as fuel, and human excreta are considered impure. However, the alluvial soils of Uttar Pradesh have been yielding moderate harvests for six hundred years without being manured. They are very carefully cultivated, it is true, but the yield would be very much greater if the Indian peasant would consent to the use of human excreta and did not burn the cow dung. It is of course possible that the human manure gets to the fields in the end, for the rain will wash it there, or into the streams. Despite the existence of some 200 million oxen and buffaloes, the Indian population has an almost exclusively vegetarian diet; high population densities are thus, as in Vietnam, accompanied by a low standard of living.[2]

India is a country with a very long history of civilization, which has given time to develop appropriate techniques for the development of the Deccan plateau. The scarped mountains within the plateau (Vindhya, Mahedeo and the Eastern Ghats for example) are sparsely populated, and are given over to *jhum* (ladang). But the crystalline plateau itself, where of moderate relief, as in Mysore, carries populations of as much as 310 to the square mile, thanks to the rice crop which is irrigated with waters ponded up behind earth dams thrown across small valleys. The soil is but mediocre, and the interfluves are of little value, but the valleys with their ricefields support the population. The case of the *regur* soils of the north-western part of the pre-Cambrian plateau is different; these black earths, formed in a climate with a moderate rainfall (20 to 40 inches) that has not leached them, are cultivated without irrigation; they grow cereals and cotton.

The density of the rural population in India, already at a high level, is increasing. The census of 1961 showed that every administrative divi-

1. On malaria in India see the following papers by A. T. A. Learmonth, 'Medical geography in Indo-Pakistan', *Indian Geographer*, 1958, p. 1–59; 'Medical geography in India and Pakistan', *Geog. Journ.* 127, 1961, pp. 10–26.
2. For further information on India see N. Krebs, *Vorderindien und Ceylon, eine landes-kunde* 1939, O.H.K. Spate, *Indian and Pakistan*, London. 1954; S. P. Chatterjee, *Bengal in Maps*, 1949; and pp. 367–450 of P. Gourou's *L'Asie*, 1953.

sion had a higher density than ten years earlier. Overpopulation has become a menace. If by overpopulation we mean that every increase entails a reduction in the standard of living, then it is possible to say that such a state has been reached in Travancore, where several areas have rural densities of over 3,000 to the square mile. Here the threshold of impoverishment was crossed in 1920, for from that time a population that produced and consumed rice as the essential part of its diet has depended increasingly upon cassava. The traditional landscape of Travancore has been transformed; formerly the valley bottoms were set apart for swamp rice, which formed the principal food, whilst the slopes were covered with coconut palms, under which the attractive dispersed houses sheltered. In contrast with this smiling landscape were the poverty-stricken terraces in between the valleys, deforested and with a lateritic crust that was seldom cultivated. From 1920 onwards the poorer folk began to cultivate these areas in order to grow cassava, the only food crop that would grow and give a reasonable return in such poor conditions; these carefully tilled plots, looking like the floor of a dark red gravel pit, prevented a large part of the population from dying of starvation. Probably the consumers have lost on the deal, for cassava is less rich in protein than rice and the quality of the food intake has thus declined. As for the cassava terraces, they are becoming eroded and there is fear that they will not yield harvests much longer. In the same way the lateritic terraces near Goa (which was a very large city in the sixteenth century) have been stripped of their surface soil and are mostly now covered with slabs of crusty laterite.

A somewhat similar situation is to be found in certain parts of Java,[1] particularly in the limestone areas where the poverty and scarcity of the soil have not prevented the population from so multiplying that a state of overpopulation (as defined above) has been reached. The limestone areas of Java support 6 million people; we may select for study the Gunong Kidul regency which had 520,000 people (in 1960) on its 500 square miles, at an average density of just over 1,000 per square mile. This is a very high figure, for about half the area is bare rock and quite uncultivable; such soil as there is, is thin, stony and easily eroded. It is difficult to establish an agricultural system based on terrace cultivation, for the permeability of the limestone deprives the terraces of their essential function. Irrigation is obviously impossible, though it would be very useful, for whilst the total rainfall is fairly heavy (70 inches a year) the period May to

1. K. V. Bailey, 'Rural nutrition studies in Java. I. Background to nutritional problems in the cassava area', *Tropical and Geographical Medicine*, 1961, pp. 216–54.

October is dry and can yield no crop without irrigation. The land is so permeable that even drinking water is difficult to get in the dry season, and the people often have to go several miles to get water from artificial ponds, and use of this water, which is heavily polluted, spreads many diseases. The lack of water is perhaps harder to bear than the inevitable annual food shortage. Assuredly these limestone hills of Gunong Kidul are grossly overpopulated, much more so than the fertile plains of Jogjakarta, where a density of over 2,500 to the square mile is supported by swamp rice cultivation. But of the plain of Jogjakarta every inch is cultivable, compared with under one-half in Gunong Kidul; whilst the yield per acre on the plain is at least three times what it is on the limestone hills, for a single harvest—and two harvests in twelve months are quite normal around Jogjakarta.

We may conclude, therefore, that the role of soil fertility as a causative factor in high population densities must be regarded with due caution. Certainly the plain of Jogjakarta is both more fertile and more densely peopled than the upland of Gunong Kidul, but the quantity of foodstuff produced per inhabitant is very much greater around Jogjakarta. The population is very uncomfortably crowded amongst the poor limestone hills of Gunong Kidul, which form a particularly hostile environment in their northern and southern parts, where the limestones have been so weathered as to form a chaos of bare hills (known as Gunong Sewu, the Thousand Mountains), forming the kind of karstic landscape that is typical of the tropics. The central part, forming the plain of Wonosari, is of softer relief, and is less inhospitable. It is no exaggeration to say that the limestone terrain of Gunong Kidul cannot really support more than 250 people to the square mile, and yet its actual density is four times this figure. In order to equalize the standard of living in the two areas the plain of Jogjakarta should have more people than it supports at present, whilst Gunong Kidul should have many fewer.

The inhabitants of Gunong Kidul are desperately poor; 99 per cent of them are devoted to subsistence cropping, and eat nothing but what they grow. Cassava was introduced about 1900; before this they lived on rice and maize. The yields are very low—715 lb of dry rice to the acre, 855 lb of maize, and 1150 lb of cassava (and cassava will grow on the poorest soils, on which maize and rice would not). There is a shortage of food from October to January, before the maize is harvested. The poorest of the poor, who have neither rice nor maize, stave off their hunger until July by eating the boiled skins of dried cassava tubers, the tubers of canna and yam, minced banana stalks and boiled leaves which give them diarrhoea. Many of the people have literally no food stores at all; they live from day to day, with not a morsel of food to put between their teeth in the morning

36. A *shaduf* worked by two persons. In this as in the scoop shown facing page 113 much ingenuity has been displayed to save muscular effort.

37. Planting out young rice shoots on the Tongking delta. This is hard work, but by ensuring good crops it enables a high civilisation to be built up.

38.

A *seringueiro* near Gurupá in Braz[il?]
white ball at his feet is the rubber [he has]
collected. The black ball is the ves[sel]
holding the latex. An open fire i[s used]
for coagulating the latex.

39.

The results of bad cultivation. A f[ormer]
coffee estate on the north-east [of the]
State of Sao Paulo. The hillsides [were]
once covered with coffee bushes [but]
as no care was taken of the soil, it [is]
exhausted. The coffee bushes hav[e died]
out, and new ones will not grow. [Apart]
from small patches in the valley bo[ttoms]
the whole area is now covered [with]
grass which serves merely as pastu[re for]
cattle.

and no money to buy any. They eat whatever they can find or whatever they can buy if the opportunity arises to earn some money. Better-provided households might have a few pounds of cassava tuber skins to last a week or two, and a 'well-to-do' family might have a few pounds of dried cassava.

The diet is even more deficient than it might be because the wretched peasants actually sell in the towns the handfuls of soya beans and ground nuts that they have grown, in order to get money. The standard meal for the mass of the people consists—except during the months of shortage—of cassava porridge and a sauce made of leaves and beans, with no meat (many families only eat meat once a year, on the village feast-day), no vegetable protein and no fat. The calorie deficiency is serious, for the average daily intake per person during the years 1952–58 was only 1,233 calories, whereas the mean for the whole of Java was 1,860 calories, and even this is but a meagre total. The lack of protein is also very pronounced—only 14·4 grammes per person per day of all kinds of protein, or no more than one-half of what is considered necessary. The consumption of cassava aggravates the situation, and if maize could be substituted it would give a much better protein content to the diet.

It is not surprising that the oedema or swelling brought on by hunger affects five per cent of the population and about one-half of the nursing mothers; not surprising either that kwashiorkor is of frequent occurrence. What is surprising is that the health of the people is not worse than it is; the adults are active and tough, and the men are capable of carrying loads of more than a hundredweight over long distances; the children are no less healthy than those of the miserable shanty-towns outside Djakarta. The birth rate, alas, is high, and the demographic pressure will inevitably increase.[1]

The examples of Travancore and Gunong Kidul shows that the menace of overpopulation exists in tropical monsoon Asia, whereas it is unknown in other parts of the tropical world. The explanation must be sought not in the physical peculiarities of Monsoon Asia but in the history of civilization. A closer study of Indonesia will make this clear.

Indonesia exhibits very markedly the contrast, typical of south-east Asia, between areas that are densely peopled and those that are almost empty.[2] Whilst Java and Madura in 1961 had the very high figure of 1,230 people to the square mile, the 'Outer Provinces' had but 50;

1. For further studies of this problem see M. Timmer, *Child mortality and population pressure in the D.I. Jogjakarta, Java*, Rotterdam, 1961 (mimeographed).
2. K. J. Pelzer, *Pioneer Settlement in the Asiatic Tropics*, New York, 1945; Ch. Robequain, *Malaya, Indonesia, Borneo and the Philippines*. 2nd English edn. London, 1957.

Kalimantan (the Indonesian part of Borneo) had only 18 to the square mile, and the Moluccas 20. A map of the distribution of population in Sumatra shows clearly the empty spaces on this island, which in an earlier period of history had an advanced civilization (Fig. 14). Certainly Java possessed very great physical advantages: its mountains are not compact, but consist of a series of separate volcanoes; the climate is wet, and there is an abundance of basic volcanic soil of great fertility. We should be unwise, however, to draw too simple a conclusion as to the causal effects of favourable environmental conditions on population density. The example of Gunong Kidul has already shown that there is great density in areas that are clearly unfavourable, and we found there a density of 1,000 to the square mile where we might have expected a few score. A study of history shows that though Java is a very old centre of advanced civilization, it was not very densely peopled a century and a half ago; the density in 1817 was only 96 per square mile as against 1,230 in 1961.[1] This enormous demographic expansion has been possible because in the first place the traditional Javanese civilization possessed excellent agricultural techniques which enabled the steep slopes to be carefully terraced for flooded ricefields, and secondly because its political organization for the control of the land was adequate. Then also the Dutch occupation favoured population growth, for it put an end to the wars between the various states, improved communications and the irrigation system, oriented agriculture towards the production and export of tropical products, and materially lowered the death rate.

Recognizing then the importance of the traditional civilization and the nineteenth-century history, we may examine in more detail the distribution of population density in Java.

It is tempting to seek correlations between the fertility of the soil and the density of population, and to say for example that in western Java the Bantam region owes to the acid volcanic soils its low density, which in the district of Tjibaliyung is only 50 to the square mile. It is interesting too to trace the basic ash from the volcano Merapi and to note that the southern flank of the mountain is more densely peopled than the north because there is more ash on the south side, blown there by northerly winds. These examples suggest a deterministic explanation. But it would need an exhaustive soil survey of the whole of Java to confirm this determinism, and at the present time we cannot

1. This is the generally accepted figure, but its basis is probably inadequate and there is good reason to suspect that the population in 1817 was underestimated. See K. J. Pelzer, *Indonesia, Physical and Human Resource Pattern*, Yale University, South-east Asia studies, 1964. The point made in this paragraph takes on a greater degree of probability if we accept a figure for 1817 of twice that given above; the population growth thus becomes slower and more credible.

do this; we can but record that the highest rural density of all was found in 1931 in the Adiwerno district, on the northern coastal plain not far from Cheribon—4,240 to the square mile over an area of 36 square miles! And yet here the soils are not derived from basic

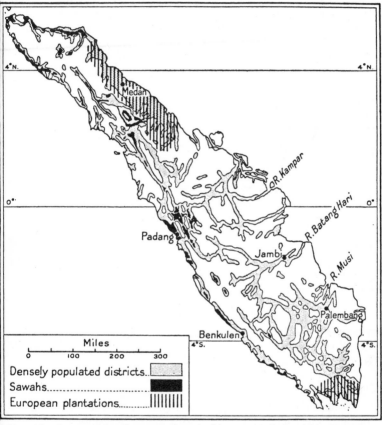

FIG. 14. Sumatra, showing areas cleared of forest and distinguishing inhabited strips and European plantations.
The unshaded portions have not been cleared of forest, for human settlement is discontinuous here as always in an equatorial region.

(After Herbert Lehmann, 'Die Bevölkerung der Insel Sumatra', *Petermanns G. Mitteilungen*, 1938)

volcanic ash at all, they are river alluvia. Such soils, developed on old alluvia, are often quite impoverished, and they are cultivated because they are so easily worked. All the soils of the Adiwerno district, whatever their quality, are cultivated, and they give at least one and often two harvests a year, thanks to a well-organized irrigation system.

Rice is the main crop, and sugar cane, which had been encouraged by the Dutch, is now declining; a domestic cotton industry adds to the peasants' resources.

The low densities in the Bantam region are not adequately explained by soil poverty, for the soils are certainly not poorer than those on the limestone of the Thousand Mountains, where the density reached 1,000 to the square mile. Madura island, which has no volcanic rocks and only a relatively poor irrigation system, had a density of 800 in 1940, which had risen to nearly 1,300 by 1962. It is surprising that the great deltas of Borneo and of eastern Sumatra have not been tamed by man; the natural conditions for rice cultivation are certainly much more favourable there than on the slopes of the Javanese mountains, where the maintenance of the terraces—the prevention of erosion and the provision of irrigation water—is a costly business. If the great Indonesian deltas had been conquered by the rice cultivators, so that they had become populated like the deltas of the Red River, the Mekong and the Menam, should we have hesitated to say that their dense population was due to the favourable natural conditions—recent alluvium, plenty of water, easy communications by inland waterway and by the sea, and the use of the tidal flow in the irrigation of the ricefields?

The high population densities in Java do not appear to have been prevented by malaria, although the disease is widespread throughout the island at altitudes below 6,000 feet. In the densely peopled coastal belt the 'tambak' (ponds in which fish are bred) are the cause of violent malarial fevers brought on by the bite of *Anopheles sundaicus*; around the town of Chilachap nine-tenths of the children have enlarged spleens. The terraced ricefields are excellent lodgings for the larvae of *A. aconitus*; their water is always flowing (for percolation through the banks is balanced by irrigation water) and so has just the right quality for this particular variety of mosquito. It appears that the plains in the middle of northern Java, in which the highest population densities occur, are relatively free from malaria, at least away from the zone of fish-ponds. But the distribution of malaria in Java is by no means simple, and we can only put forward the following hypothesis: Java is not a country of great plains of recent alluvium in which it has been possible (albeit unintentionally) to create almost complete freedom from malaria; the alluvial plains are small and never beyond the possible flight of mosquitoes from the neighbouring older terraces or hills; and the staircases of ricefields on the mountain slopes provide shelter for the larvae of dangerous mosquito species. The balance-sheet is thus clear—below 6,000 feet the whole of Java is malarial, which means that the colonization of sparsely populated areas from those more densely peopled has not had to take account of the incidence of malaria, for the lands from which the people come are just as malarial as those to which they go. In these circumstances malaria, although a nuisance, does not play a decisive part in population movements. It is however noteworthy[1] that modern methods of malaria control by the use of DDT have made an important contribution towards the success of the spontaneous colonization by the Javanese of the Lampong region at the southern end of Sumatra. The Javanese example shows that malaria is not an insuperable bar to demographic expansion.[2] This is not to contradict what was said above about malaria in Vietnam; but the conditions are not the same. When people live in freedom from malaria they obviously hesitate to go into malarial districts—as happens in Vietnam. But freedom from malaria has not been attained in Java below 6,000 feet, so that the Javanese have not shown any reluctance, at least for health reasons, to colonize the hilly areas.

The Igorots of the Philippines have made irrigated ricefields extending many hundreds of feet up the mountain sides in the northwest of the island of Luzon. The construction and maintenance of these narrow floodable terraces, on slopes so steep as to be more suitable for forest, requires infinite care,[3] but though the Igorots are not lacking in this respect, their techniques are somewhat archaic, and this seems to show that they are refugee people, occupying the mountain areas, and different from the people of the plains. The Igorots have no iron implements, and their hoes are wooden, yet they know how to forge weapons. The plough and harness are unknown to them. They skilfully irrigate their ricefields by using the gradients of streams but have no means of raising water. If a ricefield cannot be irrigated by means of a conduit, it is watered laboriously by carrying the liquid to the field in small pots. The Igorots were formerly head-hunters; they are ignorant of writing and have no political organization higher than that of the village. All the evidence points to their having been familiar with irrigated rice cultivation before the use of the plough spread among the cultivators of southeast Asia. Thanks to their paddy-fields the Igorots reach a density of 180 to the square mile, which is remarkable for such a mountainous area; and the rice secures them against food problems in their isolated

1. W. F. Wertheim, 'Sociological aspects of inter-island migration in Indonesia', *Population Studies*, 1959, pp. 184–201.

2. It remains true, however, that a better understanding of the geography of malaria in Java would be of the greatest value. Of course the anti-malaria campaign might cause such a study to lose much of its interest; but it is assumed that in former times Java was never free from malaria.

3. F. M. Keesing, 'Population and land utilization among the Lepanto', *C. R. Congr. Internat. de Géographie*, Amsterdam, 1938, *Geographie coloniale* pp. 458–64.

situation. Yet the Igorot system of rice cultivation must not be taken as a pattern which should be copied in other tropical mountain areas for it demands an enormous outlay of human effort over many generations. It is possible only if the standard of living is very low and man's labour is regarded as of little worth; in other words it can exist only in an isolated environment.

Within its sparsely peopled areas tropical Monsoon Asia presents landscapes that are identical with those in other parts of the tropical world. The emptiness of the interior of Borneo resembles that of the Congo Basin, and that of eastern Cambodia resembles the northern Mato Grosso. The hot, wet parts of Asia differ from those of the other continents, however, in having the human possibility of exploiting the empty quarters, for there are many overpopulated areas at hand. All that is needed is encouragement in the shape of communications to break down the isolation, an efficient medical service, schools and a simple property system. If these things are provided, the people do not need much direct encouragement in the form of subventions, food, materials or houses, for their innate peasant ingenuity will provide the answer to these problems. The conquest of malaria is already opening new horizons for the colonization of the empty spaces of Asia, and the pioneers need no longer be victims to the new environment.

The densely peopled areas of tropical Monsoon Asia confront us with very different problems. These regions, already teeming with rural people, see their population increasing at the rate of at least one per cent a year. Such a rate of increase will double the population in seventy years, and an area that has 1,000 inhabitants per square mile now will have 2,000 in seventy years; and 4,000 in one hundred and forty years. If the annual rate of increase is two per cent, the doubling will take place in thirty-five years and quadrupling in seventy years. It is abundantly clear that the population simply cannot go on increasing indefinitely, for the local agriculture will not be able to produce sufficient food.

Monsoon Asia has taught us that low population densities are not a necessary result of tropical conditions. The tropical environment certainly provides many obstacles, but these can be overcome; the vast areas of dense population in tropical Asia contain peoples with a well developed civilization, whilst the sparsely peopled areas of the tropical world are occupied by civilizations whose techniques of production and political organization are rudimentary. The exceptional character of Monsoon Asia is not due to physical advantages, it is explained by the happy coincidence of geographical and historical factors which have enabled it to participate in the progress of Eurasia. India and China, which bequeathed to tropical Asia the elements of their superior civilization, have also been deeply involved in the development of the human relations that have produced the mature civilizations of Eurasia. The other parts of the tropical world are much more isolated. The human geography of Indonesia is of great interest, in that towards the east the density of population and the local civilizations are less and less well equipped to form great agglomerations. The civilizing influences which came from the west—the last pale reflections of the civilization of India—peter out eastwards, ending in the solitudes of New Guinea and the even more empty spaces of tropical Australia. No more swamp rice, no more writing, no more political states.

CHAPTER 11

Problems due to European Intervention in The Tropical World

EUROPEANS were attracted to the tropical world from the moment when geographical knowledge and the means of navigation enabled them to enter it. Until the end of the fifteenth century spices, in which they had traded with avidity, were obtained only through Levantine intermediaries. The double obstacle of the Sahara and Islam separated Europe from the hot, wet parts of Africa, and in any case the latter did not produce spices. And as a result of the isolation of tropical Africa from its American and Asiatic counterparts, the hot, wet parts of Africa had absolutely nothing to sell to Europeans at the end of the fifteenth century. The Europeans' first acquaintance with the humid tropics was made in Africa, and they found there none of the spices which had aroused their greed; no sugar, no pepper, no nutmeg, no cinnamon, no cloves. Africa did not even offer any unknown plant products, as America did later with its cocoa and tobacco. The malagretta, or 'grains of paradise', that the Portuguese tried as a substitute for pepper, achieved but little success.[1] In order to establish fruitful commercial relations with the humid tropics, the Europeans had to push as far as southern Asia, where they found not only the products which they coveted but also local merchants capable of conducting trade negotiations. The poverty of Africa in traders and in objects of trade was certainly not due to adverse natural conditions. The more advanced civilizations of southern Asia had been able to discover, select and cultivate a great variety of plants, the products of which were valuable enough to stand the cost of transport to far distant destinations. Tropical Africa at the end of the fifteenth century had not yet reached this stage of development, and it had not yet received from Asia the plants which generated trade. Even Ethiopian coffee did not owe its export to African initiative. True, it was known to the local inhabitants in its native area, and they ate the beans either boiled or as a puree mixed with butter; but it was left to the Arabs and then to the Europeans to use it as a drink and to make it an article of commerce.

China was separated from the humid tropics neither by a desert nor by Islam. Chinese relations with the tropical world were thus much earlier, more direct and more important than those which the

1. The plant is an *amomum*, the seeds of which have a warm and camphor-like taste; it was obtained wild in the Guinea area and not cultivated.

Europeans developed by such a circuitous route after the great age of maritime discovery. The Chinese obtained from tropical Asia much larger quantities of more varied products than did the Europeans. In addition to the spices which the Europeans bought, the Chinese took cardamoms (which had but a small sale in Europe), sandal-wood, aloes-wood, birds' nests, deer antlers and rhinoceros horns and many other products used in Chinese medicine-chests.

It was the Europeans, however, who had most impact on the tropical world, for the results of Chinese intervention were slight, mainly because Chinese trade with the Asiatic tropics was so easy and so well developed—whereas the Europeans, in Africa, and in America, were obliged to start from scratch, and to impose their commercial activity on people who were unprepared for it; and this often led to bloodshed which gave the European intervention in the tropics a most unfortunate aspect.

From the moment when they achieved all-round technical superiority and began to develop trade in tropical produce, the intervention of the Europeans in the tropics became irresistible. One of the first results was the diffusion of cultivated tropical plants. Until this time the tropical world had consisted of three separate regions, in America, Africa and Asia—with perhaps a fourth recognizable in Oceania, for despite the proximity of New Guinea and the East Indies, Oceania has cultivated plants that are strikingly different from those of Asia.

Africa received rice (*Oryza sativa*) from Asia, and cultivated it both with and without irrigation (there is a native African swamp rice *Oryza glaberrina*, but it is inferior to *O. sativa*). Africa also received from Asia the banana (the ensete—*Musa ensete*, the Abyssinian banana—which is of African origin, has remained purely African; it is cultivated in southern Ethiopia for the starch which can be extracted from its leaf-veins), the yam (though there are African species) and taro. Perhaps it is as well not to speculate on the exchanges of the various sorts of millet (eleusine, sorghum) between Africa and Asia; it is simpler to assume that these plants were domesticated on both continents. The transfer of cultivated tropical plants from one continent to another was either non-existent—owing to the complete isolation of America—or very slow, prior to European intervention. After this however, the process speeded up enormously. Africa gave little, for it had but little to give; we have seen how coffee made its exit, and the oil palm, though introduced by African slaves into the Bahia region of Brazil, only spread to the plantations of Sumatra and Malaya at a much later date. Many African-cultivated plants are of little value and could not compete with new importations; such were voandzu, coleus, teff, fonio, and many others which were not worth taking elsewhere.[1] The colanut tree has remained exclusively African. On the other hand, Europeans were responsible for spreading throughout the tropical world a great many American plants. Of prime importance are maize (of Mexican origin), cassava and haricot beans; but other examples include the groundnut, tomato, pawpaw, nazeberry, pineapples, custard-apples, capsicum (red pepper) and cacao. The rubber tree (*Hevea*), which was not a cultivated plant, has made triumphal progress outside South America. These American plants were all taken to Asia by Europeans; but Asia gave rice, and the methods of growing it, to tropical America, and also sugar cane and the technique of sugar extraction, together with citrus fruits and mangoes. Europeans also took the breadfruit tree from Polynesia and spread it (though with less success than had been anticipated) throughout the appropriate latitudes.[2] The results are clear: sugar cane is now produced in every country that has a suitable climate, rubber is much more widely cultivated in south-east Asia than in its native America, coffee, of African origin, is mainly produced in South America, whilst West Africa is the principal exporter of cocoa. The needs and the tastes of European consumers (including all areas of European civilization) were responsible for this diffusion of cultivated plants, which created the intercommunication between the tropical countries for which they had been kept waiting so long. This all enables us to put our finger not only on the principal cause of tropical backwardness, namely isolation, but also on the main remedy for this state, which is to reduce the dependence of the tropical lands on the demands and the technical skills of the advanced countries, which are all to be found in the temperate zone.

In the Asiatic tropics the Europeans found local tradesmen who sold them the spices they were seeking. Things were much less simple in Africa and America. We have already noted that in Africa, and particularly in West Africa, European greed found nothing to satisfy it, because both the products and the local tradesmen were lacking. Could they not have established plantations, or encouraged the natives to do so and to sell the produce to European merchants? Neither course was possible, for though they succeeded in making contact with the small states along the Guinea coast, the Europeans

1. *Voandzeia subterranea* is the Bambarra groundnut; *Coleus rotundifolius* is the 'fra fra potato', cultivated for its edible tubers; teff grass (*Eragrostis abyssinica*) was used as a cereal by the natives of Bornu; fonio (*Digitaria exilis*) is another grass used as a cereal.
2. The sweet potato (*Ipomea*) is apparently of American origin, but the story of its spread has some peculiar features, and it seems likely that it was known in Polynesia and New Guinea before the discovery of these areas by Europeans.

were not strong enough to conquer them; the mere handful of men constituting the Portuguese expeditions could hardly overcome by force of arms one of these Guinea coast kingdoms in order to create plantations, or to demand the cession of land to European colonists, or to force the inhabitants to hand over the produce required. Moreover, these Guinea kingdoms, though they may have been very difficult for the tiny European forces to conquer, were yet of small extent, and the conquest of one of them would not have provided the key to the control of a large empire. It was very different in America: the Tupi of Brazil, fragmented into tiny groups, could not provide the organized resistance of the Guinea kingdoms; and on the other hand the Spanish seizure of the administrative machinery of the Aztecs, Mayas and Incas enabled them to control a vast area. The horse, which contributed so much to the success achieved by Cortez in Mexico, was of no use in Guinea, for the forests were too dense and the trypanosomiasis carried by the tsetse fly proved fatal to horses; and the Africans were not in any case frightened by horses, for they had seen them or at least had heard of them. In addition, the unhealthiness of the Guinea coast decimated the Europeans, who were rapidly killed off by malaria and intestinal infections, so that the death rate was fantastically high. The Europeans simply could not contemplate the creation of agricultural systems worked by African or European labour, neither could they envisage the imposition of such systems on the natives or the employment of slaves on plantations, for slaves could not have been kept on such plantations. It is easy to understand why the Portuguese established tropical agriculture not on the African continent but in the Azores islands, Madeira and the Cape Verde group. Besides, very soon the fields in the Cape Verde islands were worked by African slaves, and these islands became entrepôts for the traffic in slaves destined for America; small islands make excellent prisons.

The New World offered the European conquerors a very different set of circumstances. In Brazil the resistance of the fragmented Tupi was but slight, and its occasional prolongation simply reflected the feebleness of the Portuguese aggression. Once established, however, the Portuguese found themselves helpless: there were no precious metals and no local labour supply, for the native population was not numerous and showed no willingness either to work for wages or to resign itself to slavery. There were no spices either; the '*drogo do sertão*' (Brazil wood for example) was of little value, but even so it was necessary to force the Indians to collect it, and this entailed atrocities and violence for very meagre results. The real economic development of Brazil began with the sugar plantations—but for these it was necessary to import slaves from Africa.

The Spaniards had better luck, for they benefited from several advantages. Much gold was placed at their disposal as conquerors, and the native hierarchies and governments were willing to continue to function under their European masters; in areas where such highly-developed Amerindian political organizations did not exist, as in the Llanos or in the Orinoco basin, the Spaniards were unable to administer effectively the territories that they had so easily conquered. Besides, the really hot and wet parts of their American domains did not interest the Spaniards, whose attention was riveted on the cooler highlands, where the climate was pleasanter and more healthy, the native population more numerous and better organized, and precious metals were to be had. There were some exceptions, areas which were both hot and wet and densely peopled, like the Maya country in the north of Yucatan, the territory crossed by Cortez before approaching the mountains towards Mexico, and the Totonac country on the Gulf coast of Mexico. Elsewhere, over the whole of their vast American dominions, the Spaniards could only create plantations by using European labour or African slaves, for the native population was sparse, unwilling to work for wages, and too elusive to be caught and enslaved. It was the same when the English, French, Dutch and others started to establish plantations in those West Indian islands that Spanish indifference to non-metalliferous territories had allowed them to annex; Carib and Arawak labour could not be used, and it was necessary to use Europeans, and soon after, African slaves.

We must now examine this white colonization in its three aspects of settlement, slavery and the plantation system. There have been many attempts at white colonization in the tropics,[1] involving white agricultural labour in the production of tobacco, sugar and coffee for the European market. These attempts have often ended in failure. The first obstacles to white settlement were tropical diseases; this is not to imply that the Europeans were fundamentally more vulnerable to these diseases than the natives of the tropical world, but simply that the Europeans were not equipped to combat them. These tropical maladies took a terrible toll of the Europeans who landed on tropical soil, though the native peoples appeared to be less susceptible, either because the weaker individuals had already been weeded out during infancy or childhood, or because they had acquired a certain degree of immunity. Thus yellow fever did not attack the rural African people because they had acquired immunity thanks to a slight attack at an early age. Another example is provided by the population groups that contain many individuals who carry 'sickle cells' in their blood,

1. Grenfell Price, *White Settlers in the Tropics*, New York, American Geog. Soc. Spec. Publ. no. 23, 1939.

which are resistant to malaria; amongst such groups the ravages of malaria are much reduced, whilst newly-arrived Europeans are (or were before modern means of prevention and cure became available) tortured and demoralized by malarial attacks. Some degree of protection against malaria also exists amongst individuals whose mothers were subject to malaria and who have been constantly bitten by infected mosquitoes from an early age. European colonists could benefit in none of these ways. Some colonial enterprises were monumental failures. The Guiana affair of 1765 was catastrophic, for in a few months eight thousand out of ten thousand colonists died. Guiana could not be colonized, though it received in all more colonists than French Canada, which had barely received eight thousand before its abandonment by France in 1763, and which has received no more since. The utter failure of Guiana and the huge demographic success of French Canada are thus of immense significance. The English attempt in 1792 at colonizing the coast of Portuguese Guinea was no less striking a failure,[1] though the numbers involved were smaller. The group comprised 279 people, who landed on the African coast on 3 June 1792; overwhelmed by their first contact with the reality of tropical life most of them returned to Europe on 19 July. Ninety-one hardy (or care-free) individuals remained, under the command of Captain Philip Beaver, whose lack of authority equalled his incompetence. The result speaks for itself; of these ninety-one, sixty-six had died of fever by 29 November 1793, when Beaver evacuated Bolama island, attributing the failure of the enterprise not to the failure of his methods or supervision but to the lack of resolution amongst his companions (his own energy, he wrote, had enabled him to overcome the attacks of delirium to which he had been subject). More effective remedies than mere will-power are now available to overcome malaria and the anopheles mosquito, but malaria and many other tropical diseases were very severe obstacles to European colonization before the modern advances in scientific medicine.

If they are not ravaged by diseases, European colonists maintain a good state of health in the tropics, and contrary to what has been so often written, do not degenerate in a hot, wet climate. A vast literature has accumulated on the disastrous effects of this climate on the white races, the burden of which is that Europeans will lose their physical energy and moral fibre, and so on. But in fact such a result seems unbelievable and it cannot be demonstrated. The European who has not suffered from tropical diseases enjoys abundant health in the humid tropics, and of this there are inumerable examples, such as the white Americans of Hawaii and the Panama Canal Zone, the Scots

1. Philip Beaver, *African Memoranda*, London, 1805.

and Irish established in the seventeenth century in Saba island in the Lesser Antilles, the English and Scots in the Cayman Islands,[1] the French of Saint-Barthélemy, the Germans of Seaford Town (in Westmoreland county, Jamaica), the English in Brownsville (in the Cascade sector of Hanover district, Jamaica), the Dutch of Surinam, the Germans of the state of Espiritu Santo in Brazil, and the English and Italians in the sugar belt of Queensland. The last case is particularly noteworthy, for the European settlement of this hot, wet region (near Cairns) has taken shape only in the present century. Today the population is exclusively white, with no Australian aboriginals and no labour force from Melanesia or Asia; the sugar cane plantations are worked only by Europeans. There were and are no tropical diseases—no malaria, no dysentery, no hookworm—and the demographic conditions and the standard of life are just as good as in the temperate parts of Australia.[2]

The black African slave provided the solution to the labour problem of the Europeans who started agricultural enterprises in the American tropics; European labour was expensive and not very amenable; besides, why should Europeans emigrate as agricultural labourers when the wages they could expect would be less than what they could get in Europe? Furthermore, the Amerindians were becoming extinct. The European 'planters' came to believe that Africa had been created to provide them with labour and America to provide them with land. So began a population transfer which had the effect of giving the hot, wet lands of America a population in which the African racial element was dominant. From Virginia in the United States to Bahia in Brazil, the whole eastern face of the Americas became a black New World. The slave-traders bought slaves on the west coast of Africa and sold them in America, and some 12 million persons were the victims of this detestable traffic. In America the planters preferred to buy slaves rather than rear them on the spot, for it was cheaper to do so; thus Jamaica had 45,000 slaves in 1703 and 205,000 in 1778, though during this time some 359,000 Africans were imported.

1. J. H. S. Billmyer, 'The Cayman Islands', *Geog. Rev.* 1946, pp. 29–93, writes that they 'have a better physique, better health and a more lively intelligence than the average American', though the latitude is only 19° 20′ N; but there are no tropical diseases, and the inhabitants derive a good livelihood from the sale of turtles to the United States and from the servicing of British and American shipping.

2. This list has omitted the white colonization of the Kenya highlands. Although the Europeans who occupied the highlands had every intention of staying there and raising families, we have omitted them partly for physical reasons (for altitude moderates the heat of the climate) but mainly for human reasons—for these colonists did not till the soil themselves but employed African labourers. With the independence of Kenya these European enterprises will disappear. We shall examine the cases of Brazil, Colombia, Puerto Rico and Hawaii later on.

It was slavery that permitted the growth of the plantation system in tropical America; in Africa and Asia, the system was of much later development, and depended on a wage-earning labour force. Whether employing slaves or paid labour, however, the plantations represented a very aggressive form of European intervention in the tropics. They have not caused the settlement of many Europeans, but they have transformed vast areas and have introduced new techniques and new plants; they have also created human situations that today strongly influence the political and economic evolution of many tropical countries. The plantation system certainly merits our especial attention by reason of the importance of its geographical consequences.

The word 'plantation' is perhaps a little unfortunate, for it conjures up a picture of a countryside planted with rows of fruit or rubber trees; and there are, or have been, plantations of such things as cotton, sugar cane and tobacco. It has been suggested that the characteristic feature of the plantation is the industrial treatment to which its crop is submitted; thus the plantation sells sugar and not sugar cane, it sells crepe and not latex (though in fact it may also sell latex), it sells tea and not raw leaves. But this is not necessarily always so, and the cotton plantations of the 'Deep South' of the United States would be excluded by such a definition, the ginning not being regarded as an industrial operation (any more than wheat threshing or the husking of maize would be).

It is simpler and more useful to characterize the plantation as something foreign introduced into the geographical environment. The plantation is (or was) 'foreign' in respect of its cultivated plants, which were often brought from other continents, e.g. Asiatic sugar and African coffee in America, American rubber, cocoa and tobacco in Asia and Africa. The plantation is also 'foreign' in the economy that it creates; in unexploited areas or in areas devoted to subsistence agriculture the plantation is a foreign enterprise, a response to the demand of a far-off buyer for a commodity that he cannot produce; the consumers are in the temperate world, the plantations in the tropics or subtropical belt. The 'foreign' character of the plantation shows itself in the regimented landscape that contrasts so markedly with the surrounding untouched countryside or with the deforested patches produced by the native 'slash-and-burn' cultivation and fallow. The strangeness is further marked by the buildings which are necessary to prepare the harvest for market, by the agricultural techniques, and by the personnel of managers and labourers. There are black Africans in the West Indies, in the United States and in Brazil, Asiatic Indians in British Guiana, in Fiji, Mauritius, Natal and Ceylon. The capital is foreign, and the profits are exported. The plantation is thus a feature of the cultural landscape that results from the actions of a foreign, a European civilization in a tropical environment with a non-European civilization. The object of the enterprise is to deliver to the temperate lands of European civilization vegetable commodities that those areas need and cannot produce, and the characteristic element in the system is the clash of civilizations. The plantation is an enclave of another form of civilization. There is no need to talk of 'plantations' when the clash of cultures does not occur. The spice gardens of southern India before the Europeans came, the coconut groves of Polynesia, and the cola groves of the Guinea coast are not plantations. The cola nuts are used by the producers or sold on the local market as well as being exported to the Sudan, and the cola groves are cultivated by the native people and have not required foreign capital. There is no 'foreign' element either in the cocoa groves of Ghana and Nigeria or in the neighbouring oil-palm groves; the palm oil of the 'Oil Rivers' is not the product of plantations. Plantations cease to deserve the name when, integrated into the geographical pattern, they are no longer intrusions of a foreign civilization into the local cultural landscape. The Queensland sugarfields are local in respect of their capital, ownership, labour supply, techniques and much of their market. The sisal cultivators of the Merida region at Yucatan cannot be called 'planters'; they produce for export, but are native Mayas, small proprietors growing a local plant.[1]

The true plantations have often left a heritage of difficult problems. They have indeed provided the basis for two kinds of problem, the first concerned with the high density of population and the second involving the juxtaposition of different kinds of people who come into conflict. Both problems have a common origin in the desire of the planters, after the abolition of slavery, to have an abundant labour supply so that the wages would remain low. The planters of Réunion, for example, demanded that labour should be imported, even though the original slave population was already large;[2] they were unsuccessful, but even so Réunion has a very serious demographic problem, which shows how unreasonable the planters' demands were. The Mauritius plantations imported labour from southern India, and now these Mauritians of Indian origin form a majority of the superabundant population. The planters of Guadeloupe[3] succeeded in introducing Dravidian Indian workers into an island whose demographic future was already threatening. Jamaica in 1961 had 1,631,000

1. R. E. P. Chardon, *Geographical aspects of plantation agriculture in Yucatan*, New York, Nat. Acad. of Science, 1961.
2. J. Defos du Rau, *L'île de la Réunion*, Bordeaux, 1960.
3. G. Lasserre, *La Guadeloupe, étude géographique*, Bordeaux, 1961, 2 vol.

inhabitants on 4,400 square miles; but of this area some 1,500 square miles are barren limestone of no agricultural value, so that the density of population in the cultivable part of the island is 554 per square mile. The congestion on some parts of the island is considerable— 620 per square mile on the slate hills of Clarendon and St Catherine districts, where the density in relation to the cultivated area rises to 3,729 per square mile. One remarkable geographical consequence of the plantation system is that the coastal districts, formerly as at the present time occupied by plantations, have a lower rural density than the inhabited parts of the interior, which have in fact a less favourable environment. This inversion of density is explained by the fact that the interior was peopled first by 'marrons' or runaway negro slaves, and later, after the abolition of slavery, by liberated slaves who refused to remain on the plantations and preferred to set up home on a patch that they cleared for themselves.[1]

British Guiana is really like a West Indian island, sandwiched between the sea and the unoccupied interior. Its 81,000 square miles are divided between a coastal strip of 3,800 square miles supporting 540,000 inhabitants in 1960, and an interior zone covering 77,000 square miles with only 40,000 people; a density of 140 per square miles on the coast and 0·5 in the interior. The coastal strip is West Indian in its economy and its problems, which are heritages of the days of slavery. The emptiness of the interior is of long standing, for the Amerindians were very sparse in this region before the European intervention—but were they as few as they are today? The forests and the continental savannas are not without their possibilities, but the European colonists confined themselves to the coastal strip which offered the advantages of fertile alluvial soils, good navigable rivers (which further inland are interrupted by great cataracts) and a relative and very welcome freedom from malaria. This last was due to the fact that the coastal waters do not shelter the larvae of *Anopheles darlingi*, which is the principal malaria carrier in South America, or other species of anopheles. Political events brought Dutchmen here, who were experts in creating the polders which were a necessary prelude to the utilization of these marshy areas; they laid out large estates in dyked strips perpendicular to the rivers. The very meagre resources that this enterprise was able to employ in its early years makes it easier to understand why the Europeans colonized the eastern coasts of equatorial America and neglected the west coast of Africa. When it was founded in 1627 the Dutch colony on the Berbice river (now British Guiana) numbered sixty persons; in

1. G. V. Roberts, *The population of Jamaica*, Cambridge, 1957; E. Paget, 'Land-use and settlement in Jamaica', *Geographical Essays on British Tropical Lands*, London, 1956, pp. 181–224.

1763 the Dutch colony on the Essequibo had sixty-eight plantations with 2,571 slaves and twenty-one soldiers, whilst the Demerara colony had ninety-three plantations with 1,648 slaves and eighteen soldiers. Some Europeans were able to hold forts or trading posts on the Guinea coast with the connivance of a local chief who shared the profits of the slave trade, but they could not establish agricultural colonies with such slender defences as those in Guiana; for how could they have kept their slaves and resisted the territorial claims of the neighbouring villages? Even in Guiana they were menaced not by the natives but by escaped slaves.

So the planters bought African slaves, and after the abolition of slavery, called in Asiatic Indians. The present day sugar plantations are worked by paid labour of African or Indian origin. Of the 540,000 people in the coastal belt, 190,000 are of African descent, 270,000 Asiatic. The Indians, who are more prolific, have now out-numbered the Africans. They will soon be an absolute majority, for the rest of the population comprises only 11,000 Europeans, 3,000 Chinese, and between 60,000 and 70,000 mestizos. The Indians have shown more initiative than the Africans; they are no longer merely wage-earners but also entrepreneurs and owners of irrigated ricefields which supply local demands and a considerable export. The coastal belt of British Guiana is not menaced by the overpopulation that threatens Barbados; the population density is only 140 to the square mile in the coastal belt as against 1,370 in Barbados, whilst the density per square mile of cultivated land is only just over 1,000 compared with 2,360 in Barbados; yet only 13 per cent of the surface of coastal Guiana is cultivated as against 58 per cent of Barbados. Guiana, however, is afflicted with an unhappy political situation caused by the juxtaposition of Africans and Indians who are in bitter opposition and not yet ready to join together as one nation.[1]

In the Fiji islands, the sugar planters, unable to draw workers from the native population, had recourse to indentured labour from India. The Indians are now more numerous than the native Fijians; they produce almost all the sugar, which forms a very important export from Fiji. The two peoples do not mix; the Indians have a much higher growth rate, and adopt new techniques much more readily, but they cannot extend their land holdings, for land which is not already in Indian ownership is reserved for the Fijians. Commercial cupidity created the sugar plantations without waiting for the Fijian people to acquire either the habit of working for wages or the practice of commercial agriculture with its requirement of standards of quality fixed by the sugar factories; thus the financial gain has been

1. R. T. Smith, *British Guiana*, London, 1962. M. Swann, *British Guiana, the Land of Six Peoples*, London, H.M.S.O., 1957.

offset by the creation of an inextricable and unhappy political situation.

Ceylon is a typical plantation island, with all the advantages and drawbacks that accrue from such a history of development. The balance is a favourable one, for the economy of Ceylon derives great benefit from the plantations. Though the natural environment explains why the tea and rubber plantations have been developed in the south-western part of the island, it does not explain why the growth of the plantation system should have been so much faster and more pronounced than in southern India. Nor can this contrast be explained by any superiority of the Cingalese in either techniques or enterprise. The plantations in Ceylon are the result of European initiative in an island where political control was easy, and in which the south-western mountains offered land favourable to plantations in juxtaposition with valleys inhabited by friendly people. The mountains of southern India, from the very fact of their being part of a huge peninsula, presented greater difficulties of political control, and they were also less easy of access. In Ceylon, which was one of the spice islands of antiquity, British capital has established 550,000 acres of tea plantations, 650,000 acres under rubber, and 1,100,000 acres under coconuts, which together provide 90 per cent of the island's exports. Foreign trade, indeed, is entirely due to the plantations, for Ceylon imports half its food supply, which is paid for by the labour of the 200,000 workers employed on the plantations; the production of the locally grown half of the food supply occupies nearly 1,500,000 people. The plantations ensure for Ceylon an annual income per head of population which is twice that of India, a higher level of savings, a smaller proportion of the population engaged in agriculture, a valuable source of revenue from export taxes (15 per cent in the case of tea), the finest road and railway systems in southern Asia, and a good educational system. If, during the Ten Year Plan (1961–71) Ceylon succeeds in industrializing itself, it will be thanks to the exports which have provided the money for the purchase of equipment.[1] The plantations of Ceylon have come in for much local criticism; they are regarded as foreign enclaves, playing a minimal part in the local economy and exporting their profits; but perhaps the critics do not take sufficient account of the export duties, the taxes, the commercial agreements and foreign exchange. In any case, the land-ownership of the plantations is largely in the hands of the Cingalese, who in 1952 owned 88 per cent of all the plantations of more than 20 acres and 52 per cent of the area occupied by such plantations. In the case

1. B. H. Farmer, 'The Ceylon ten-year plan 1959–1968', *Pacific Viewpoint*, 1961, 123–136; 'Peasant and plantation in Ceylon', *ibid.* 1963, p. 9–17.

of plantations of under 20 acres the ownership is entirely Cingalese, and these small ones produce quite a large proportion of the total crops (77 per cent of the coconut products, for example). At the present time Cingalese interests and capital predominate in the plantations, and the people who produce for export are better off than those who produce for the local markets.[1]

In sum, the plantations, which are being increasingly brought under Cingalese control, have been and still are of great benefit to the island. But they have not been without their disadvantages, for they present land problems as well as political ones. The plantations were established during the nineteenth century on land which was un-cultivated but which belonged to peasant communities. At the time when the plantations were laid out the peasants had more land than they could cultivate; they used the valley bottoms for flooded rice-fields, constructed rice terraces on the lower slopes, near to their houses and gardens, but used little of the upper slopes, the forests and the plateaus except for the occasional burnt patch or *chena*. The British administration had no qualms in 1840 about declaring these apparently unoccupied highlands Crown lands; and here the planta-tions were established. Today, however, the population has greatly expanded and the peasants find themselves constricted; their eyes turn towards the lands over which they once held the sole rights. On top of this land problem is the political one. The Cingalese will take part in the establishment of plantations by undertaking the deforesta-tion and clearance, but refuse, from pride rather than laziness, to help with the maintenance and harvesting. So the planters called in the Tamils, who are satisfied with low wages, and thus came into existence a population of some 800,000 Tamil workers and families, who do not mix with the Cingalese. Since the island attained its independence in 1947, the Cingalese have refused to allow the Tamils to own plantations or to have Ceylon citizenship (apart from the Tamils long since established in the Jaffna peninsula), and are minded even to deny them the right to live in the country. Since the Indian government refuses to regard the emigrants as Indian citizens, we have here, as a result of the plantations, 800,000 stateless persons. Perhaps further negotiations between India and Ceylon will provide a more humane solution to this problem.

Plantations, then, in the usual sense of the term, have had an immense influence on the human and economic geography of the tropical world, extending even into the regions in which they have never existed. In black Africa the purchase of slaves for the American plantations gave rise to political entities—such as the kingdoms or

1. See, for example, a study by E. R. Leach, *Pul Eliya, a village in Ceylon*, Cambridge, Mass., 1961.

republics in the Niger delta and Cross River areas—that would not otherwise have existed; and on the other hand the slave trade de-populated certain areas, such as, in all probability, the territory fringing the mouth of the Congo.

In order to gauge the geographical role of the plantation system in the context of its historical development, no better example could be found than Hawaii.[1] This group of islands owes its earliest economic development to the sugar and pineapple plantations, for which the local labour supply was insufficient. At this time, however, it was no longer a question of importing slaves, for slavery had been abolished. So Hawaii, contrary to what happened in the West Indies and the islands, does not bear the heritage of the slave trade. Instead, it was necessary to recruit wage-earning labour under contract, from the Philippines, Japan, China, Korea, Puerto Rico and even Portugal, with the result that the native Polynesians were reduced to a feeble minority. Here is a repetition on a larger scale of the situation already described in British Guiana and Fiji, though without unpleasant consequences. The political and social evolution of Hawaii resulted in the rapid up-grading of the immigrant workers; the general prosperity (not only due to the plantations), the abundant employ-ment opportunities, and the action of the American syndicates gave the immigrants the status of free men, without any of the paternalism of the planters in other countries, and with high wages. Furthermore, both the Polynesian Hawaiians and the immigrants are becoming converted to the American way of life, with all its prestige, wealth, and technical power, for the local circumstances do not offer any social or political obstacles to this conversion. Assimilation through prosperity is certainly the quickest, best and most respectable way, and Hawaii provides a unique example of this type of geographical development engendered by the plantation system.

The effects of the migrations resulting from the plantation system and slavery are many, and they cannot be examined here in all their diversity. But two more examples may be quoted. The first is from Colombia, where the attraction of placer gold on the Pacific littoral brought black slaves and their masters from the interior and also escaped slaves (*marrons*) from the plantations of Panama. These two classes of slaves, after the abolition of slavery, were free to redistribute themselves over the country; they drove out the Choco Indians, who abandoned the valleys and took refuge in the mountains. In so fleeing, the Choco were not bowing to a superior race but to invaders who were better equipped, both technically and in general experience of the world. Face to face with the Choco, the blacks were the bearers of

1. P. Gourou, 'Hawaii 1960', *Cahiers d'Outre mer* (Bordeaux), 1963, pp. 1–14.

European civilization. The second example is the islands of San Andrès and Providencia, which were originally peopled by liberated black slaves from Jamaica, English-speaking and Protestant in religion.[1] By a political chance the islands came under Colombian sovereignty, and administrators were sent in who spoke Spanish and were Roman Catholics. The islanders regarded these Colombians as dirty, ignorant and vulgar, in other words as 'inferior'—whilst the Colombians thought the islanders obtuse and backward, and since they were darker skinned than themselves, looked upon them as 'blacks', and, so, as 'inferior'!

In Brazil, though the plantations have played a large part in moulding the human geography of the country, many other factors have also been at work, and Brazil could not be described as a simple example of the effects of the plantation system. The first wave of Brazilian prosperity was set in motion by the sugar plantations in Pernambuco and the tobacco plantations in Bahía; these plantations employed African slaves whose descendants have given a very distinctive character to the racial composition of the population in the coastal belt of north-eastern Brazil. The coffee plantations of São Paulo started a nineteenth-century wave of prosperity and population growth in the southern part of the country.[2] But the Brazilian plantations have always had a somewhat unstable character; after a peak of prosperity the plantations moved elsewhere, and peace reigned once more in areas that had been a hive of activity. In general one may say that the decline is most obvious in the coastal regions that were first colonized and exploited. The coastal areas in the state of São Paulo, for example, are now inhabited by poor and backward people who combine fishing with a little cultivation and give no hint of the former prosperity of the region. The wave of coffee planting in São Paulo state has moved westward, leaving behind it areas deprived of their forest cover and with worn-out soils; this is particularly evident in the Paraíba valley in the eastern part of the state. One reason for all this is that the Brazilian plantations were run by great landowners, and they did not fix the population to the soil. It is very instructive to compare the cocoa 'plantations' of Ilhéus (in north-eastern Brazil) and of Ghana. In Brazil there are real plantations, with large estates, absentee landlords, and a miserable collection of paid workers living in isolation; in Ghana, there are tiny groves of cocoa trees exploited by their owners, who live in villages which are alive with social activity. The African system is

1. J. J. Parsons, *San Andrès and Providencia, English-speaking islands in the western Caribbean*, Univ. California Publ. Geog. no. 12, 1956.
2. P. Monbeig, *Pioniers et planteurs de São Paulo*, Paris, 1953.

more humane and more conducive to the stability and well-being of the population. The feeble attachment of the Brazilian peasants (*caboclos*) to the land explains why they so easily pack up and go if the rumour spreads that greater prosperity is to be found elsewhere: the call of a 'bonanza' will set crowds of them on the move. After the discovery in Minas Gerais, in the eighteenth century, of rich deposits of gold, diamonds and emeralds, five hundred thousand people left north-eastern Brazil, not only from Ceará state which then as now was constantly under the threat of drought, but also from the coastal belt. Migration from the *sertão* of the north-east to São Paulo has sometimes taken the form of a panic-stricken rush. Such things would not have happened if the peasants had been prosperous with their own homes, fields, and cattle. But the Brazilian *caboclo* is poor, lives in a mud hut with a thatched roof, easily built but easily destroyed, and has no land of his own, merely cultivating temporarily the patch that has been provisionally assigned to him by the estate owner; he has no cattle, no furniture, no household linen, and no clothes but what he stands up in. All this is certainly not a necessary consequence of the tropical environment; it is the land-ownership system and the plantations that have deprived the peasant of any right to the soil. Over vast areas in the interior of Brazil the dreadful state of the roads prohibited commercial agriculture, and the peasants in these areas were condemned to mere subsistence, with a minimum of equipment. They cultivated Indian plants—maize, beans and cassava—in the Indian fashion by *roça* (slash-and-burn).[1] European immigrants, established under such unhappy conditions as these, were condemned to isolation and to economic and technical backwardness; such was the lot of the Germans in the state of Espirito Santo.

Brazil is often called the greatest white nation of the tropical world. This is a statement that contains a good deal of truth but needs qualification. It is true that there is some degree of homogeneity engendered by the Portuguese language, and by customs and general outlook on life, and Brazil's greatest success is to have created a new and coherent nation of 90 million people spread over 3,288,000 square 19 76 miles, and to have put a common imprint on a population that has grown, in large measure by immigration, from 8,800,000 in 1863 to 70 million in 1963. But if the Brazilian nation is homogeneous in its civilization it is certainly not so in the racial composition of its population. It is impossible to give precise figures, but it is certain that the number of Portuguese origin was never large; however, they intermarried freely with the native people, for they much appreciated the Tupi women, of whom the early colonists have left some delightful

1. R. E. Crist, 'Cultural cross-currents in the valley of the Rio São Francisco', *Geog. Rev.*, 1944, pp. 587–612.

descriptions.[1] The Indian males having been killed off, the inter-marriage of the Portuguese and the Indian women resulted in a population of mixed blood, in the *sertão* of Ceará, Maranhão, Rio Grande do Norte and Paraíba. In the Amazonian region there are also people of mixed Portuguese and local Indian blood, and these have been added to by many people from Ceará. On the coastal belt, from Rio Grande do Norte to Bahía, as we have already seen, there are many people of African descent. The pure-blooded whites form the bulk of the population in the southern parts of the country (23 million, in São Paulo, Paraná, Santa Catarina and Rio Grande do Sul). These 'pure' whites are of diverse origin—Portuguese, Spanish, Italian, German, Polish, Syrian and Lebanese. To all these various races we must add the Japanese, who are to be found in Amazonia but more especially in southern Brazil.

The races of Brazil pose an interesting problem in tropical geography: is their distribution determined by climate? Are the whites particularly 'pure' and numerous in the south because the climate there is the nearest Brazilian approximation to a temperate climate, by reason of latitude and altitude? It is indeed remarkable that the Brazilians are whiter the further south one goes; though one must also note that most of the immigrants are of Mediterranean origin and so more accustomed to heat. But this is really no more than an illusion. It is true that the European immigrants who came in such large numbers in the nineteenth and early twentieth centuries preferred to establish themselves in the southern states, where they mingled with the old Portuguese stock (albeit with some Indian admixture) who were already in the region. But the destination of these immigrants was not determined by a desire to seek the cooler climate, but simply by the existence of large areas of available land, in regions which were rapidly developing (as in the coffee areas of São Paulo state) and in which there were already large and prosperous cities (São Paulo, Santos, Porto Alegre). The immigrants could hardly have been directed to the already densely peopled plains of old colonial Brazil, nor towards the poverty-stricken and overpopulated *sertão*, nor towards the scarcely explored solitudes of Amazonia and the Mato Grosso.

Europeans can live and do physical labour in all parts of Brazil. Malaria is widespread but is not unduly serious except in a few

1. Orlando Ribeiro, *Aspectos e problemas da expansão portuguesa*, Junta de Investigações do Estudos politicos e sociais, no. 59, Lisbon, 1962; on p. 19 is a description written by one of the first Portuguese visitors to north-eastern Brazil of the scantily-clad Indians that he met: '. . . tres ou quatro moças e bem gentis, com cabelos muito pretos compridos pelas espáduas, e suas vergonhas tão altas e tão cerrandinhas, e tão limpas das cabeleiras. . . .' (three or four maidens, very shy and very gentle, with very black hair, long about the shoulders; their breasts were so prominent and firm, and their hair so clean . . .).

particularly unhealthy spots. A map of malaria in Amazonia shows healthy and unhealthy areas in juxtaposition. It so happens that the chief vector in Brazil, *Anopheles darlingi*, is very exacting in its physical requirements for breeding, and in any case it is not one of the more dangerous varieties. An experimental verification of this was made in the 1930s when through an unhappy accident the terrible *A. gambiae* was introduced into the Natal region. At once the picture changed, and endemic malaria was replaced by a violent epidemic. By 1938 nine-tenths of the inhabitants of the Natal neighbourhood had been infected, and in the region of Baixa Verde (Rio Grande do Norte) 20,000 out of 100,000 patients died. Happily, however, *A. gambiae* had been introduced into a region that is arid for part of the year, and it proved possible to exterminate it in its dry-season hideouts.

It is reasonable to suggest that the uneven distribution of racial elements in Brazil is due entirely to historical factors. If, for example the negro element is well represented on São Sebastião island, near Santos, this is simply because there were sugar plantations there during the age of slavery. The blacks of São Sebastião are the descendants of the former slaves, and are no more explicable by present conditions than are the ruins of the *engenhos* which litter the countryside. To the south of Santos, some thirty miles from São Sebastião, the *caípiras* of the Itanhaem neighbourhood are Portuguese-Indian mestizos without a trace of negro blood; whilst to the north of São Sebastião the people of the Caraghatatuba and Ubatuba districts are also devoid of any negro element. These are accidents of the history of settlement, from which it would be rash to draw any general conclusions.

Brazil offers one further problem in tropical geography, of the first importance: more than half its vast territory (1·85 million square miles out of 3·29 million) is almost uninhabited (only 2·7 million, at a mean density of 1·3 per square mile). The area includes the states of Amazonas, Pará and Mato Grosso and the territories of Rondônia, Acre, Rio Branco and Amapá; and these areas are by no means deserts. We shall return to this problem in the next chapter.

Brazil provides an excellent example of European civilization in the tropics. Similar examples are to be found in Spanish America, resulting from the feeble resistance of the Amerindian populations and the greater healthiness to be found here than in other parts of the tropical world. Cuba, with 6,500,000 inhabitants on 44,000 square miles, is predominantly white, as also is Puerto Rico, with 2,500,000 people on 3,400 square miles.[1] Mexico (30 million on 760,000 square

1. P. Gourou, 'Porto-Rico. Île exemplaire pour le monde tropical?' in *Hommage à Lucien Fèbvre*, Paris, vol. 1, 1953, pp. 419–28.

miles) is more mixed, but the lower and more genuinely tropical parts have sometimes a greater proportion of Europeans than the high plateaus, which have remained largely Indian. The plateaus of the San José da Costa Rica region have the most purely white population in Central America;[1] altitude may be the explanation, but the western slopes of Costa Rica have a population which is only slightly mixed,[2] particularly in the Valle General recently opened up by the pan-American highway, where the Italian colony of San Vito appears prosperous.[3] The peninsula of Nicoya, colonized much earlier, has a mixed population of whites, negroes and Amerindians.[4] As in Brazil, the historical circumstances of the settlement are responsible for these variations. The population of the Antioquian area of Colombia, which claims a pure European origin, is a very interesting subject for study,[5] that we only ignore here because the considerable altitude of Antioquia takes it beyond the climatic limits of the tropical world.

European intervention in the tropical world has transformed the landscapes and the people. Considerable areas (albeit minute in comparison with the total area of the tropical world) have been given over to the plantation system and to commercial cultivation; whole races and civilizations have been almost obliterated (like the Indians of the Amazon basin and Brazil); black Africans have through the slave trade peopled large parts of tropical America, and new populations have come into being as a result of the mixture of these 'races' in America. European civilization has annexed a large part of the tropical world, and it has profoundly penetrated those regions which have managed to conserve their traditional culture. Brazil is European, and though India remains Indian it willingly becomes more and more impregnated with European civilization. Many aspects of European intervention are matters of history; it is most unlikely that slavery, with its far-reaching geographical consequences, will ever be re-established; never again will nations of mixed races be formed, as in Brazil, though this does not exclude the successful outcome of situations that are still in the melting pot, such as the making of a nation in British Guiana and political modifications in the West Indies.

1. L. Waibel, 'White settlement in Costa Rica', *Geog. Rev.*, 1939, p. 529.
2. R. E. Nunley, *The distribution of population in Costa Rica*. Washington. Nat. Acad. Sci., 1960.
3. G. Sandner, *Agrarkolonization in Costa Rica: siedlung, wirtschaft und sozialgefüge an der Pioniergrenze*, Geogr. Inst. Univ. Kiel, 1961.
4. P. L. Wagner, 'Nicoya, a cultural geography', *Univ. of California publ. in Geog.* Berkeley, 1958, pp. 195–250.
5. J. J. Parsons, *Antioqueno colonization in Western Colombia*, Berkeley. Calif., 1949.

Also belonging to the past are the disastrous medical consequences of European intervention staged at a time when the spread of infectious diseases was not understood. In Fiji, for example, in 1875, 40,000 persons, or 28 per cent of the population, died from measles which spread from a European ship. Lung diseases and smallpox of European origin spread like wildfire amongst the Polynesians; whilst smallpox and influenza spread by prospectors and missionaries contributed very largely to the depopulation of Amazonia. In many parts of the tropical world railway-building operations have been the focus of intense epidemics of malaria and yellow fever; and the story of the Panama Canal provides a similar example. It was in all probability the arrival of the Europeans that spread yellow fever, which is of African origin, in America; and some experts believe that the most severe forms of malaria ('tropical' malaria due to *Plasmodium falciparum* or *praecox*), were carried from Africa to America, which before the Columbian discoveries was either non-malarial or only affected by mild varieties due to *Plasmodium malariae* ('fourth fever') and *Plasmodium vivax* ('third fever'). Finally the population movements resulting from European intervention in Africa in the early twentieth century were responsible for the spread of sleeping sickness.

One inevitable result of European intrusion into the tropical lands was the rise of the porterage system, which involved undernourished people in hard physical effort, exposed the porters to unaccustomed infections whilst spreading the germs that they already carried, subjected them to maltreatment by their gangers, and diverted them from their necessary agricultural activities. Here is an example: it was long the practice to start for the French Chad territory from Brazzaville, and to travel by river boat up the Congo, the Ubangui and a right-bank feeder of the latter as far as Fort Sibut; then overland with porters for 150 miles as far as Fort Crampel, whence at high water the journey would be continued by boat on the Gribingui, a tributary of the Shari. The sparse population of the district between Fort Sibut and Fort Crampel could not cope with the task of porterage. Actually, though the journey was not very long and there was little merchandise to be taken to Lake Chad (only 300 tons a year), the carriage of this small amount divided into 9,000 loads of between 60 and 65 lb required 100,000 days' porterage on the Congo–Chad road. The excessive demands of this work would have been realized, had there been better knowledge of the state of health of the people and of their irregular and vitamin-deficient diet. As it was, the people just fled, and the district was deserted. The recruitment of porters became a never-ending task which became the chief anxiety of the officials. The practical results were lamentable; the carriage of goods from Bordeaux to Fort Lamy, the chief town of the Chad territory, sometimes took eighteen months, was very expensive and was accompanied by losses that might run to 90 per cent.

In Tanganyika Territory, in the 1920s, a considerable part of the labour force was occupied in porterage. In the district of Kilosa 400,000 days' porterage were required to meet Government needs alone; and the demands of private trade were far greater. Native porters carried 7,000 tons of goods a year to the railway station at Tabora. Each load amounted to about 90 lb, and the 90 mile journey took three days. Raw cotton travelled for fourteen days in this fashion. This squandering of human labour, now happily supplanted by motorized road transport, greatly hindered the development of tropical Africa.

There are many other consequences of European intervention in the tropical lands: soil erosion resulting from ill-advised deforestation and inappropriate methods of cultivation has ruined many plantations; the urge towards commercial cropping has led many a native cultivator to shorten his fallow and increase his tilled area. This development has been made possible by the use of the plough—but it has ruined the fragile soil. We need not lay too much stress on this, however. Usually the damage can be repaired by a period of forest fallow. If it is irreparable, the damage is on slopes that should never have been deforested, for whether eroded or not, such slopes would never have been cultivable. We shall develop this and other related points in the next chapter on 'prospects for the tropical world'.

CHAPTER 12

Prospects for the Tropical World

HUMAN geography does not modify its aims and objects according to climatic regions; it is always concerned to examine the relationship between civilization and environment. However, the physical peculiarities of the hot, wet lands give a certain character to tropical geography, and it is both convenient and necessary, when studying afresh the geography of a tropical country, to make use of the experience gained of other countries with a similar climate.

The outlook for the hot, wet parts of Asia will not be examined in this chapter; the human masses and the menace of overpopulation are aspects of civilization which are only loosely connected with the nature of the tropical environment. The latter makes its presence felt at the boundaries of the densely peopled areas and in the wide open spaces of the Asiatic tropics, where the problems are the same as in other tropical lands. Likewise, the prospects for industrialization, and the vistas opened thereby, will not be dealt with, for in this field the tropical lands do not differ from other parts of the world that are poor in capital resources and technical equipment. We may pose one question, however. Given the particular conditions of the tropical environment that favour certain types of agricultural activity, is it reasonable to devote capital to the creation of artificial rubber factories in India or in Brazil when these countries are already producers of the natural material, and when this production, scientifically and democratically organized, could contribute to the well-being of many people and initiate the economic development of large areas? Would not the capital invested in this type of industry find better employment in the production of agricultural raw materials?

Outside Asia, the tropical world, sparsely inhabited and with a low standard of technical equipment, includes 350 million people, though it could without difficulty support ten or twenty times as many. In all aspects of technology, whether it be in various forms of production or in organization, it is backward and lagging. The retarded development is due above all to the fact that technology and science have made their modern advances in the temperate world, and progress on similar lines was not possible in the tropical world without modification. These adaptations are made but slowly, and the time they take represents the degree of backwardness of the tropics. The traditional civilizations, particularly if they are without

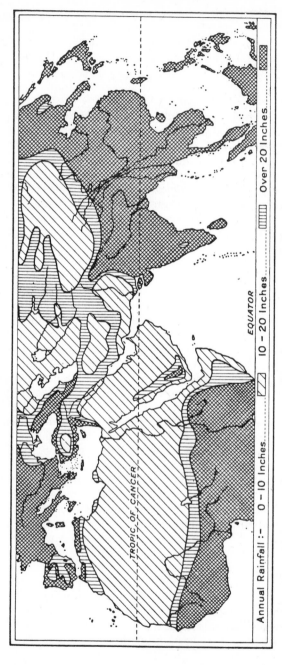

FIG. 15. Rainfall in the Old World, showing that Africa south of the Sahara is isolated, whilst India and South-east Asia are connected with the temperate belt by zones of high rainfall.

literacy, change little and at a very slow pace. Modern civilization, armed to the teeth with techniques and inventions, is ready for the rational development of the tropical world, but the tropical people have scarcely begun to master the science and technology that provide the key to progress.

One of the causes of the backwardness of the tropical world is its separation by the ocean into three parts, which have had little or no relationship with each other (Fig. 16). Agricultural techniques are easily transmitted within the climatic region in which they originated, and so they tend to move along lines of latitude; transfer to another climate is more difficult. This is not to say that each climatic variety determines particular forms of agriculture. The example of ladang makes this quite clear, for this elementary culture has developed in all the tropical climates, including those which favour it least, as in Borneo, where the Iban persist in trying to burn the forest in a typical equatorial climate in which the felled trees often refuse to ignite. Such agricultural techniques are the expression of civilization rather than climate, but the fact remains that they are spread most easily within one climatic zone. It is therefore important that the zone should not be interrupted by vast expanses of ocean. It would have been of great advantage to the tropical world had sugar cane, rice and cassava been more widely diffused, and it has been both important and unfortunate that intercontinental relations within the tropical world have been so slight.

Contacts and cultural exchanges of all kinds have been difficult between the various tropical regions, and this has had a paralysing effect, for technical progress results largely from borrowings between human groups whose techniques do not greatly differ. When one group borrows a hitherto unknown technique from a neighbouring group, the chances are that the technique in question will get modified in the process. It may not be accurately copied, or it may be improved, but there will always be some modification, and in course of time this may be so great as to be regarded as a new technique. Progress is first of all a change, and nothing is more favourable to change than contact between groups in similar environments, with no natural obstacles which would prevent the use of the techniques that are acquired during the course of the contact. Exchanges of this kind lead to modifications which all add up to progress.

By their territorial cohesion and the similarity of their climates, the temperate lands of Europe, Asia and Africa presented the greatest opportunities for cultural exchanges and the mutual fertilization of the civilizations which developed within them. The tropical lands with the greatest cultural development were those that not only had easy relationships between themselves but also the most frequent and continuous contact with the temperate world. Within the Asiatic tropics, India and the area influenced by India and China were excellently placed for exchanges of technique with the temperate lands of Asia, for the tropical and temperate climates merge into each other both in the Indian peninsula (where there is no climatic barrier between the Punjab and Ceylon) and in the Far East (where the summers are hot and wet at Shanghai and at Bangkok). There was thus considerable contact between the tropical and temperate lands of Asia. The advanced civilization of India was an amalgam of northern and southern elements, Chaldean, Aryan and Austrasiatic. Indian cultural influence spread to the Môn, the Khmer, the Sumatrans and the Javanese. China helped to mould Vietnam, and Chinese influence on the Cham was appreciable. The culture of the Thais (Laotians, Siamese, Chan and Ahom) shows a remarkable mixture of Indian and Chinese elements. The isolation of the fragments of the tropical world is a thing of the past; the great age of discovery, the colonial period, slavery and trade have resulted in abundant contacts. But the backwardness persists and can only be remedied slowly. Very exceptionally, some parts of the tropical world have been able almost completely to overcome their economic backwardness; but is their example significant? Hawaii is the most prosperous of all tropical territories (p. 153), but in 1960, $437 million out of a total revenue of $1,400 million came directly from the American government (the cost of administration and defence), and the revenue from sugar was only $127 million! A similar economy to that of the Hawaiian islands might develop in other tropical countries if outside financial assistance were available on this scale; but this example should put us on our guard against undue optimism. Somewhat similar is the case of Puerto Rico, though the standard of living here is much lower than in Hawaii. The relative prosperity of the Puertoricans is one of the advantages that they derive from their incorporation into the American economy; their sugar is sold at a good price, there is an enormous American expenditure on the island, and an inflow of cash sent back by Puertoricans who have emigrated to the United States.

One of the most important prospects in view in the tropical world is the development of the vast sparsely populated areas. Does this represent a serious hope for a human race that is beginning to ask if one day it will not run out of cultivable land? Let us first consider Amazonia, almost deserted by man, whether it be in its Brazilian part or in Bolivia, Peru, Ecuador or Colombia; and the adjacent parts of the Orinoco basin in the interior of the Guianas, which are similarly unpopulated. In sum these regions amount to almost 2¾ million square miles, yet they have scarcely 3 million inhabitants.

One very striking example is provided by the Gradaús district, in the Altamira municipality of the state of Pará, which has but one person to 25 square miles. This huge neglected area lies between 8° N and 10° S, in equatorial and subequatorial latitudes. It is always hot, but not so overwhelmingly so as in many other parts of the tropical world. Rainfall is everywhere abundant, and the dry seasons, which vary in length according to latitude, are not very severe. Evergreen equatorial forest holds sway over immense areas. There are no relief obstacles, and the climate which favours the development of luxuriant vegetation is also conducive to the existence of large rivers which are navigable over very long stretches. The Marañon, for example, is navigable right up to the Pongo de Manseriche, where it leaves the Andes, 2,800 miles from the sea. The Amazon itself is navigable without any interruption for ocean-going vessels of 10,000 tons, right up to Manaus, and for vessels of 3 to 4,000 tons as far as Iquitos in Peru; and from there river steamers can ascend to Pongo de Manseriche. The Amazon has a much larger flow than has been generally recognized: figures of 120,000 cubic metres a second have been quoted, but 200,000 is more likely, as an annual average.

The causes of this vast human vacuum provide a problem that has more than mere scientific interest. If these $2\frac{3}{4}$ million square miles of Amazonia and its borderlands are to be regarded, either as a whole or in part, as a huge potential reserve of agricultural land, it is obviously necessary, in order to avoid errors in planning its development, to discover the origin of the existing situation. From what has already been said it is clear that climate and relief do not provide the explanation; perhaps other aspects of the natural environment may be more helpful. The Amazonian region is not exempt from serious tropical diseases like malaria, yellow fever, leishmaniasis, dysentery and ankylostomiasis. Nevertheless, it could not be called a particularly unhealthy region. Malaria is of a mild type, and a map of its incidence in Amazonia shows the juxtaposition of malarial and malaria-free areas, the former mainly around water surfaces—large, deep and exposed to sunlight—that are suitable for the larvae of *Anopheles darlingi*, which is the main vector. The Congo forest is no healthier than Amazonia, but its population density is ten times as great (ten people to the square mile as against one). Similarly the Benin forest has never offered such healthy conditions as would explain a population density twenty or thirty times that of Amazonia. On the contrary, both the Congo and Benin are much more unhealthy than Amazonia. Furthermore, the most densely populated part of Amazonia, the Belém-Bragança country, is no more healthy than the rest of the region; there are healthy areas, like the plateau served by the Belém-Bragança railway, but there are also malarial parts like the banks of the Guama and its tributaries, and until quite recently, the city of Belém itself.

Do the soils of Amazonia offer any explanation? In the Brazilian section, which covers 1,350,000 square miles, tertiary and quaternary rocks occupy 620,000 square miles, the remainder being underlain by palaeozoic rocks. The tertiary areas are sandy rather than clayey, and are arranged in terraces at different levels with steep bounding slopes that often represent the outcrop of lateritic crusts. To the south of Santarem, for example, there are various terrace levels between the river Tapajos and the 'Planalto de Santarem' which is some 300 feet above. Outliers capped with lateritic crusts indicate the former extent of the terraces. The tertiary sediments have been trenched by the rivers, which have all reached a state of erosional equilibrium. The valleys are relatively narrow and bounded by the scarped edges of the tertiary formations. At Gurupa, just above the delta, the Amazon, some six miles wide, washes on its southern bank the foot of a lateritic scarp that keeps the place above flood level. Here the tidal river has really no flood plain at all. In total the flood-plains covered with recent alluvium (*varzeas*) represent no more than 23,000 square miles in Brazilian Amazonia. Some valleys are simply river channels, in which the river occupies the whole area between the scarped sides. These are fresh-water 'rias'; the lower valleys of the Xingú, the Tapajos, the Rio Negro, the Urubu and the Trombetas are of this type. The city of Manaus lies on the banks of a ria shaped like a goose-foot.

The terraces or low plateaus of tertiary rocks in Amazonia occupy huge areas, sandy, permeable and almost devoid of water in the dry season. Are these the cause of the low population density? It is not possible to give a short and simple answer to this question. True, some parts that were deforested long ago, like the southern outskirts of Santarem, have a most unpromising appearance, consisting as they do of savannas in which the discontinuous bush leaves expanses of white sand that offers but little hope of fertility; the bushes (*barba de bode*) are in any case characteristic of exhausted soils. The very small charge of dissolved matter, and the preponderance of silica in this dissolved matter, are indications of the small content of fertile elements in the soils of the region. The first floods after the dry season bring down more dissolved matter than enters the river during the rainy season, and the plankton flourish for a while before declining again to their normal low level; these floods have released the soluble elements (arising from decayed vegetation, for example) which have accumulated during the dry season, and once the rains have started there is no more available (see above, p. 19).

There are great soil inequalities within short distances. Not far from the poor savannas of Santarem is an agricultural experimental station on the Planalto, that certainly cannot complain of poor soil; whilst the rubber plantations of Belterra, a little further south, have soil of indifferent quality. We need go no further; the soils of Amazonia are not in general so poor as to be solely responsible for a density of population of less than one per square mile. Even as they are, these soils could carry a much larger population. In the Belém-Bragança district some fifty people to the square mile (excluding Belém city) cultivate by *roça* (slash-and-burn) the sandy soil that has no lateritic crust; and the soils of this district are no better and no worse than those of the remainder of Amazonia.

Does the explanation lie in the forèst? The Amazonian selvas have been something of a bogy in tropical legend, a green hell, an impenetrable forest, with trees that spring up again soon as they are cut down, giant snakes that crush the unwary traveller, and piranha fish that lie in wait and in a few seconds reduce to a skeleton the unfortunate individual who falls into the water. In its natural and primitive state the forest simply indicates that man has not taken possession of the territory; it is a witness simply to the absence of man and is not necessarily an obstacle to human occupation. The fronts from which the forest may be attacked are convenient and of immense length, viz. the river banks. The Amazonian forest does not burn naturally while it is growing; in order to clear a patch it is necessary as elsewhere to cut it down and leave the trees and undergrowth to dry out. Examples are not lacking of areas of forest cleared by slash-and-burn methods; the example already quoted from the Santarem area is repeated around all the towns. The best example is the area that feeds Belém; this Amazonian metropolis of 400,000 inhabitants receives cassava and wood fuel from the Belém-Bragança area. Some 8,000 square miles of primeval forest have here given place to cultivation and fallow.

So the forest is just as unable as the other elements in the physical landscape to explain the characteristic feature of the human geography of Amazonia, which is a very sparse and poor population, eking out a meagre livelihood by collecting rubber and nuts, and producing no food of their own. The Brazilian part of Amazonia has to import foodstuffs and does not export any; it harvests none of the coffee, sugar, beans, onions or rice that it consumes. The population is affected by a remarkable incapacity for production.[1] This is linked with but is not the result of the natural conditions. Only the history of the peopling and economy of Amazonia can account for the surprising condition in which this territory now finds itself.

1. Earl Hanson, 'Social regression in the Orinoco and Amazon basins', *Geog. Rev.*, 1933, pp. 578–98, describes this situation very effectively.

The first description of Amazonia is contained in the account of explorations of Orellana, whose amazing descent of the river thrust a spearhead of Spanish influence from Peru to the Atlantic. This account is of an Amazonia that was more densely peopled in the seventeenth century than it is today; there were villages strung out along the banks, sometimes for many miles, close to the rivers but sited on natural banks above flood level or on the tertiary scarps; cultivation occupied the most fertile alluvial areas, there was much fishing, and giant turtles were kept in enclosures; thanks to the rivers there was some trade, including gold ornaments. Beyond a few hundred yards from the rivers the forest was apparently unexploited. The Indian population of pre-Columbian Amazonia thus comprised a series of narrow strips along the rivers, and the overall density cannot have been high. There was apparently no political organization more elaborate than that of tribes and chiefs. But perhaps the civilization of Marajo island, which was destroyed before the arrival of the Europeans, may have had a more elaborate control of the territory.

The Portuguese actually took possession of Amazonia in 1616; they were soon penetrating it by means of the rivers. It is relatively easy to ascend the 'Rio Mar' (literally, the sea-river, which is what the lower Amazon is) when the easterly trade wind is blowing strongly, and easy to descend with reefed sails. The Portuguese were deceived in their search for gold and for the fabulous kingdom of the Amazons. There was almost nothing to export. So it was necessary to make the Indians supply—freely of course—the *droga do sertão*, and as they showed no enthusiasm for such business, punitive expeditions were mounted, which had a disastrous effect on the population, which was massacred, infected by common European diseases to which they had no resistance, carried off as slaves or scattered as refugees into the recesses of the forest, away from the rivers used by the Portuguese. Efforts by missionaries to rescue these people had but little effect, even when such an energetic and forceful personality as the Jesuit Viera took matters in hand; and the population continuously declined, whilst the territory controlled by the Portuguese remained extremely poor. In the eighteenth century there was so little business done in the town of Belém that there was no money in circulation; the few soldiers were paid with cocoa beans. A comparison of easily-entered Amazonia and the Congo, which was inapproachable at its lower end, is perhaps significant. The Portuguese had discovered the Congo one hundred and fifty years earlier than the Amazon, but the rapids in the last 200 miles of the Congo's course had prevented ships from penetrating the African fastnesses, which remained unknown until the end of the nineteenth century.

In the mid-nineteenth century the fortunes of Amazonia, despite the fact that the area was well enough known, were at their lowest ebb; the Indians were fast disappearing, and white immigration was insignificant, whilst the absence of plantations had prevented the influx of a negro population. Some small colonies of Azores islanders, fleeing from the catastrophic volcanic eruptions, had been created in the Belém-Bragança area, and the present population of this exceptional Amazonian area is derived from this modest foundation.

The second half of the nineteenth century witnessed the rubber boom. The high price obtained for this product caused an influx of population which brought the area few benefits. Thousands of *borracha* collectors spread out along the rivers and streams where the *Hevea* was to be found; many of these unfortunates were killed off by disease and by the lack of preventive measures, or were massacred by the Indians. They were urged on by extortionate masters who assumed all kinds of imaginary rights over these unoccupied lands, and by merchants who bought their rubber very cheaply and sold them food at high prices. The Indian population meanwhile continued to diminish as a result of infectious diseases and of punitive expeditions that were staged as reprisals for the killing of *caboclos*; it was a case of rifles (*espingarda*) against bows and arrows. The labour for dealing with the rubber was obtained by calling on the local population of Indian–Portuguese mestizos, Portuguese and people from Ceará. During this period of prosperity due to rubber, the Indian population disappeared from the river banks, and the Indian languages were replaced by Portuguese.

The reduction in the price of rubber occasioned by the competition of the plantation product caught Amazonia unawares, and from that time the unfortunate effects of its historic heritage began to be felt. The population, which had become accustomed to the collecting habit and had neglected agriculture, was completely lacking in modern techniques, and instead of turning to the cultivation of the rubber tree, poured tirades of abuse on the competitors who had stolen their seeds, and proclaimed loudly that Para rubber was superior to plantation rubber (which was not true): they sincerely believed that the collection of wild rubber was a more economic operation than the cultivation of the *Hevea*, because it involved no investment of capital! Thus today Amazonia has few inhabitants, and its economy languishes not because the natural conditions enforce this but by reason of the disastrous historical record, in which the Indian population has been largely destroyed without being replaced by an influx of colonists. No important economic activity, capable of expansion, has been substituted for the mere collection of products, which had a debilitating effect both on general economic activity and on technical progress.

The river Amazon could perhaps one day carry convoys of boats laden with merchandise, if the inhabitants, at all social levels, could acquire better techniques and a more imaginative conception of economic progress. Amazonia lends itself to the establishment of cocoa, coffee and rubber plantations, and there is space enough for the cultivation of enormous quantities of foodstuffs. The results of the rubber plantations at Belterra are far from being negative; they have suffered from the difficulty of recruiting labour, for the population of Amazonia has no liking for regular work. Japanese colonists have achieved excellent harvests of jute near Santarem. The Instituto Agrônomico do Norte at Belém has established ricefields in the floodable alluvial areas whilst the *caboclos* get only poor results on the terraces. Here, as elsewhere in the tropics, the cultivation of annual crops needs to descend to water level. Groups of cultivators established along the banks of a navigable river and producing by their combined efforts (without necessarily abandoning the principle of private land-ownership) foodstuffs on the alluvial lands, commercial crops on the best plateau lands and timber on the remainder, could certainly achieve prosperity. Amazonia is admirably adapted by its climate to silvi-culture, and has plenty of water for paper making, and navigable rivers. If only the Brazilian part of the Amazon basin were populated to the level of the Belém-Bragança region, there would be 70 million instead of 2 million. But the population of Brazilian Amazonia is increasing rapidly as a result of the decline in the death rate. Without recourse to immigration, Amazonia has a labour force which was formerly deficient, but which will become too numerous to be employed merely in the business of collecting.

The forests of the Congo and of Kalimantan (Borneo) are more populated than those of the Amazon, but they too have a population that is small in relation to their possible development, and that would be inadequate to exploit these possibilities. New Guinea has at the most 2 million people on its 330,000 square miles; a few small areas have densities above the average, reaching 130 to the square mile in the Balim valley and the Chimbu territory. An analysis of these areas of greater density shows that they are not due to any specially favour-able natural conditions; similar densities could exist in other places. The greater density seems to result from purely human factors and to be unstable both in space and in time. The generally low population density of the tropical world can be presented in another way: of the 6 million square miles of hot, wet Africa, only 200,000 are effectively cultivated each year. Even if we allow a figure of 40 per cent for the uncultivable areas, it is clear that a modification of the agricultural system by shortening or abolishing the period of fallow could redeem enormous areas.

A modern characteristic of the tropical lands is the existence of large empty or half-empty areas that could support human life; but in the eighteenth century there were also large areas in the temperate lands with only a very sparse population, such as the Argentine pampa, the prairies of Canada and the United States, south-eastern Australia, New Zealand, the black earth belt of western Siberia, and Manchuria. These areas lay open to receive wave after wave of immigrants from Europe (or in the case of Manchuria, from China). The occupation was a relatively simple process, for the open spaces were healthy, and the immigrants were supported by political powers interested in expansion. The colonization of the vacant lands in the humid tropics poses problems the true nature of which is brought out very clearly by a comparison.

The unoccupied tropical lands were until recently much more unhealthy; but on the other hand, can one really imagine that millions of Asiatic Indians could have colonized Amazonia, or the Congo forests, or New Guinea, as millions of Europeans in the nineteenth century occupied the United States, Canada and Argentina? India at this time was not in a state of political and economic expansion which would have permitted such an enterprise. Though the Chinese overran Manchuria, Indian colonists have not even been able to maintain themselves in Burma; and the Javanese, despite all the favourable circumstances, have scarcely begun to colonize the empty lands of Indonesia. Human circumstances, in other words, allied to the obstacle presented by tropical diseases, have not been favourable to the occupation of the unpopulated areas of the tropical world, and yet these latter are the agricultural trump cards that the human race must play in the struggle for survival. For the moment, the conditions under which these empty lands could be occupied remain uncertain. Have the states that control Amazonia and its borderlands the means to undertake the development? There are political problems here that are perhaps more difficult and even more important than the technical ones.

The main prospect for the hot, wet lands of the tropics is the expansion of agriculture over wide areas at present unused. Industrialization may be necessary, but this problem will not be examined here, for the tropics do not provide special conditions that are not present elsewhere (apart from the inability of the tropical forest, in the present state of technology, to provide the raw material for paper manufacture).

The cultivation of crops for export merits our attention, for the money that is thus earned (provided it remains in the country) primes the economic pump and effectively counters isolation and stagnation. It is an advantage to produce an export crop under good conditions and to buy low-priced food from outside. Réunion, for example, despite its poor sugar yield (500 lb per acre in twelve months), can purchase with the product of one acre of sugar cane a quantity of maize that would require five acres to grow locally.

During the last century or two these export crops were provided by the plantations, the geographical effects of which we have already examined (p. 148). But at the present time plantations in the proper sense of that term, being foreign enclaves, are becoming less and less possible to maintain, for obvious social and political reasons. Many of the so-called plantations which still survive deserve but little commendation. As an example of the unfortunate economic condition of such cropping for export, in which unsuitable methods of exploitation (in this case large estates worked by many small share-croppers) are combined with absence of control and lack of technical progress, we may cite the Venezuelan Andes, where the provinces of Tachira Mérida and Trujillo have a population density much greater than the average for Venezuela (72 per square mile as against 13) and a lower standard of living; the coffee plantations, which provide the main export crop, have very low yields.[1] In Guatemala the coffee exports are the main prop of the economy, but for the coffee *fincas* to survive it was necessary to introduce forced labour; by the application of laws against vagrancy, Indians were made to work in the plantations.[2] In Brazil the babaçu palm produces a nut that contains an oil-yielding seed of commercial value; in the Maranhão region the wild palms are cared for by what is almost a form of agriculture, but it suffers from being run by large landowners and small share-croppers, and from the complete absence of technical equipment.[3] Brazil could furnish many more examples of the unfortunate consequences of plantations which have ignored technical progress; in the *mata* of Minas Gerais, in the south-eastern part of this state, coffee plantations were established early in the nineteenth century; they were badly managed and ruined the soils so that yields declined by two-thirds between 1870 and 1910; the plantations eventually gave way to a poor savanna cultivated only at intervals with food crops, as in the

1. *Problemas economicos y sociales de los Andes venezolanos*, Parte I and Parte II, Caracas, 1957.
2. G. and M. McCutchen McBride, 'Highland Guatemala and its Maya communities', *Geog. Rev.*, 1942, pp. 252–68.
3. O. Valverde, 'Geografia economica e social do babaçu no Meio Norte', *Revista Brasiliera de Geografia*, 1957, pp. 381–420.

Rio Novo area of the north of Leopoldina.[1] A similar decline is to be seen in the plantations of the island of São Tomé, where there are large estates, wage-earning labourers, and low yields.[2]

Plantations, in the old sense of the term, can be justified in the modern world only if, through their high degree of technical development, they can act as experimental stations; but even in these circumstances the social and political disadvantages may be very great. Is it possible to retain the advantages of the plantation system within a new régime of native small holdings? To answer this question we must first examine the 'good' plantations (as opposed to the 'bad' ones of Brazil) in south-east Asia, and particularly in Malaya, where the only real survivors remain. Before the plantation era the Malay Peninsula was sparsely peopled (Fig. 16); as most of the land was unutilized, the establishment of plantations gave rise to no territorial problems. Through the perfection of the techniques of both agriculture and sanitation, these plantations helped to convert tropical agriculture from empiricism to a science. This success was not just accidental. Though Malaya has but ordinary soils and an equatorial climate without exceptional qualities, it was favoured by its geographical situation and its state of civilization. Singapore provided the economic incentive and the Chinese population provided both the labouring and the trading classes. Maritime communications were easy. The combination of European capital, techniques and trade, and Chinese skill and tenacity, worked wonders. The establishment of the plantations took place at a time and in circumstances in which the planters could no longer get their profit from the exploitation of slaves or forced labour and so had to engage in scientific research into the improvement of yields.

The Malayan plantations have perfected agronomic techniques that have both increased yields and helped to conserve the soil; it was here that the former widespread practice of clean weeding was realized to be inappropriate, since it kept the soil bare and encouraged rapid leaching and the erosion of the surface layers; experience gradually showed that it was important to retain a cover of vegetation. So with new plantations neither deep ploughing nor complete deforestation was practised, the young rubber trees being planted in holes and only the biggest of the forest trees being removed. The original vegetation was thus gradually eliminated, while conserving the least objectionable of the plants, such as *Leguminosae* of moderate size, the presence of

1. O. Valverde, 'Estudo regional da zona da mata de Minas Gerais', *Revista brasiliera de geografia*, 1958, pp. 3–82. For the situation in São Paulo state see above, p. 154.
2. F. Tenreiro, *A ilha de São Tomé*, Lisbon. Junta de Investigacões do Ultramar, 1961.

which helps to retain nitrogen in the soil. By a gradual transition the original forest becomes the undergrowth of the plantation, the soil is never without a cover and does not suffer erosion. Plantations of trees do not exhaust the soil; the losses of humus and soluble salts that occur are mostly due to erosion. Patience and a scientific approach

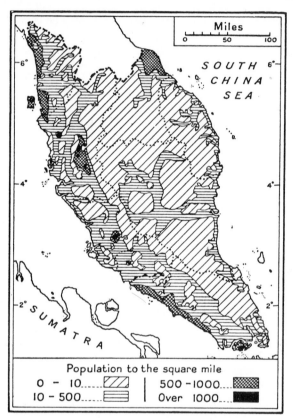

FIG. 16.   Density of population in Malaya
(After C. A. Vlieland, 'The Population of the Malay Peninsula'
Geog. Review, 1934)

have thus perfected a technique which gives the least possible offence to nature.

The plantations have also developed the profitable use of chemical fertilizers. This was a long process, for some tropical soils do not respond to chemicals as temperate soils do: thus phosphatic fertilizers may give rise to aluminium phosphates that are actually harmful. The scientifically-run plantations of Malaya and other parts of south-east Asia have thus helped to drag tropical agriculture out of its routines that were based largely on guesswork. One example, taken from outside Malaya, is the plantation of Soukamendi in Java, where sisal and cassava were cultivated in rotation; the plantation had two factories, one producing sisal fibre and the other tapioca. Sisal and cassava were chosen because they do not make the same demands on the soil; sisal needs a fertilizer mainly composed of phosphate and potash, whilst cassava needs nitrogenous fertilizer. The spreading of fertilizers was done in response to the needs of the crops; and the large quantities of effluent from the factories was carefully led back on to the fields by means of ditches. Thus almost nothing was lost to the soil through the harvesting of these two crops.[1] Whilst the plantations of the pre-scientific age have done the tropical world more harm than good, those of more recent date present a very favourable balance sheet. It will be most unfortunate if the agricultural techniques perfected by these plantations are forsaken by the native cultivators amongst whom they are divided up.

The Malayan plantations succeeded in overcoming the mosquito problem before the advent of modern insecticides such as DDT. For the suppression of the anopheles species whose larvae prefer running water, a very effective technique was devised: the streams were enclosed in concrete channels carefully shaded by bushes, so that the water continued to flow (thus discouraging those species that like stagnant water and shade), but lost its sunshine. All pools and puddles, however small (for even a tin can filled with rain-water could make an excellent home for some larvae) were rigorously suppressed; and particularly difficult sites were treated with oil or 'Paris green' (a compound of cupric arsenite and acetate).

The great problem of the moment is how to maintain this heritage of scientifically run plantations under the new régime of independence that most tropical countries are now experiencing. It is easy to understand that the newly independent people wish to suppress the plantations because they represent colonialism. With the foreign owners eliminated, the plantations will lose their enclave character and will become an integral part of the national economy. But the plantations played a dual role, for they provided a money income and were in the forefront of agronomic progress. The 'commercial cultivation' that succeeds the 'plantations' must continue to maintain this position by ensuring equal or greater production, continuous technical progress and an increasing productivity in terms of labour. This is an essential condition of future prosperity in the tropical world. That it is by no means easy is evidenced by many examples, in particular in Indonesia, of the decline in technical standards since the end of the

1. G. Oudot, *Bull. écon. de l'Indochine*, 1940, pp. 76–91.

plantation system. May not the same thing happen in Malaya, where the small farms of the Malays have so far had yields far below those of the large plantations?

The break-up of the large plantations, however, may not have a bad effect on yields if the small-holdings, once established, are not parcelled out still further, and if the occupiers continue to benefit from common services such as the provision of tractors, combating of plant diseases, and the transport, treatment and sale of the products; and provided that they are under an obligation (with the penalty of eviction) to respect a common discipline regarding the maintenance of works and the elimination of inferior trees. In the Fiji islands the plantations have been divided into small farms of seven to twelve acres, under conditions that are favourable to the cultivators, who are guaranteed security against further subdivision of the holdings, but who in return have to conform to a strict control designed to maintain and increase the yields. Something of the same kind is planned for the sugar plantations of Hawaii. A revival of coffee planting has taken place in the São Paulo region, towards Campinas, in an area that had seen both its plantations and its coffee production declining; a new generation of farms, small in size but intensively worked by their owners, is getting high yields by up-to-date methods which include spray irrigation. Small coffee farms in the vicinity of San José in Costa Rica obtain good yields of high quality coffee, and a population of European stock derives a decent living therefrom. It is too soon as yet to say whether the new organization of sisal cultivation in the neighbourhood of Mérida in Yucatan, Mexico, will give reliable yields greater than those of the old private estates, but the prospects appear good.

Concern for high yields and the necessity of selling good produce involves the introduction of measures of control and supervision of the small farmers. The essential thing, however, is that the export of agricultural products should take place; better to have commercial crops produced by poor techniques than an agricultural system that is not oriented towards exportation, as the examples show of commercial cropping developed by native peoples without the prior existence of plantations. Even though the methods of production are poor, this export cropping resulting from local initiative offers the possibility of gain, gives rise to a trading class and presents opportunities for mastering improved techniques. A necessary condition for the development of this kind of native initiative is the absence of large estates and of monopolistic foreign enterprise which deprives the natives of the opportunity for technical advancement that cultivation for export offers.

The existence of a class of people with experience in exporting and in preparing agricultural products for export might easily form the basis of the industrialization of the tropics. There are of course other ways of achieving the same end, but this one is too often forgotten. If the inhabitants of the tropical world were more experienced in the business of exporting and competent in all the financial, commercial and industrial processes to which it gives rise, the much desired industrialization of the tropics would make good progress. All things considered it would cost less to bring this about by international agreements to stabilize the price of tropical products than to donate capital for the establishment of factories that run the risk of failure through the absence of a social environment into which they can be integrated.

With this in mind, the development of certain parts of West Africa merit our attention. Here, in Ghana and in the Yoruba territory of Nigeria, the inhabitants have created a cocoa culture that is the most successful enterprise in black Africa. They did this in the early years of the twentieth century without any encouragement from the colonial authorities; no agronomist came to their aid for many years, and no lawyer helped them to resolve the delicate territorial problems posed by the creation of permanent cocoa groves in an area where land was in common ownership. The Yoruba territory supports 2,400,000 people on 8,000 square miles, and the annual export of cocoa averages 100,000 tons; cocoa represents 60 per cent by value of the agricultural output of the Yoruba territory and 23 per cent of the value of all Nigerian exports. Cocoa gives a net income per acre three times that of the subsistence-crop areas, and for a much smaller expenditure of labour (215 hours per acre for cocoa, 305 hours for food crops). It is not surprising, in these circumstances, that the Yoruba farmers are the most comfortably off in Nigeria, as their greater purchases of cloth, bicycles and motor cars bear witness.

This successful enterprise is not particularly favoured by the natural environment: the rainfall is barely sufficient, varying from 60 inches in the south to 46 inches, which marks the northern limit of the cocoa belt; this is not the best climate for the cocoa tree, particularly in view of the November dry season and the desiccating blasts of the harmattan in February. The soils are not bad, compared with those of neighbouring regions; in fact the southern limit of the Yoruba cocoa belt corresponds to the junction of the crystalline rocks of the Yoruba massif, which yield 'good' soils, and the Benin sands which give 'bad' soils. The climate further south, with its more abundant and more evenly distributed rainfall, would be more favourable for cocoa, but the soils are too poor. The success of the Yoruba cocoa culture is neither due to exceptionally favourable natural conditions, nor to a high degree of technical skill. It results from the good judgment of the Yorubas in taking up an interesting type of agriculture. They practise no selection of trees, they have no seedbeds or plant nurseries; they provide no shade trees for the cocoa, and use no manure. New plantations have far too many trees (as many as 1,600 to the acre), but twenty years later there are too few (only 160) for the farmers do not bother to replace dead trees. With such a poor cover the soil is not sufficiently shaded; it dries out, becomes compacted, and grows grasses. The Yorubas even indulge in practices that are clearly injurious, such as keeping the soil bare under the cocoa trees (they do this to keep down the weeds, but this could better be done by growing bushes and shade trees). The cocoa trees are needlessly pruned, and the harvests are too widely spaced (which lowers both quality and quantity).

This Yoruba example shows that the establishment of native export cultures needs in the first place not so much a high level of skill as a desire to have something to sell. The development of cocoa production has engendered the construction of a good road system (often paid for by the cultivators themselves), and the rise of a class of cocoa-dealers and cocoa-carriers.[1] The economic and technical advancement of the Yorubas, of which cocoa is the expression as well as being both the result and the cause, is manifested in Lagos, an essentially Yoruba town, where a purely African bourgeoisie, engaged in commerce, industry and finance, constitutes a phenomenon that in size and variety is unique in black Africa.[2]

Other interesting and encouraging examples may be found in the cocoa cultivation of Ghana[3] and the Ivory Coast.[4] And however poor the quality of the methods employed, the creation of coffee groves in the tropical valley of Tambopata is probably the best thing that could be done for the people of the Puno area, on the Peruvian shores of Lake Titicaca, who are undoubtedly suffering from over population (cf. p. 131). For the cultivation of export crops to get off to a good start, the local population must have acquired an urge to have a regular money income through trade. The Land Dyaks of the Sadong basin in Sarawak have created rubber 'plantations'; but in 1954

1. F. Galleti, K. D. S. Baldwin, and I. O. Dina, *Nigerian Cocoa Farmers*, Lagos, 1956.

2. P. Marris, *Family and Social Change in an African City; a study of re-housing in Lagos*, London, 1962.

3. W. H. Beckett, *Akokoaso: a survey of a Gold Coast Village*, London School of Economics, Monographs on Social Anthropology, 1943; P. Hill, *The Gold Coast Cocoa Farmer*, Oxford Univ. Press, 1956; J. M. Hunter, 'Akotuakrom, a case study of a devasted cocoa village in Ghana', *Trans. Inst. Brit. Geog.*, 1961, pp. 161–86.

4. M. A. Kobben, 'Le planteur noir', *Inst. français d'Afrique noire. Études éburniennes*, 1956, pp. 7–100.

they still regarded these as a money-box, only tapping the trees when they had a desire to buy some particular object which was not an immediate necessity—such as a bicycle, a lamp or a gun.[1]

However poor may be the methods used, commercial cropping is always preferable to mere gathering. The case of Amazonia has already been used to illustrate this point. When gathering, through an unfortunate chain of circumstances, retains pride of place in the commercial activity, the country in question cannot fail to suffer, for economic expansion will inevitably be very limited, and the population will have no opportunity of acquiring knowledge of better methods. This was so in Amazonia, and until recently in the Kwilu region of Congo-Léopoldville. Situated south of the river Kasai and east of Léopoldville, this latter region, with its sub-equatorial climate, is favoured by a system of navigable rivers, tributaries of the Congo, and by relative proximity to the sea. A vigorous attempt at exploitation was made by the government and by private enterprise; but the results are very deceptive. After sixty years the territory is still economically and technically backward, for all the activity was directed towards the collection of natural products, and so was very ill-balanced. The lure of something for nothing has in this case also done a great disservice to the people.

In the Kwilu region, grassy plateaus overlook wide valleys which contain long ribbons of equatorial forest. Oil palms abound in the million acres of these forests, and there is also the savanna plant *Landolphia* which has long roots containing a latex that can be used for rubber. The Kwilu region is more densely peopled than its neighbouring territories, so it had the manpower to exploit these natural resources. It had been transformed by its inhabitants before the arrival of the Europeans—for neither the savanna nor the oil palm groves are natural occurrences—and had thus set the trap into which a modernized economy was to walk.[2] The opening up of the country to modern trade began by the people selling lumps of *Landolphia* rubber to European factories; round about 1910 Kwilu exported 1,400 tons of rubber a year, but the collapse of prices between 1910 and 1912 put an end to this traffic. The Europeans might have planted *Hevea* trees in order to compete with the Malayan plantations, but it was possible to collect palm nuts instead of rubber, and so, taking the easiest way out of the difficulty, one form of gathering was replaced by another, and a grave economic mistake was made. The oil palms in the forests of Kwilu owe their existence to

1. M. W. R. Geddes, *The Land Dyaks of Sarawak*, London, H.M.S.O., 1954.
2. A. Nicolai, *Le Kwilu, étude géographique d'une région congolaise*. Brussels, 1963.

the cultivators of old, who cut down the primeval forest and opened up sunny clearings in which the palms could take root and grow. The palms have but a small yield, and the collection of nuts is a quick operation that teaches the collector nothing. The organization on a large scale of the collection of wild products is an attempt to escape from technical progress. There is an annual export of 60,000 tons of oil and 40,000 tons of palm kernels, but no real attempt to establish palm plantations. The people have learnt absolutely nothing of modern progress and remain mere collectors of wild fruit. If the sale of palm products ceased, the people would find themselves in the same economic condition as they were in 1893.

Though the superiority of export cropping over collecting, in the creation of an active economy, is not in doubt, it is important not to encourage just any type of cultivation. Trees and shrubs are much better than annual plants, for with the latter there is always the risk of soil erosion. It was certainly not a happy inspiration that prompted the authorities of the Central African Republic to force the population to grow cotton as a commercial crop over large areas of the former Belgian Congo and Ubangi-Chari territories. This has led to the destruction of forests and the deterioration of the soils; the temporary arable areas give way to a poor savanna. It is unavoidable that man must destroy the forest in order to get at the cultivable soil, but this should only be done for perennial crops with a high yield. The forests of Ubangi-Chari were destroyed in great haste to make way for cottonfields that produce a mere 450 lb of cotton-seed per acre; for this meagre return the fertility of the soil has been sacrificed, for the cotton plant requires careful cultivation of the soil and does not provide any cover to protect the surface layers from the ravages of erosion.

The Kenya province of Nyanza has an interesting economic history.[1] The British administration was anxious to establish cotton as a commercial crop, for this had been successful in Uganda. The population resisted this development and took to maize growing, which became very important. An analysis showed that maize brought the cultivator a money income nearly three times that from cotton; and from this an important general point arises, that the economic progress of the tropical farmer must be sought in ways that will give him the greatest financial return. Advice and encouragement will be readily accepted if it is clear that they will result in profit. Paternalism must be avoided, and before spreading a new commercial crop, time must be taken to find out what the local cultivators think about its

1. H. Fearn, *An African economy, a study of the economic development of the Nyanza Province of Kenya*, 1903–1953, Oxford Univ. Press, 1961.

profit-earning capacity. That too much attention was focused upon cotton in the Belgian Congo is one of the causes of the failure of these schemes.

Despite the success of maize in the province of Nyanza, it is not proven that this type of cultivation is the most advantageous. Maize does not protect the soil any more than cotton does, and in this area of accidented relief this is a serious drawback. Possibly coffee groves, planted and maintained by the native people under expert guidance, would give an even higher return than maize. There is some evidence pointing in this direction in both Nyanza province and Uganda. Tree and bush cultures undertaken with a view to exporting the crops have a much more beneficent effect on the economy, on the agronomy and on the social life of the people; they have much more chance of finding a place in the world's markets, they lead to the rapid acquisition of better techniques and they give locational stability to the population.

The development of export cropping is limited by the selling prices of tropical products; a lowering of the price may result either from tropical over-production or through the competition of extra-tropical products, natural or synthetic. Amongst the tropical agricultural products, some are a monopoly of the tropical world (and so are exposed only to the danger of competition between tropical producers), some are liable to competition from temperate products, whilst a few are exposed to the competition of chemically synthesized substances.

The tropical world has an outright monopoly in the case of only a few crops; the list comprises coffee, cocoa, bananas (the extra-tropical production of which is negligible), pineapples (despite the forced crops of the Azores), pepper, nutmeg, cinnamon, cloves and clove oil (produced by distilling the buds and leaves of the clove-tree).[1] Tea does not figure in this list, for the production of China, Japan and Caucasia is obviously extra-tropical. Indeed, the only products of real economic importance are coffee and cocoa.

Coffee is in most years the agricultural export that brings in the greatest revenue to the tropical world. The $2\frac{1}{2}$ million tons of coffee that are put on the world market are vital to the prosperity of many

1. We hardly dare place the cashew (*Anacardium occidentale*) in the list of irreplaceable tropical products, because it is in competition with almonds and nuts; whilst in the cake trade the cashew fruits compete with grated coconut. Similarly with ginger (*Zingiber officinalis*), though it is true that the roots of tropical ginger are not exactly replaceable by the ginger of China and Japan, for tropical ginger is a spice whereas Chinese and Japanese ginger is a sweetmeat; ginger for spice comes from Jamaica, Sierra Leone, Nigeria and India, and the total export amounts to 5,000 tons a year.

countries: Brazil, Colombia, Angola, El Salvador, Guatemala, Costa Rica, Nicaragua and Haiti all have trade balances that depend largely on coffee exports. Despite the tropical monopoly of coffee, the price of the commodity is ruled by markets situated in the temperate lands, especially New York; that is, by the consumers. Prices are low, and to prevent them falling still further, exports are limited by international agreements. Customs and other duties, levied by the consumer countries on what is considered to be a luxury, are not without their effect on sales. The coffee producers, who are all in tropical countries, need to be guaranteed against a drop in price and against the restriction of consumption by fiscal means. The future for coffee producers is really very bright, for whilst the United States consumes 13 lb a year per head of population, and France 9 lb, the U.S.S.R. only buys one ounce, India less than three ounces, and China less than one-thirtieth of an ounce. It is much the same with cocoa, for the annual consumption per person in the United States is 2 lb 10 oz, but only 2 ounces in U.S.S.R. and less than one-thirtieth of an ounce in China. We can safely say without exaggeration, therefore, that the tropical countries could greatly increase their sales of coffee and cocoa.

Amongst the tropical crops exposed to the competition of similar products grown in the temperate lands, the most important is sugar, which plays a vital role in the economy of many tropical countries. All the sugar that enters international trade (16 million tons) is of tropical origin; it is the weightiest of all tropical agricultural exports, though usually its value is only equal to or less than that of the $2\frac{1}{2}$ million tons of coffee. By reason of its high yields, sugar gives the greatest income per acre. It comes into competition with sugar beet grown in temperate latitudes, and we may consider its relative advantages.

Sugar cane was grown in 1961 on 22 million acres, which yielded 32 million tons of raw sugar, or 3,150 lb per acre planted (not per acre harvested); sugar beet was grown on 17 million acres, yielding 23 million tons of raw sugar, or 2,950 lb per acre. The average yield of sugar cane is reduced by India and Pakistan, which have 7 million acres under sugar and a yield of only 3·2 million tons of raw sugar (excluding brown sugar which does not figure in the statistics); if these two countries are omitted, the rest of the tropical world had 15·3 million acres under cane sugar, yielding 29 million tons of sugar, or 4,200 lb per acre planted. In the case of beet sugar it is the U.S.S.R. that pulls the average down, with 7·5 million acres and a production of 6·6 million tons; omitting this, the rest of the temperate world had 9·7 million acres under sugar beet, yielding 16·1 million tons, or 3,550 lb per acre. The present superiority of cane over beet is thus hardly overwhelming, 4,200 lb/acre as against 3,550. But is not the price of cane sugar less than that of beet sugar? It is not easy to give a clear answer on this point. The unequal soil occupation of the two crops is no obstacle, for it is not difficult to calculate the twelve-month equivalent of a cane crop that may take eighteen or twenty months to mature. The comparison is hindered by the inequality of the wages paid, by the inequality in the market value of the land, by protective tariffs, by import quotas, and by the degree of utilization of the waste products of refining. These waste products are but little used in the case of cane (perhaps because insufficient technological and economic study has been directed towards this problem), but are very valuable in the case of beet. In north-west Europe an acre of sugar beet yields, besides the sugar, fodder to produce 450 gallons of milk, and an acre of beet is thus worth two acres (one of sugar and one of a fodder crop). Cane used to be regarded as easier to cultivate, but the sowing of monogerm beet seeds does away with the necessity for thinning, and this, with the use of topping and lifting machines, has greatly reduced the labour demands of the beet crop. Sugar cane probably has the greater possibility for further increase in yields. In short, is it not rather usless to debate the problem of the competition between cane and beet? The potential market is vast enough to accommodate both types of production. In 1962–3, the world output was 57 million tons of sugar for 3,000 million people, that is 42 lb a head per annum. If all the world's population ate as much sugar as the 500 million largest consumers (100 lb a head per annum) the demand would rise to 138 million tons.

Since the sale of sugar would appear to be one of the most reliable sources of income for the tropical world, it is very desirable that production and yields should be increased. Science and capital investment can help, and neither depends on the existence of 'plantations', for intensity of production and high yields can be obtained by small producers provided that there is adequate technical control. The cane plantations which existed in Cuba before the revolution were anachronistic, for they had foreign technicians, often non-Cuban labour, exported raw sugar to be refined in the United States, and paid dividends to shareholders outside Cuba. They were delicate anachronisms; but it was not necessary to reduce the output by such clumsy methods; on the contrary, it would have been possible to increase it by greater yields (for the Cuban plantations were not outstanding in this respect). A system of small farms controlled by competent managers could have achieved this end. Tropical countries must not reduce the precious inflow of money from the sale of agricultural products, for only by its aid can they diversify their economy and finance the development of industry. Plantations, in the old sense of that term, are a thing of the past; but only export cropping can assure the future.

The position of tropical countries in respect of oil-yielding plants is a very strong one; groundnuts, copra, palm oil and cotton-seed oil (not exclusively tropical) have long dominated world trade in vegetable oils. This domination, however, is not due to any particular advantages of tropical oleaginous plants; it is due rather to the fact that production in the temperate lands was not at a very high level at the time when the consumption increased rapidly (in the nineteenth century with the enormous increase in the use of soap, table oil and margarine), and also to the low wage levels of the tropical countries. Today the production of tropical oil-yielding plants is threatened, for the detergents produced by the petrochemical industry have slowed the increase in soap consumption, and, more seriously, temperate plants have reappeared on the market. The most dangerous of these is the soya bean, which with mechanized cultivation can give large yields at a low price. The soya bean can also succeed just as well in equatorial as in temperate latitudes; comparative studies have shown that with equal care it can give just as good a yield in temperate lands, where technological progress makes this possible with less human labour and certainly with less expense. The sunflower is also a serious competitor (though it is true it does equally well in tropical lands with a pronounced dry season, as in Mozambique for example). Like the soya bean, the sunflower yields, besides its oil, the raw material for cattle cake, which is eagerly sought by the animal foodstuffs industry and which helps to lower the price of the oil.

Of the tropical oil-yielding plants that have a large sale, the groundnut is the poorest. Its yields per acre remain low, and its flavour is not such as to ensure its competitive power against tasteless oils. It must retain an important place in tropical food supplies because of its richness in protein, but its place in the world market is likely to be severely contested. This is an alarming prospect for such a country as Senegal, whose entire economy depends on the groundnut, without any substitute in view. Furthermore, the groundnut has already had a devastating effect on the light and fragile soils of the central and northern parts of the country; the irregularity and violence of the rainfall, and the hot, dry winds have already ruined the soils in the Louga and Cayor regions. And now there is talk of an indestructible carcinogenic product that forms in groundnuts when they are kept in store.

Palm oil is better placed to withstand competition; in well-managed groves of selected trees the *Elaeis* palms will give two tons of oil to the acre on the clay soils of the plains of Malaya and Sumatra. The coconut palm cannot stand comparison with this: on the same soils it yields no more than two-thirds of a ton of oil. The magnificent results of careful selection on the yield of the *Elaeis* palms were planned and produced on large plantations; there is a risk, with small holdings, of lowering both the yield and the quality. If the nut-clusters are harvested too soon, the oil yield drops; if too late, the oil is too acid; and the transport of small quantities may be slow and careless, again increasing the acidity.[1]

What about the role of the tropical countries in the world markets for rice and maize? And whatever it may be, how can they compete with the temperate cereal-producing countries, which are already embarrassed by the low prices obtainable in the open market? Are we not witnessing, on the contrary, a relative devaluation of tropical rice, due to the fact that wheat surpluses are given (or sold under conditions which almost amount to a gift) to countries which, in the absence of such generosity, would have bought rice from the traditional rice exporters such as Burma, Thailand and Cochin-China? On the other hand the technological progress of the temperate lands is so great that the price of temperate cereals is no higher than that of the tropical cereals, despite the much lower wage rates of tropical countries. The tropical lands, by reason of their heat and sunshine, seem well endowed to produce tuberous plants; the tubers are not exported as such, but are used for the preparation of such products as dried chicory roots, flour, starch and tapioca. It would require a good deal of audacity to assert that the potato of the temperate lands is not equally adaptable. Somewhat similar thoughts arise in connection with tobacco, for it is very difficult to say whether, apart from the lower labour cost in the underdeveloped countries, it is better to produce this commodity in a truly tropical environment or in subtropical or even temperate lands. And as for tropical fruit, other than bananas and pineapples, is there any prospect that mangoes, mangosteens, litchis, naseberries, custard-apples, pawpaws, naranjillas (*Solanum quitoense*) or granadillas may give rise to new currents of trade?

A large part of tropical agricultural production finds itself in competition with the products of industry. This is a disaster of the first magnitude for tropical countries without being of general benefit to humanity as a whole. Many tropical products have been reduced in value and their producers have seen their incomes falling. The synthetic or manufactured products that compete with tropical commodities are not always more useful or of higher quality; but they arise from industrial activities that are already in existence and they use by-

1. B. S. Gray, 'The potential of the oil palm in Malaya', *Journal of Tropical Geography*, 1963, pp. 127–32.

products that were formerly an encumbrance. Thus, because they are complementary to industries that could exist without them, they can be produced very cheaply. Synthetic anti-malarial preparations leave no hope whatever of further prosperity for cinchona plantations (though it must be recognized in this case that the synthetic products are much more effective and reliable than quinine). Synthetic rubber menaces the production of latex from *Hevea*, vanillin has paralysed vanilla cultivation, chemical dyes leave no room for indigo, and man-made fibres are taking the place of sisal, jute and cotton. Synthetic products do not necessarily do away with the need for tropical commodities, but they impose a price ceiling and so reduce tropical incomes.

Commercial cropping for export has been given pride of place in this review of the prospects for the tropical world. It seems that the prosperity of this form of culture is essential not merely to economic progress but also to the emancipation of tropical peoples. But what are the prospects for agriculture in general, which is concerned with the feeding of the local population? Is progress towards a more prosperous future to be hindered by obstacles presented by natural conditions and by techniques inherited from the past?

The traditional cultivator of tropical lands uses the ladang system, with the sequence of forest-cutting, burning, sowing, weeding, harvesting and fallow; the yields are low, both in relation to the areas sown and to the amount of labour expended. The implements used are very simple, no animals are employed and no ploughs, and the fallow takes the place of manure (cf. p. 31–9). Shifting cultivation on burnt forest land, the 'slash-and-burn' system, is inseparable from a low standard of living and a hand-to-mouth existence; it is not conducive to economic or technical progress. Any improvement of economic conditions must involve the abolition of ladang. But what are the possibilities?

The future does not seem to lie only in an intensification of human labour, if this simply means more careful but still purely manual work. Such an intensification merely leads to lowered productivity. Some remarkable studies carried out in the Genieri region of Gambia have shown that the traditional African intensive agriculture, entailing a huge expenditure of human labour, leads to a reduction in productivity; and that the traditional extensive agriculture gives a better reward for the effort put into it. In the cocoa groves of Yoruba-land in Nigeria, an expenditure of labour of more than 300 hours per acre leads to a reduction in the productivity per hour, even though the yield may increase.

Neither is the future concerned simply with an extension of the area cultivated by the native peoples. An increase in the productivity of the tropical cultivator cannot be brought about simply by bringing in more acres, regardless of yields, through the agency of implements which diminish the amount of human toil per acre cultivated. This way lies the ruination of soils through the shortening of the fallow period without any compensating improvements. The spread of the plough amongst African cultivators has not been an unmixed blessing; it has allowed larger areas to be cultivated for a longer time, but without any increase in the yield per acre. Thus in the Teso area of Uganda there were 282 ploughs in 1923, and 15,388 in 1937—but the yields remained the same.[1]

The extension of the cultivated area reduces the length of the fallow and confronts us with the problem of manure, which is particularly acute in the case of annual or biennial crops. A tree can more easily renew its intake of fertile elements because it exploits a much larger volume of soil and because its search for nutriment can be pursued throughout the year. A cereal crop, in the same soil, would be in a much more delicate situation, particularly if the soil were thin, for its root system extends but a short way into the soil, and then only for a few months. Besides, the harvesting of the cereals removes a large quantity of material, not only the grain but also the straw, both of which contain mineral elements drawn from the soil. Thus a single cereal crop can remove more from the soil than a plantation of trees, even though it is actually exploiting a smaller volume of soil.[2] A good rubber plantation will yield 1,350 lb of latex per acre whereas a good cereal crop will remove 8,000 lb of vegetable matter in the form of grain and straw. The manuring of annual crops is thus particularly urgent if the practice of fallow is to disappear.

One important point at this stage can be made with regard to all the tropical countries. It is that even though the area cultivated by each farmer remains unchanged, there comes a time of the year when the use of an animal-drawn or motorized plough would be most useful, for at present the cultivator has to use a hoe. This is the case for example in all the savanna areas, where the rhizomes of the giant grasses are resistant to fire. A study conducted by agronomists in Tanzania showed that twenty-five man-days of hard work were necessary on a farm to prepare the soil for sowing. These twenty-five man-days must be worked during a period of forty days, and this period is critical, for many happenings may contrive to hinder the work and prevent its being completed within the forty days; it has been

1. Sir F. Stockdale, *Report on his visit to East Africa*, London, Colonial Office, 1937.
2. P. Vageler, *An Introduction to Tropical Soils*, London, pp. 224–7.

stated that the yield of millet is greatly reduced if the sowing takes place more than fourteen days after the commencement of the rainy season. The availability of a tractor would enable the sowing to take place with certainty very shortly after the first rainfall. The only question is how to make an implement pay that is in use for such a very short period in the year.

The total abandonment of fallow, particularly fallows lasting for more than one year, would put an end to deforestation and allow improvements in land management. Tropical countries must feed themselves from stable and permanent arable fields that produce one or perhaps two crops a year. The proper equipment of tropical agriculture with such services as roads, water and electricity is incompatible with shifting cultivation and a sparse population, for these things make for the instability of the environment. The cultivation of wet rice offers immense advantages, for it assures good yields, allows two harvests a year, and minimizes the effects of floods and droughts; the paddy-field also uses effectively the fertilizers that it is given, and conserves the soil by hindering erosion and preventing leaching. Rice is also a food that is universally appreciated, even by those who do not use it as the mainstay of their diet. The example of tropical monsoon Asia should be considered by the rest of the tropical world. The very densely peopled parts of monsoon Asia remind the world's tropical population of the certainty that high civilization can have its roots in a hot, wet area. They teach, too, that the regions with the richest cultural history are the low-lying plains where flooded ricefields assured mankind of a regular food supply without recourse to the practice of fallow. For in the rest of the tropical world the plains have been more or less neglected, through the fault either of the native inhabitants who lacked adequate technical competence, or of the European colonists who had no experience of wet rice cultivation.

Wet rice cultivation is certainly not the only solution to the problem of subsistence cropping; to cater for the needs of an ever-increasing population there must be other means as well. But the paddy-field has the advantage of being well-tried and without risk. How can we refrain from expressing surprise at seeing a steep African hillside deforested, burnt and sown with dry rice whilst the bottom of the adjacent valley remains an unused swamp? On the one hand an uncertain crop and the inevitability of eroded slopes, on the other a valuable resource lying idle.

The advantages of wet rice cultivation may be offered to other areas through the medium of irrigation. This seems to be the most unquestionable form of technical progress that tropical agriculture can make. All the refinements and improvements to which tropical agriculture can be subjected can be improved still further by the use of irrigation. Farming in the tropics would be much more productive if the dry seasons were not dead seasons. Dry season irrigation would not only enable the cultivated area to be extended, but it would enable plant growth to take place when sunshine is at its maximum. It is often maintained that the heavy cloud cover in the rainy season is a factor in the poor yields of crops grown in hot, wet lands, for the clouds diminish solar radiation. If this is true there is surely good reason to profit, through irrigation, from the brilliant sunshine of the dry season.

Irrigation can also be used in the rainy season, with profit. In the equatorial climate of Yangambi, in Congo-Léopoldville, five and a half inches of rain a month is a minimum below which the soil shows signs of moisture deficiency and plants begin to suffer from lack of water. Such a quantity does not always fall in each month, and irrigation would allow complete regularity of watering. Recent studies have emphasized even more the value of irrigation: chemical reactions that take place in plants as a result of photosynthesis and build up the substances that man needs, evolve gases that escape through the plant pores. For these useful reactions to take place, the pores must be open, and if the plant suffers from lack of moisture it closes its pores so that the chemical reactions cease. Under unirrigated conditions it is around midday, when the light is strongest, that the plant resents the lack of water and so closes its pores. So the paradoxical situation arises that just when the sunlight is most favourable for photosynthesis, the plant is least disposed to perform the operation. Irrigation could get rid of this bottleneck or at least reduce its effect.

The field within which improvements could take place in tropical agriculture is immense, but improvements demand the shrewd and sensible use of the natural environment and the human resources. Over-simplification of the problem may court disaster. For example, the 'Groundnut Scheme' tried brutally to revolutionize 5,000 square miles in Tanzania, by attempting to convert a sparsely-utilized savanna into an arable area closely cultivated with groundnuts. The enterprise was a complete failure, but the £36 million that it swallowed up was perhaps a small price to pay for the lessons that can be drawn from its bankruptcy. We now know much better the faults that a scheme to reorganize tropical agriculture must avoid. But what were the errors that put paid in 1948 to an enterprise that had only begun in 1946? The first undoubtedly was lack of scientific preparation. The climate was but little known, and it happens that the major area of the scheme, at Kongwa in central Tanzania, has a rainfall that is marginal for groundnut cultivation (as indeed for any other form of agriculture), with a variability involving deficiencies that would jeopardize the harvest, however careful the preparations for the crop might have been.

A careful preliminary study would also have shown that bush-clearance would be much more difficult than was anticipated. Heavy motorized equipment was thrown in, but despite this it was not easy to clear the tree stumps and extract the roots, which damaged the ploughshares. New ploughshares of special steel were ordered, for ordinary ones were quickly worn down by the quartz particles which formed the matrix of the soil. It soon appeared that complete clearance of the bush was an extremely costly operation; to rid the soil of all woody lumps that might damage a plough would cost more than the economy of the whole enterprise could stand. It is better at the first stage simply to cut down the trees; if the plantation is to be for tree crops this is all that need be done; but if the intention is to go in for annual crops such as groundnuts, sugar cane or cereals, it is better to follow the initial felling (which gets rid of most of the woody matter) by a year or two of traditional polyculture; during this period the woody stumps and roots in the soil will be demolished by termites, and thereafter powerful mechanical ploughs can move without encountering any obstacles.

The very high costs of complete forest or bush clearance are only supportable if the ground is to be used for regular annual harvests of high-value produce; they are economically intolerable if the ground, after a year or two under cereals or groundnuts, is to relapse into fallow. If the fallow lasts for several years the ground will be covered with woody plants and by grasses with tough rhizomes that require a fresh clearance which can only add to the cost of the products. Neither is it certain that deep ploughing is a good technique in many tropical soils, for such ploughing brings to the surface the lower, poor quality layers, and buries the surface soil which contains the fertile elements. At Kongwa the very costly deep ploughing certainly did not improve the soil; but the situation was aggravated by circumstances that are not peculiar to Kongwa but were surprising to the technicians who had not been warned about them. Under a tropical climate with a marked dry season, and in soils heavily charged with hydroxide of iron, the ground just before the rains is so hard that it is very difficult indeed to work it. The operators at Kongwa were obliged to clear and plough the land at the beginning of the rainy season; but having done this, it was then too late to sow the crop, and it was necessary to wait for the next rainy season. So the ground lay uncovered for twelve months, eroded by wind and rain and burnt by the sun. A careful preliminary survey would have shown that in the Kongwa area only the damper valleys lend themselves to modernized agriculture, which moreover could only have been safe from hazards if irrigation had been possible. As for the plateaux between the valleys, there were some parts that were better than others, but once again, only by irrigation could permanent agriculture be made to give a good return for the money spent on it.[1]

The motorized colonization scheme at Mokwa in Nigeria, between 1949 and 1954, was also a complete failure. But it confirmed certain important ideas about the progress of tropical agriculture: though motor-driven implements are the best weapons for the destruction of the forest, they are too expensive to use for the immediate and complete cleaning of the soil; large expenditure on the reclamation of rural land is justified only if intensive perennial agriculture is the result, and it is a mistake to undertake the mechanical preparation of an area that is too large for the local farmers to utilize, for they will be incapable of the final clearance of anything more than a couple of acres or so. The clearance ought to be done mechanically, but the traditional field arrangements would not permit the passage of the weeding machines.

Some unsuccessful experiments have also taken place in the former French colonial territories; not much has been heard about them, perhaps because they were less grandiose, but partly because in France there has been rather less criticism and rather more discretion. The disastrous affairs of the vegetable oil factories on the West African coast, or the mechanized ground-nut cultivation in Senegal, have not received the publicity that their value as lessons warranted. The experiment of reviving wet rice cultivation in the Yagoua area of northern Cameroon has been the subject of some useful studies. French government money was squandered in this region; in seven years each rice farmer cost the French Treasury Fr. 150,000, though the extra payments budgeted for were only Fr. 91,000 per farmer. It would have been cheaper for the Treasury, and would have given more pleasure to the Musgum people, if the latter sum had simply been given by the Treasury to each farmer!

Of course the employment of machines has a part to play in tropical agriculture; the productivity of human labour will reach a satisfactory level only when tropical man has large numbers of mechanical slaves. But the machines should follow and not precede scientific and technical advancement. The tractor on its own solves no problem; 'tractoritis' is a disease fatal to progress. To raise the scientific level of tropical agriculture there must be research workers from the tropical countries to do the necessary work: both the research and the researchers must be 'tropicalized'. Some examples may be given of work already done or in progress. Research undertaken in North Cameroon (by the genetics section at Guétale) have shown that it is

1. P. Gourou, 'Le plan des arachides', *Cahiers d'Outre-Mer*, 1955, pp. 105–18.

possible, by plant selection, to raise the yield of millet and sorghum by 30 per cent in three years.[1] But such work and its practical application demands that the research workers should be in close contact with the population that may benefit from it. Another example concerns cassava, the leaves of which contain large quantities of protein. A recent study has shown that the powdered leaves of cassava are as rich in protein as the leaves of lucerne; in fact the protein content of the dry matter of cassava leaves amounts to between 20·6 and 36.4 per cent. An experiment conducted in Costa Rica on dairy cows showed that dried cassava leaves could quite conveniently replace dried lucerne in a ration the remainder of which consisted of wheat bran and cotton-seed cake[2]. Cattle-raising is probably just as possible and profitable in tropical climates as in temperate ones, under certain conditions which involve the importation, full application and adaptation of all the technical progress made in the temperate lands, namely selection of fodder plants, the use of irrigation, abundant and precise application of manures, careful breeding of animals, controlled feeding, and above all, complete and lasting victory over microbic and parasitic diseases. If all these conditions were realized, tropical stock-raising would produce almost as much meat and milk per acre as in temperate lands. The opinion has often been expressed that the growth of stock-rearing in the tropics will be a slow process; but it does not seem that such observations tell the whole story, for they would appear to indicate that tropical stock-rearing suffers from so many deficiencies that it can never play a notable part in the economy. On the contrary, on condition that all the scientific and technical progress realized in the temperate world is transplanted into the tropics, the latter will no longer be a feeble producer of animal products. When such a programme is realized, we shall no longer have the spectacle of the savanna landscapes with their skinny beasts, tormented by flies and ticks, chewing in the dry season straw that is as hard as matting. But the difficulty—perhaps the tragedy— is that this technological revolution will have to take place first outside the areas inhabited at present by pastoralists, for it will be much better understood and applied by sedentary cultivators than by the traditional pastoralists who love their cattle more than what the cattle produce. A further difficulty is that this technical revolution will require a large number of qualified specialists and technicians who will have to be recruited and trained on the spot.

Geography is above all an attitude of mind towards the problems posed by the presence of a certain people, with a certain type of

1. A. Saurat, in *Riz et riziculture et cultures vivrères tropicales*, Paris, 1960, pp. 94–101.
2. D. J. Rogers, in *Economic Botany*, New York, 1959, vol. 13, pp. 216–63.

civilization, in a certain area. If the area is tropical, its description may legitimately be called tropical geography. Are the differences in the human geography of Malaya and of Denmark due simply to differences of civilization, and are the differing natural environments of no account? It would be absurd to claim that civilizations are determined by their physical environment, but it would be equally so to pretend that they are not influenced or moulded by it. Certainly the Chinese of Malaya or North Borneo remain Chinese, but the human landscape that they have created differs from that of their native land. It would seem more profitable to illuminate a study of the Niger delta by a comparison with that of the Sikiang, or vice versa, rather than with the delta of the Mackenzie or the Lena.

The present differs from the past in the sense that the realities of the tropical environment are now clearly understood; we know that between the 'inexhaustible luxuriance of tropical nature' and the formidable difficulties due to the poverty of tropical soils and the unhealthiness, there is an assured middle way, opened by scientific progress. Our civilization can at last approach the development of the hot, wet lands, by safe and certain methods. But the evolution of the tropical world has been much retarded. When the techniques of modern civilization came up against the tropical world they ran into unexpected difficulties in matters of health, the behaviour of the soil, and methods of husbandry. As a result, the peculiarities of the tropical world appeared as hostile obstacles; it was necessary to adapt the techniques to new conditions, and such adaptations were slow, because the research workers who carried them into effect were few in number, and all originated in the temperate zone and were only temporary residents in the tropics. Today the adaptations have been brought clearly into focus; tropical diseases are now for the most part easily curable, and the peculiarities of tropical soils are well understood. But the application of the adaptations requires a numerous personnel, skilled in the science and technology of the tropics. Though political independence has put an end to political colonialism, independence in the matter of technology and science is very far from being attained, and the situation is still quite colonial. The tropical peoples must not only apply for themselves in their own world the technology and science that have been developed in the temperate lands by the scientists of the temperate zone, but they must also get into the position of being able to conduct their own scientific and technical research and make new discoveries for themselves.

The tropical world is a good third of the world's surface, excluding the deserts. Outside Monsoon Asia it is sparsely peopled, and its inhabitants contribute little to the economic life of the globe. The techniques of production and medicine that permit the taming of nature in the tropics have been perfected, but the problems of a real organization, that is the political problems, are far from being solved. The organization of mankind is much retarded on both production and health fronts. Perhaps we shall reach the moon or Mars before we take a really serious interest in this very earthy enterprise of developing the Tropical World.

Index

Gourou, *Tropical World*

The more important references are printed in **bold** *type*.